THE CONFESSIONS
OF
ST. AUGUSTINE

St. Augustine
Pastor, Theologian, Mystic

The Confessions
of
ST. AUGUSTINE

REVISION OF THE TRANSLATION OF
REV. J .M. LELEN. Ph.D.

CATHOLIC BOOK PUBLISHING CORP.
NEW JERSEY

NIHIL OBSTAT: Francis J. McAree, S.T.D.
Censor Librorum

IMPRIMATUR: ✠ Patrick J. Sheridan, D.D.
Vicar General, Archdiocese of New York

ABBREVIATIONS OF THE BOOKS OF THE BIBLE

Acts—Acts of the Apostles	Jb—Job	Nm—Numbers
Am—Amos	Jdt—Judith	Ob—Obadiah
Bar—Baruch	Jer—Jeremiah	Phil—Philippians
1 Chr—1 Chronicles	Jgs—Judges	Phlm—Philemon
2 Chr—2 Chronicles	Jl—Joel	Prv—Proverbs
Col—Colossians	Jn—John	Ps(s)—Psalms
1 Cor—1 Corinthians	1 Jn—1 John	1 Pt—1 Peter
2 Cor—2 Corinthians	2 Jn—2 John	2 Pt—2 Peter
Dn—Daniel	3 Jn—3 John	Rom—Romans
Dt—Deuteronomy	Jon—Jonah	Ru—Ruth
Eccl—Ecclesiastes	Jos—Joshua	Rv—Revelation
Eph—Ephesians	Jude—Jude	Sir—Sirach
Est—Esther	1 Kgs—1 Kings	1 Sm—1 Samuel
Ex—Exodus	2 Kgs—2 Kings	2 Sm—2 Samuel
Ez—Ezekiel	Lam—Lamentations	Song—Song of Songs
Ezr—Ezra	Lk—Luke	Tb—Tobit
Gal—Galatians	Lv—Leviticus	1 Thes—1 Thessalonians
Gn—Genesis	Mal—Malachi	2 Thes—2 Thessalonians
Hb—Habakkuk	1 Mc—1 Maccabees	Ti—Titus
Heb—Hebrews	2 Mc—2 Maccabees	1 Tm—1 Timothy
Hg—Haggai	Mi—Micah	2 Tm—2 Timothy
Hos—Hosea	Mk—Mark	Wis—Wisdom
Is—Isaiah	Mt—Matthew	Zec—Zechariah
Jas—James	Na—Nahum	Zep—Zephaniah
	Neh—Nehemiah	

(T-173)

PREFACE

A MONG all the spiritual, philosophical and theological works of the Fathers of the Church, none has been more universally esteemed in all ages or read with greater profit than *The Confessions of St. Augustine.*

The word *confession* in the Old Testament has two meanings: to *confess* our *sins* and to *praise* God. Accordingly, the recurrent theme of this great work is that of penance and praise—a humble confession of St. Augustine's sins and the glorification of God's mercy. Although popularly classed as an autobiography, it is only accidentally so in the true sense of the word. The many and sometimes intimate events of his life are narrated parenthetically and are subordinated to his main purpose of encouraging penance and praise for God.

The *Confessions* cannot be considered as a book that narrates, but as one that edifies; the story not of a life, but of a soul; not a work of art, but a cry of repentance and love. Thus, the *Confessions* can be called a magnificent soliloquy before the Divine Presence, or rather, as one writer classifies it, "an Epistle to God."

The temperament of the Saint was ardent, affectionate, and excitable. In his early youth, driven by the desire for his companions' praise, he stole some fruit from a neighbor's orchard, and he later records the desolation of soul caused by the death of a friend. Whether he dwells on the characters of Alypius and Nebridius or that of Adeodatus, the son of his sin, or whether it is his conversations with Monica, his mother, and her loving and tender care of him, or his sorrow at her death, St. Augustine reveals himself as a compassionate man to whom friendship and fellowship were absolutely essential, and one in whom there was not the slightest trace of desire for personal aggrandizement.

The style of the *Confessions* bears many traces of Augustine's training in rhetoric. It is often epigrammatic, and in a stately and untranslatable way he plays on the sounds of words and balances them with extraordinary care. His familiarity with, and common use of, Scripture is remarkable. His mind was thoroughly steeped in the Bible, and its phrases had become so much a part of his vocabulary that they recur constantly in his writings.

The long struggle between Augustine's higher spiritual impulses and his lower carnal habits, the way in which his moral character and conduct act and react upon his mental clearness of vision, and his state of religious doubt—these facts are set forth in a manner that cannot fail to awaken deep interest and to manifest the intimate connection between moral conduct and ardent faith.

To the agnostic of the twentieth century *The Confessions of St. Augustine* provides a warning. His cultured intellect had sought, at the prompting of his lower nature, complete satisfaction and rest in many deviations from a Faith that demanded a purer life than he was prepared to live. Yet, the fact that he finally embraced the Creed of the Catholic Church may suffice to convince unbelievers that the religion of Christ can afford to the most logical and scientific mind a peace that elsewhere will be sought in vain.

CONTENTS

Book 5—Augustine the Catechumen

Book 6—Gravitating Toward Faith

Book 7—From Error to Truth

Book 8—Conversion

Book 11—Time and Eternity

Book 12—The Meaning of Holy Scripture

Book 13—Total Dependence on God

BIOGRAPHICAL NOTES

AUGUSTINE was born on November 13, 354 A.D., at Tagaste, at that time a small free city of Numidia, in Algeria, North Africa. His father, Patricius, a city official, was a pagan of modest means, loose morals, and a disposition easily aroused to anger. His mother, Monica, was a well-educated Christian whose admirable qualities have caused the Church to regard her as a model of Christian motherhood.

Owing to the influence and insistence of his mother, Augustine completed his elementary studies as a Christian catechumen. During a serious childhood sickness, Augustine himself asked for Baptism, but he changed his mind after the crisis had passed, in accord with the widespread custom of deferring Baptism until manhood.

Augustine proved to be a brilliant student at the schools of Tagaste and Madauros. As a result, his father decided to send him to Carthage to study rhetoric and prepare for a legal career. Unfortunately, the lack of necessary funds forced Augustine to spend a year at home in idleness and worldly pursuits. About this same time, 341 A.D., his father died after receiving Baptism.

While studying rhetoric at Carthage, Augustine devoted himself to the pursuit of pleasure and licentiousness. Accordingly, as we read in the *Confessions,* he engaged in an illicit relationship with an unnamed woman who bore him a son, Adeodatus. During all this time he repeatedly scorned the religion of his mother and eventually came under the influence of the sect of the Manichees, which claimed to possess a scientific explanation of nature and its most mysterious phenomena.

He continued in this belief for nine years, during which time Monica suffered in the knowledge that her son not only was steeped in licentiousness but also boasted of being foremost in the performance of evil deeds. His incessant proselytism drew most of his friends to embrace the errors of this fanatical sect. A saintly bishop consoled Monica with these words: "A son of so many tears cannot perish."

After completing his studies at Carthage, Augustine opened a school of rhetoric, first at his native Tagaste and then at Carthage. Near the end of his stay in Carthage, Augustine visited and questioned the celebrated Manichean bishop, Faustus of Mileve, who, instead of strengthening Augustine's belief in the doctrine, left him completely disillusioned, and as a result he abandoned that sect.

In the year 384, Augustine closed his school of rhetoric at Carthage and sailed for Rome. After a brief stay there, through the efforts of Symmachus, the prefect of Rome, he obtained the post of professor of rhetoric at Milan. During the course of this teaching assignment in Milan, Augustine listened to the sermons of St. Ambrose. At the beginning he attended these sermons because he admired Ambrose's use of the classical rhetorical form.

However, as time went on, his avid study of Neo-Platonist works, which refined his concept of God, together with the sermons of Ambrose, inspired him to a greater love for the Scriptures and a genuine love for Christ. Nonetheless, he could not bring himself to abandon his way of life and free himself from the bonds of sensuality. Thus, he still remained a catechumen.

In the Autumn of 386, Augustine abandoned his post as professor of rhetoric and requested that he be baptized. Accordingly, on Holy Saturday in 387, together with his son Adeodatus and his friend Alypius, Augustine received Baptism from the hands of St. Ambrose. A few months later, her work on earth accomplished, Monica died peacefully in the arms of Augustine.

After the death of his mother, Augustine remained in Rome for another year, occupying himself in writing. Finally, returning to Africa, he began an ascetic life in company with a group of his friends. However, his reputation for holiness and the fame he achieved as the result of his doctrinal teachings became so great that, in 391, Valerius, the Bishop of Hippo, asked him to become his coadjutor, a decision that was enthusiastically received by the faithful of his diocese. A short time afterward, Augustine was ordained a priest, and he immediately began preaching to the faithful of Hippo.

In 396, Valerius consecrated Augustine a bishop, and when Valerius died, Augustine succeeded him as Bishop of Hippo. As a priest, so now as a bishop, Augustine continued to lead a monastic life together with his priests. He was indefatigable in preaching to the poor and doing whatever he could to alleviate their wretched condition.

However, it was as an apologist and defender of the Faith against the principal heresies and schisms of the time that he achieved his greatest renown and provided inestimable help to the Church. His activities in this endeavor were divided in three directions—the Manichean heresy, the Donatist schism, and the Pelagian heresy.

At first Augustine continued the controversies with the Manichees that he had initiated at Rome; then, by preaching and writing, he fought against the Donatist schism that held sway over the African Church throughout the fourth century.

At a solemn religious conference at Carthage in 411, attended by 286 Catholic bishops and 279 Donatist bishops, Augustine as the spokesman of the Catholic bishops scored a glorious victory over the Donatists. He upheld the thesis that the Catholic Church can tolerate sinners for the purpose of converting them without losing its mark of holiness.

In the following year, 412, Augustine began his battle with the Pelagians, which was to last up to the time of his death and for which he merited the title of "Doctor of Grace." Augustine died at Hippo on August 28, 430, while that same city was being besieged by the Vandals.

Book 1—Early Years

After invoking and praising God, Augustine relates the beginning of his life, from his birth to his fifteenth year. He acknowledges his sins of youthful misconduct, idleness, and abuse of his studies. Finally, he gives thanks to God for gifts bestowed upon him.

CHAPTER 1 — Made for God Himself

YOU are great, O Lord, and highly to be praised (Ps 145:3); *You are mighty in power, and there is no limit to Your wisdom* (Ps 147:5). Yet man, who is only an infinitesimal part of Your creation, desires to praise You. He fully realizes his mortality, bears witness to his sinful nature, and is aware that You, O God, *resist the proud* (1 Pt 5:5).

And yet this man, this minute part of Your creation, desires to praise You. You have made us for Yourself, and our hearts are restless until they rest in You. Grant, O Lord, that I may know and understand which is my first obligation—to call upon You or to praise You, and whether first I must know You or call upon You.

But who can call upon You without knowing You? For if someone does not know You, he might call upon something else instead of You. Yet, are we to call upon You so that we may know You? *How then are they to call upon Him in Whom they have not believed? How are they to believe Him Whom they have not heard?* (Rom 10:14).

Certainly *they who seek the Lord shall praise Him* (Ps 22:27). They who seek shall find Him (see Mt 7:7), and they who find Him shall praise Him.

Let me now seek You, O Lord, calling upon You; and let me call upon You, believing in You, for You have been preached to us. My faith calls upon You,

O Lord—a faith that You have given me and that You have breathed into me by the Incarnation of Your Son, by the ministry of Your preacher.

CHAPTER 2 — Call for God To Come

AND how shall I invoke my God and my Lord? For if I should invoke Him, that would mean that I call Him to come into me. And what room is there in me where my God may enter——where God, *Who made Heaven and earth* (Gn 1:1), may come into me?

Is there then, O Lord my God, anything in me that can contain You? Or can even Heaven and earth, which You have made and in which You have made me, contain You? Or is it the case that since nothing that is could exist without You, therefore whatever is must contain You?

Since then I also am, why do I ask that You come into me—I who could not exist if You were not in me? For I have not yet sunk to the depths of the abode of the dead, and yet You are even there also—for *if I go down into the abode of the dead You are there* (Ps 139:8). Therefore, I would not be, O my God, I would not exist at all, if You were not in me—or, rather, I would not exist if I were not in You, *from Whom and through Whom and in Whom are all things* (Rom 11:36).

So it is, O Lord, so it is. Why then do I call You into me, inasmuch as I am in You? Or from where should You come to me? Where shall I go beyond the bounds of Heaven and earth that my God should come to me? For You have said, *I fill Heaven and earth* (Jer 23:24).

CHAPTER 3 — God's Immensity

DO THEN Heaven and earth contain You because You fill them? Or do You fill them, and yet still more remains of You because they cannot contain You? Where then do You pour forth what remains of Yourself after You have filled Heaven and earth? Or have You no need of anything to contain You, Who contain all things, because the things that You fill, You fill by containing them?

The vessels that are filled with You do not restrict You, and even if they were broken You would not be spilled. And in pouring Yourself out upon us, You are not cast down, but we are raised up by You. You are not scattered, but we are gathered together by You.

But You Who fill all things, do You do so with Your whole being? Since all things cannot contain Your whole being, do they contain only a part of You? If so, do they all together contain the same part of You, or various things, various parts—the greater holding more, the lesser holding less? And is there then one part of You greater, and another less? Or are You wholly everywhere, and yet nothing can contain You wholly?

CHAPTER 4—The Attributes of God

WHAT then are You, O my God? What, but the Lord God? For *who is Lord but the Lord, or who is God but our God?* (Ps 18:32). O most high, most good, most powerful, almighty, most merciful, and most just; most hidden and ever-present; most beautiful and most strong; stable and incomprehensible; unchangeable and changing all things; never new, never old; renewing all things, bringing age upon the proud and they know it not; always in action and always at rest; gathering, and never wanting; supporting, filling, and overshadowing all things; creating, nourishing, and perfecting; seeking and yet lacking nothing.

You love, yet are not inflamed with passion; You are jealous without concern; You repent without grief; You are angry yet always calm; You change Your works, yet never Your design; You recover and find what You never lost. You are never needy, and yet are pleased with gain; You are never covetous, and yet exact interest; men pay You more than they owe as if to obligate You, and yet who has anything that is not Yours? You pay debts, and are a debtor to no one; You forgive debts and lose nothing.

And what is all this that we have said, O my God, my life, my holy joy? What can anyone say when he is speaking to You? And woe to those who say nothing of You, since even the most eloquent seem to be mute.

CHAPTER 5 — Prayer To Repose In God

OH THAT I might rest in You! Oh that You would come into my heart and inebriate it so that I might forget my unworthiness and embrace You, my only good!

What are You to me? In Your mercy let me speak. What am I to You that You should demand my love, and, if I do not love You, should be angry and threaten me with grievous woes? Is it then a slight woe not to love You?

Show me Your mercy and tell me, O Lord my God, what You are to me. *Say to my soul: "I am your salvation"* (Ps 35:3). So speak that I may hear. Behold, my heart is listening, O Lord. Open it, and *say to my soul: "I am your salvation."* I will run after this voice and take hold of You. *Do not hide Your face from me* (Ps 143:7); I would gladly die in order to see it, for not to see it would be death itself.

The mansion of my soul is too narrow to receive You; let it be enlarged by You. It is all in ruins; be pleased to repair it. It has within it such things as will offend Your gaze; I confess and know it, but who shall cleanse it? To whom besides You shall I cry out, *From my secret sins cleanse me, O Lord, and from those of others, spare Your servant* (Ps 19:13-14)? *I believe, and therefore do I speak* (Ps 116:10).

O Lord, You know that *I have confessed before You the guilt I bear for my sins and You,* my God, *have forgiven the wickedness of my heart* (Ps 32:5). I do not *contend in judgment* (Jer 2:29) with You Who are the truth, and I do not want to deceive myself, lest *my iniquity lie to itself* (Ps 27:12). Therefore, I contend not with You in judgment, for *if You, O Lord, mark iniquities, O Lord, who shall stand it?* (Ps 130:3).

CHAPTER 6 — Questions About Infancy

YET allow me to implore Your mercy, *I who am but dust and ashes* (Gn 18:27); allow me to speak, for behold, it is to Your merciful heart that I speak and not to scornful man. Perhaps You too will laugh at me, but when You turn to me, You will have pity on me (see Jer 12:15).

What do I wish to say, O Lord my God, but that I know not where I came from, when I came into this mortal life, or shall I say living death? I do not know. And the comfort of Your tender mercies attended me, though I remember nothing of this, but I have been told so by the parents of my flesh, from whom and in whom You did fashion me in time.

The comforts then of a woman's milk were prepared for me. Nor did my mother or my nurses fill their own breasts. Rather it was You, O Lord, Who through them gave me that food of my infancy, according to Your ordinance and the riches of Your bounty that reach even to the roots of things. You also ordained that I would desire nothing in excess of what You gave to my nurses who willingly passed on to me what You gave them: and they, with an affection inspired by Your providence, willingly gave me what they abounded with from You.

The good I received from them was their good, which in reality was not from them, but through them, since all good things are from You, O God, and from You, my God, *comes all my salvation* (2 Sm 23:5). This I have learned afterward from Your voice speaking to me through all these things that You give me both within and without. Then I knew how to suck, and to lie quiet when pleased, and cry at what offended my flesh; but nothing more.

Afterward I began to smile, first when asleep, and then when I was awake. This custom of mine has been told to me and I believe it, because we see that this is true with other infants, though of myself I remember it not.

Thus, little by little, I began to perceive where I was, and I wanted to declare my wants to those who might satisfy them, and I could not; for my wants were within me, and the people were outside me, nor could they by any sense enter into my mind.

Therefore, I made motions and sounds as signs to express my wants, the few that I could with my limited ability, but they bore very little resemblance to what I wished.

When my will was not complied with, either because I was not understood, or because what I desired was potentially harmful, I grew angry with my elders for not submitting to me, and with those who did not offer me any help even though they had no responsibility to do so, and I took my revenge upon them by crying. Such have I found to be so with other infants. That I was such, these other infants themselves, without knowing what they were doing, have shown me better than my nurses who did know it.

Behold, my infancy is only a distant memory, and I am living. But You, O Lord, are always living and nothing dies in You. Before the beginning of time and before anything that can be said to go before, You are, and You existed, the God and Lord of all things that You have created. With You the causes of all impermanent things stand fixed forever, with You the origins of all changeable things remain unchanged, and with You the reasons of all unreasoning and temporal things live eternally.

Tell me, Your poor suppliant, O God, You Who are merciful to me so in need of mercy, tell me whether my infancy succeeded another age of mine that had already died. Was it the time that I passed within my mother's womb? Of that life also some information has been revealed to me, and I have seen women in their pregnancy.

What was I before even that life, my God, my joy? Was I anywhere, or anything? I have no one to tell me these things; neither my father nor my mother could inform me, nor the experience of others, nor my own memory. Or do You deride me for asking You such questions, You Who only require that I should praise You and confess to You the things that I know about You?

I confess to You, O Lord of Heaven and earth (Mt 11:25), and I offer praise to You for my creation and for my infancy, which I do not remember; for You have determined that man should make conjectures about his earliest days from what he observes in others, and to believe many things about himself from the testimony of women. At that time I had being and I had life, and toward the end of my infancy I searched for ways by which I could make my feelings known to others.

Whence could such a living creature derive its being but from You, O Lord? Could anyone be the source of his own being? Does there exist any channel, by which being and life can flow into us, that can derive from any other source than You Who created us, O Lord? In You being and life are identical, because Supreme Being and Supreme Life are one and the same. You are the Most High, and You *do not change* (Mal 3:6).

Nor does "today" come to an end in You, and yet each "today" truly ends in You, because in You all these things have their being. They would not be able to pass away unless You contained them; and because *Your years fail not* (Ps 102:28), Your years are a single "today." How many days of ours and of our fathers have already passed through Your "today," and from it have received their form and the being they possessed? And how many more will pass and receive their form and being?

But *You are ever the same* (Ps 102:28). All the things of tomorrow and beyond it, and all the things of yesterday and whatever is behind it, You do and have done "today." What does it matter to me if anyone does not understand this? Let him also rejoice, saying, "*What is this?*" (Ex 16:15). Let him rejoice even so, and let him be content to not understand this and to find You, rather than to understand this and not to find You.

CHAPTER 7 — Infantile Willfulness

HEAR me, O God. Woe to men for their sins! Man says this, and You have mercy on him because You made him, but You did not make the sin that is in him.

Who will remind me of the sins of my infancy? For no one is pure from sin in Your sight, not even the infant that is but a day old. Who will give me an account? Does not any small child do this, in whom I now see what I do not remember of myself? What then was my sin at that time? Was it crying greedily as I sought nourishment from the breast? For if I should at my present stage of life thus greedily cry not for the nourishing milk of the breasts but rather for the food suitable to my years, I would most justly be the object of laughter and scorn.

Therefore, at that time I did reprehensible things, but because I could not realize that these acts were reprehensible, neither custom nor reason permitted that I should be reproved; in fact, as we grow up, we root out such acts and cast them aside. Nor have I ever seen anyone who, when eliminating bad habits, knowingly also eliminates what is good. Yet was it good at that age to demand with tears what would have been harmful if granted, to rage and rant against those who were not subservient to me, against my elders, and my parents, and, by striking at them, to try to hurt those who, far wiser than myself, refused to comply with my whims and to obey my commands, which, had they been obeyed, would have done me harm?

Thus it is the weakness of infants' bodies and not their will that is innocent. I have myself seen and had experience of such a little one already possessed with jealousy; it had still not learned to speak, and yet its face would be pale and envious as it looked at a brother being fed at a breast.

Who is not aware of this occurrence? Mothers and nurses say that they know how to forestall these problems by various solutions of which I am unaware. Yet, how can an infant be called innocent when it does whatever it can to prevent another child to share in a rich fountain of milk flowing in abundance, even though that child is in great need of such sustenance to survive? Such actions are quietly tolerated, not because they are small faults or not faults at all, but because they will disappear as the years pass. Though they are tolerated at that time, they would be considered intolerable in an older person.

Therefore, O Lord my God, You have given life to the infant and a body that You have furnished with senses, equipped with limbs, and beautified with a comely form. Moreover, for the maintenance of its integrity and for its safety, you have endowed it with all the powers of a living being.

For all these things, You now command me *to praise You, and to sing to Your name, O Most High* (Ps 92:2). For You are my God, omnipotent and good, and would have been so even if this had been the only thing You had ever done for me—this which no one else could have accomplished but You alone, from Whom all things derive their existence. You are the supreme Form Who gave all things their form, and by Your Law You govern all creation.

Therefore, O Lord, this stage of infancy is one about which I do not have the slightest memory, but concerning which I have accepted the word of others and conjectured from observing other infants that I also passed through it, even though such conjecture is completely credible, and I am still reluctant to count it as part of the life I have lived in this world. For it pertains to the darkness of my forgetfulness, no less than that period which I passed in my mother's womb.

But if *I was also conceived in iniquity, and in sins my mother nourished me in her womb* (Ps 51:7), where, I beseech You, O my God, where or when, O Lord, was I Your servant innocent? But, behold, I now will pass over that period of time. For of what importance is that stage of life to me now about which I cannot recall anything?

CHAPTER 8 — Learning To Speak

PASSING on from my infancy I advanced into my childhood, or rather childhood came into me and succeeded my infancy. Nevertheless my infancy did not truly depart, for where could it go? And yet, it was now no more; for I was no longer a speechless infant, but a prattling child.

This I can remember, and I have since reflected on how I first learned to speak. I was not taught various words by those who were my elders, by means of a set method of learning, as a short time later I was taught to read and write.

But by using the mind that You, O my God, had given me, I strove by various cries, sounds and motions to make known my thoughts and my desires.

I was not able to explain myself in all things as I wished, nor to everyone I wished. However I recorded it in my memory when I heard people name something, and when they pointed to the object so designated, I observed and perceived what they called by that word.

Such things were also made clear from their bodily motions. Such is the natural language common to all nations, spoken by the countenance and the glance of the eyes, by the gestures of the other parts of the body, and by the sound of the voice, expressing the inward state of the mind when it desires, enjoys, rejects, or flees from things.

And so, little by little, I grew acquainted with the meaning of words by hearing them repeated frequently and arranged in their proper places in a variety of sentences, and by their use I began to make known my wishes, the process of speech having been subjected to the necessary training and discipline. Thus, I communicated the signs of my will to the people among whom I lived, and so ventured still farther out into the stormy society of human life, although still completely dependent on the authority of my parents and the will of my elders.

CHAPTER 9 — Schooling

O GOD, my God, what intense miseries and impositions I now began to experience when it was made crystal-clear to me as a child that the only acceptable mode of conduct for me was to obey those who taught me. In that way I would be able to flourish in this world and excel in oratorical arts that lead to honors and riches, with all the dangers they pose.

Thus I, a poor wretch, was sent to school to learn various subjects the usefulness of which I did not comprehend. And yet, if I was negligent in learning, I was whipped. This method was judged the most efficacious by my elders, many of whom had trod that path before us and had approved the use of those cruel methods that we were forced to endure, multiplying toil and sorrow upon the sons of Adam.

Meanwhile we discovered, O Lord, that there were men who prayed to You, and we learned to do the same, thinking of You, according to our capacity, as some great person Who, though invisible to our senses, could hear us and help us. I began, therefore, when yet a child, to pray to You *my only help and my refuge* (Ps 94:22), and trained my unskilled tongue to invoke Your Name.

Moreover, when still quite small, I begged You, with a great deal of intense fervor, to save me from being whipped at school. And when You did not hear me, which was *not reputed as folly in me* (Ps 18:3), my elders, and even my parents who did not wish me any evil, made light of my punishments, which I then looked upon as a great and grievous evil.

O Lord, is there any soul so great, and that cleaves to You with such intense love, as to deem of no consequence racks and hooks and other tortures from which the whole world with so much fear prays to You to be delivered? Is there any soul so great that it can laugh at those who are grievously afraid of these things, as our parents laughed at the torments that we boys suffered from our masters? Yet neither did we have less horror of these tortures than others did of greater torments, nor did we pray less earnestly to be delivered from them.

Our only sin was in not writing, reading, or paying careful attention to our lessons as intensely as was required of us. O Lord, we were not lacking in memory or intelligence, which You granted to us in proportion to our age. But we were fond of play, and we were punished for it by those who were acting in the same way. However, the idling of grownups is business, while the idling of boys is punished by those adults, and no one pities either group.

Is there anyone of sound discretion who will justify my being beaten as a boy for playing ball, because as a result I was hindered from learning so quickly, when as a man I would engage in less honorable pursuits? What did the man accomplish who beat me? Yet, if he was involved in some petty dispute with a fellow teacher, he was more racked with anger and envy than I was when beaten by a playmate in a ballgame.

CHAPTER 10 — Love of Playing and Plays

YET I sinned, O Lord my God. You are the Judge and Creator of all things natural, but of sin only the Judge. I sinned, O Lord my God, in disobeying the commands of my parents and those of my teachers, in that I might afterward have put to a good use that learning, whatever their motives might have been in desiring me to acquire it.

It was not from the desire to achieve something better that I was disobedient, but from love of play. I loved to experience the exultation of besting my playmates in a game, and I desired to have my ears tickled with vain flattery while seeking even more.

And with the same curiosity flashing more and more through my eyes, I began also to attend the shows and plays of my elders. Now those men who produce these entertainments are held in such high repute that almost all parents would wish as much for their children. Yet parents are very willing that children be whipped, if by attending these shows they forsake their studies, by which studies the parents hope their children may one day be able to produce similar forms of entertainment.

Look with mercy upon these things, O Lord, and deliver us who do now call upon You. Deliver also those who do not yet invoke You, so that they may call upon You for help and You may deliver them.

CHAPTER 11 — Baptism Deferred

I HAD heard, O God, even as a boy, of that life eternal promised to us by the humility of Your Son, our Lord, Who descended to earth to cure our pride. I had already been signed with the sign of His Cross and seasoned with His salt, as soon as I emerged from the womb of my mother who placed such great trust in You.

You saw, O Lord, when as yet I was a child, how one day I was stricken with stomach pains so severe that I was about to die. You saw, O my God, for even then You were my guardian, with what earnestness and with what faith I asked for the Baptism of Your Christ, my God and Lord, imploring the mercy of my mother and that of Your Church, the mother of us all.

The mother of my flesh was seized with fear, because with a heart chaste in Your faith she was more lovingly in labor to effect my eternal salvation. As she was taking care that with all speed I should be initiated and washed by the wholesome Sacraments, confessing You, O Lord Jesus, for the remission of sins, I suddenly recovered. Thereupon my cleansing was put off because of the likelihood that I would become more sinful if I lived longer, and because the guilt of sins contracted after that cleansing would be greater and more dangerous.

Thus, at that time, did I believe and so did my mother and all the family, except for my father. Yet he was unable to overcome in me the strength of my mother's piety to cause me to disbelieve in Christ, even as he at that time disbelieved in Him. For she was determined that You, my God, should be my father more than he. And clearly You assisted her to overcome her husband, to whom she, though a superior person, was subservient, because in so doing she was serving You Who commanded her to do so.

If it be Your will, O my God, I would like to know for what reason my Baptism at that time was put off? Was it for my good that the reins of sin, as it were, had been left loose? Or were they not left loose?

How is it then that on every side we hear it said of this or that person: "Let him alone, let him do what he wants to; he is not yet baptized"? And yet with regard to the welfare of the body, we do not say: "Let him be wounded worse, for he is not yet healed."

It would have been far better for me to have been quickly healed, and that care should have been taken by my friends and my own diligence so that the health of my soul thus recovered might be safe under Your protection Who gave it. This surely would have been much better.

But many and great waves of temptation threaten men after childhood. This my mother already knew, and she chose rather to expose to them the clay, from which I was afterward to be molded, than the image already formed.

CHAPTER 12 — Compelled To Study

ACCORDINGLY, in my childhood, during which I was in less danger of sin than in the years of adolescence, I did not love to study, and I hated to be forced to do it. Yet I was forced to study, and it was beneficial for me that this was true, but I myself did not do well, for I only learned when compelled to do so.

Now no one does well what he does against his will, even though what he does is good in itself. Neither did those do well who compelled me. Rather it was You, my God, Who did well in my regard. My teachers could discern no way I could put to use this compulsory learning other than to satisfy the insatiable desires of wealthy indigence and ignominious glory.

But You, my God, by Whom *the very hairs of our heads are numbered* (Mt 10:30), made good use, for my good, of the error of those who forced me to learn.

Moreover, my own error, in being unwilling to learn, You used for my punishment, and I well deserved to be punished, being so small a boy and so great a sinner.

Thus You were of great help to me through the agency of those who were not helpful, and You justly turned my sin to my own punishment. So You had decreed it, and so it always happens that every disordered soul shall be to itself its own punishment.

CHAPTER 13 — Greek and Latin Studies

BUT as to why I hated Greek, which I was taught when I was a little boy, I don't even now quite understand. For I liked Latin very much—not the parts handled by our first teachers, but that which is taught by those who are called grammarians.

The first stages of our education—reading, writing, and arithmetic—I regarded as no less troublesome and aggravating than Greek. And whence was this also, but from sin and the vanity of life, because I was flesh, *and a wind that goes and does not return* (Ps 78:39)?

Those first lessons were indeed better and more certain, for by them I acquired and still retain the facility of reading whatever I find written and writing myself what I want to express, whereas in later studies my head was filled with the wanderings of Aeneas, while I forgot my own wanderings. And I also shed tears for the death of Dido, who killed herself for love, while I endured my wretched condition with dry eyes, oblivious to my failings and far from You, O God, my life.

What can be more wretched than a miserable man who fails to pity himself, who weeps over Dido dying for love of Aeneas and bewails not his own death caused by not loving You, O God, the light of my heart, the bread of the inner mouth of my soul, and the power espousing my mind and the bosom of my thought?

I did not then love You, and I strayed far from You, and in the midst of my fornications the words were echoed on every side: "Well done! Well done!" The love of this world is fornication against You, yet others cry out, "Well done! Well done!" so that a man may be ashamed not to be such.

And although I did not lament these things, I did weep for Dido and the extent of her passion of love that drove her to suicide. Meanwhile I myself was following the lowest of Your creatures, forsaking You, I a creature of earth seeking the earthly.

If I had been hindered from reading these books, I would have grieved because I was not able to read that which might make me grieve. Such madness as this is accounted a more honorable and fruitful study than that by which I learned to read and write.

But now let my God cry out within my soul, and let His truth say to me, "It is not so! It is not so! That earlier learning is far better." For I would much rather forget the travels of Aeneas and all such tales than not to be able to write and read. They hang up veils, it is true, before the doors of the grammar schools, but these could just as well signify a cloak to cover up error rather than to preserve some honorable mystery.

Let not these men, of whom I stand in fear no longer, cry out against me, while I confess to You, my God, the desire of my soul, and how pleased I am to condemn my evil ways so that I may love Your ways that are good. Let not the sellers or buyers of books raise an outcry against me if I ask them whether it is true that Aeneas came to Carthage, as the poet affirms. The uneducated will answer that they do not know, and the learned will say that it is not true.

However, if I should ask how Aeneas' name is spelled, all those who have learned to read and write will answer correctly, in accordance with that agreement by which men have among themselves established these signs. If, again, I should ask which of the two it would be a greater inconvenience to forget, how to read and write or those poetical fables, is there anyone who does not realize what every man must answer who has not completely lost his senses?

Therefore, when a boy, I sinned in having a greater love for those silly stories than for those studies that were more profitable, or, rather, in hating the latter and loving the former. In like manner. "One and one make two, and two and two make four," was an odious singsong to me, while the wooden horse full of armed men, the burning of Troy, and the ghost of Creusa provided a scenario that was of far greater interest to me.

CHAPTER 14 — Dislike for the Greek Classics

BUT why then did I hate Greek literature that is full of such tales? Homer had a facility for weaving together such tales in an agreeable way, yet he was bitter medicine to me as a boy. And so, I believe, would Virgil be to the boys of Greece if they were forced to learn him with difficulty, as I did Homer.

For therein lay the difficulty of learning a foreign tongue, sprinkling with gall, as it were, all the delightful nuances of the fabulous Greek narrations. I knew none of the words, but cruel threats and punishments were employed to force me to learn them.

It is true that there was a time when as an infant I knew no Latin either. Yet I learned this tongue by observing others, without being frightened into it or forced by the rod, amid the flattering praises of my nurses, and the humorous comments of those who smiled upon me, and the mirth of those who played with me.

I learned those Latin words without any threat of punishment from others, but rather urged by my own heart to bring forth its thoughts. This I could not have done without learning words, not just from those who taught me, but also from those who simply talked with me, and into whose ears I also poured forth my thoughts.

Thus it seems clear that in learning a language the basic wish to succeed is far more influential than the threats of others. But by Your laws, O God, such threats hinder the pursuit of knowledge, as can be discerned from the history of the schoolmaster's cane and the earthly trials of the martyrs. Your laws know how to make what is bitter seem wholesome and call us back to You from that deadly pleasure whose allure caused us to depart from You.

CHAPTER 15 — Offering to God the Fruits of Learning

O LORD, *hear my prayer* (Ps 61:2); let not my soul falter under Your discipline. Never let me grow weary in confessing to You Your mercies, by which You have delivered me from all my wicked ways. May You become sweeter to me than all the allurements to which I have succumbed. May I love You with the greatest possible ardor and embrace Your hand with all the affection of my heart, so that You may deliver me from all temptations, even to the end.

For behold, O Lord, You are *my King and my God* (Ps 5:3). May every useful thing I learned when a child be used in Your service; may it be for Your service that I speak, write, read, and calculate.

For when I was learning vain things, You instructed me, and You forgave me the sins that I committed by taking delight in such vanities. In these studies I learned many useful words, but they could also have been learned from things that were not vain, and that surely is a safe way for children to tread.

CHAPTER 16 — Denunciation of Lascivious Fables

BUT woe to you, O torrent of human custom! Who shall impede your inexorable progress? How long will it be before you are dried up? How long will you carry down the children of Eve into that great and frightful sea that even they can hardly cross?

Have I not read of both a thundering and an adulterous Jove? And certainly he could not be both these things, but so it was feigned so that men might be permitted to imitate true adultery cloaked over by false thunder.

Now which of these cloaked masters will hearken with a sober ear to a man of the same profession, crying out and saying, "Homer feigned these things, ascribing human attributes to gods. Would that he had instead ascribed divine attributes to us!"

But it is more true to say that, though he made up these stories, he attributed divinity to wicked men, in order that such crimes might not be considered as crimes, and that whosoever committed them might not seem to have imitated wicked men, but heavenly deities.

And yet, O hellish river, the children of men are daily cast into you, paying dearly that they may learn these things. And there is a great outcry when some of this is done publicly in the forum, sanctioned by the laws that approve salaries in excess of reasonable earnings.

And you dash your waves upon your rocks and make a roar, saying, "Here words are learned, here eloquence is acquired; these are truly necessary to convert others to your point of view and express your thoughts clearly." Without this we never would have understood those elegant expressions, "the golden shower," and "lap," and "deceit," and the "temples of heaven," and the others written in the same place, unless Terence had introduced us to a wicked young man who took Jove as his model for lewdness.

All the while he looks at a picture on the wall that shows how Jupiter, once upon a time, sent into Danae's lap a golden shower by which to beguile the woman. Now observe how he arouses himself to lust, as if taught from heaven!

"And what god was it?" says he. "Was it not Jove who with his thunder shakes the high temples of heaven? And should I, a mere man, hesitate to do it? Indeed I have done it, and do so willingly."

It is entirely false to assert that these words are learned more easily as a result of this lewd scene; rather this vileness is more confidently perpetrated because of these words. I do not blame the words, which are, as it were, choice and precious vessels, but the wine of error, which in them is offered to us to drink by drunken masters.

And we were beaten, if we did not drink, nor could we appeal to any sober judge. But I, O my God, in whose presence I can now recall it without fear, learned these things willingly, and, poor wretch, I took delight in them, and for this reason was considered a boy of great promise.

CHAPTER 17 — Lament for Misusing Mental Powers

PERMIT me, O my God, to say something also of my mental powers, Your gift to me, and on what foolishness I wasted that gift. A task was set before me that I regarded as troublesome, for which I would either be rewarded with praise or punished with disgrace and a flogging.

I was asked to render the words of Juno raging and grieving that she "could not divert the Trojan prince from Italy." I had heard that Juno never uttered these words, but we were forced to go astray and to follow in the footsteps of these poetical fictions and to deliver something in prose similar to that which the poet had expressed in verse. And the one who received the greatest acclaim was the one who, speaking in accord with the dignity of the person represented, most perfectly expressed the relevant passions of rage and grief, clothing them in proper words and sentences.

What did it avail me, O God, my true Life, that my declamation was applauded far more than those of many of my schoolmates and other boys of the same age? Behold, are not all such things nothing but smoke and wind? And was there not some other pursuit in which my talents and my tongue might have been better exercised?

Your praises, O Lord, yes, Your praises, sung in Your Scriptures, might have held up the tender branch of my heart, preventing it from being dragged along the ground, merely one of so many empty trifles, a filthy prey to birds. For there are more ways than one of sacrificing to the fallen angels.

CHAPTER 18 — More Concern for the Rules of Grammar Than for God's Laws

WAS it any wonder that I was thus caught up in vain practices and strayed so far from You, O my God? Sometimes men were proposed for my imitation, but if they related some of their deeds, though not evil in themselves, with some barbarism or grammatical error, they were censured for it, causing them great shame. But if they recounted their acts of lust with proper and well-chosen words and in an extravagant and florid style, they were applauded and glorified.

You see these things, O Lord, and yet You hold Your peace, being *long suffering, and very merciful, and truthful* (Ps 86:15). But will You always hold Your peace?

Even now You continue to draw out from this bottomless pit the soul that seeks You and thirsts after Your delights, and the heart that says to You, *I have sought Your face; Your face, O Lord, I will still seek* (Ps 27:8).

However, by that time I had strayed far from Your countenance as a result of my shameful passions. For it is not by foot, nor by movement from place to place, that men go from You or return to You.

Did Your "younger" son (cf. Lk 15:12-32) procure himself horses or chariots or ships, or fly away with visible wings, or make his journey on foot when, living in a far country, he riotously wasted away what You gave him at his setting forth? You were a loving father indeed for giving him so much, but even more loving to him when he returned so poor to You! His going forth from You was the result of lustful passions, for these are dark, and therefore far from the light of Your countenance.

Behold, O Lord God, with patience, how carefully the sons of men observe with complete exactitude the laws of language received from their teachers, and yet neglect the eternal laws of their everlasting salvation received from You.

If someone who accepts or teaches the usual rules of pronunciation should, contrary to the laws of grammar, drop the "h" and say "uman being," he would displease his compatriots more than if, contrary to Your commandments, being himself a man, he should hate a man—as if the hatred that he bears to anyone was not a more pernicious enemy than the one whom he hates, or as if another by persecuting him could do him more harm than his own heart does by bearing malice. And certainly, no learning is more deeply imprinted in the soul than that law written in our conscience, *not to do to another what we would not be willing to suffer from another* (Tb 4:16; cf. Mt 7:12).

How hidden You are, O God, You Who who dwell on high in silence, Who alone are great. People remain blind to Your admonition against unlawful lust.

When a man seeks to be renowned for his eloquence and finds himself standing before a human judge and surrounded with a crowd of men, in attacking his enemy with implacable hatred, he takes extreme care lest by a slip of the tongue he chance to use an incorrect form for "from among men" (i.e., *inter hominibus* instead of *ex hominibus*). However, he takes no care lest by the fury of his mind he happens to destroy a man "from among men" *(ex hominibus)*.

CHAPTER 19 — The Faults of Childhood

THIS was the moral world upon whose threshold I lay, unhappy, as a boy. This was the stage of my life when I was more afraid of committing a grammatical error than, having committed one, of enjoying those who had made none.

O my God, to You I declare and confess these things for which I was complimented by those whom I thought it a virtue to please. I did not see the whirlpool of filthiness in which I then lay, *cast forth from Your eyes* (Ps 31:23).

What could be more filthy in Your eyes than my-self at that time? In addition I was the source of displeasure for others. I deceived my tutor, my teachers, and my parents with innumerable lies through my love of play, my desire to see frivolous shows, and my frenzy for imitating such follies depicted in those entertainments.

I was also guilty of stealing from my parents' cellar and from their table, either to satisfy my gluttony or to have things to give to other boys, who, in exchange for them, sold me their playthings, thus giving delight to them no less than to myself. In playing games I also often sought to win by cheating, for I myself was miserably overcome by the vain desire to excel.

What was there that I was more unwilling to suffer, and which I more sharply reproved when I discovered it in others, than that which I did to others? And when I was caught doing something and criticized for it, I would rather quarrel than yield.

Is that the innocence of childhood? It is not, O Lord, and for this I implore Your mercy, O my God. For these same practices are simply transferred from our first subjection to tutors and teachers, and our playing with nuts and balls and sparrows, to our subjection afterward to magistrates and prefects, and gaining gold and manors and slaves.

Thus our childhood toys, as we grow older, pass into greater toys, just as our rods are replaced by greater punishments. It was, therefore, the stature of children that You, our King, commended as a symbol of humility, when You said, *Of such is the Kingdom of Heaven* (Mt 19:14).

CHAPTER 20 — Thanksgiving for God's Gifts

AND yet, O Lord, thanks be to You, the most excellent and best Creator and Ruler of the universe, our God, even if You had destined me only for childhood. For even then I existed, blessed with life and feeling, and I cared for the well-being of my person which was a faint shadow of that mysterious Unity from which I derived my origin.

I watched over the integrity of my outer senses with an interior sense. Even in little things, and in the thoughts about little things, I was delighted with truth. I was unwilling to be deceived; I had a powerful memory and facility of speech, and I delighted in friendship. I fled from pain, meanness, and ignorance. What was there in such a living being that was not wonderful and praiseworthy?

But all these things are the gifts of my God. It was not I who gave them to myself. They are good, and they comprise my being. Therefore, He Who made me is good, and He is my God.

In God I rejoice for all those good things that made up my boyhood. For my sin was in this, that not in Him but in His creatures—myself and others—I sought pleasures, honors, and truths, and so fell into sorrows, confusion, and errors.

Thanks be to You, my God, my sweet delight, my glory, and all my trust! Thanks be to You for Your gifts. But be pleased to keep them for me, for thus will You keep me. And the things You have given me will grow and be perfected, and I shall be with You because my very existence is Your gift.

Book 2—Augustine at Sixteen

Augustine experiences further ills of idleness, bad companions and lustful pleasures during his sixteenth year, and with his companions commits theft.

CHAPTER 1 —Pursuit of Creatures

I WILL now relate the wickedness of my former life and the carnal corruptions of my soul. I do this not because I love them, but so that I may love You, my God. I do this for the love of Your love, reviewing my most wicked ways in the bitterness of my remembrance so that You may become sweet to me, You Who are a sweetness without deceit, a sweetness happy and secure, gathering me from my dissipation in which I was rent piecemeal, while I departed from You, the one Good, lost in the pursuit of many creatures.

For there was a time in my youth when I burned with fire to experience base pleasures, and I ventured to spread and branch out into various forbidden loves. As a result the beauty of my soul was consumed, and I became putrefied in Your sight, desiring only to please myself and to be pleasing to the eyes of men.

CHAPTER 2 — Unruly Lusts

A ND what was it that delighted me but to love and to be loved? But in this love the due measure was not observed between mind and mind, as far as the lightsome bounds of friendship go. Rather, black vapors were exhaled from the muddy concupiscence of the flesh and from the bubblings of puberty; these so overclouded and darkened my heart that I was not able to distinguish the serenity of love from the fog of lust. Both boiled together within me, sweeping my unsettled youth down the cliffs of unlawful desires and plunging me into the whirlpool of evil actions.

Your wrath had grown strong against me but I did not realize it. I had been deafened with the noise of the chains of my mortality, the punishment caused by the pride of my soul. I wandered still farther from You, and You left me alone. I was tossed hither and yon, consumed in my fornications, aimlessly driven by my burning lust.

Yet You were silent, O my Joy, Whom I did not find for so long. You were silent then, and I strayed still farther from You, sowing more and more barren seeds of sorrows, with a proud baseness and a restless weariness.

Oh who was there to lessen my misery and render useful the fleeting beauties of these evil lusts, and to set bounds to their allurements, so that the tides of my youth might have broken themselves upon the shore of lawful marriage? And if these tides could not otherwise be calmed, could I not have been made content at least with the end of bringing children into the world, as Your Law prescribes, O Lord?

In this way, You fashion the offspring of our mortality, and are able with a gentle hand to blunt the sharpness of these thorns that are foreign to Your Paradise. For Your omnipotence is not far from us, even when we are far from You.

Or, again, I myself might have more vigilantly heeded the voice from the clouds sounding to me from above, *Such will have tribulation of the flesh.*

But I spare you that (1 Cor 7:28). And, *It is good for a man not to touch a woman* (1 Cor 7:1). And again, *He who is unmarried is concerned about the things of the Lord, how he may please God, whereas he who is married is concerned about the things of the world, how he may please his wife* (1 Cor 7:32-33). I might therefore have listened to these words with greater attention, and thus, in making myself a *eunuch for the Kingdom of Heaven* (Mt 19:12), looked more joyfully for Your embraces.

But, wretch that I was, I broke away, following the violent course of my own passions. In leaving You, I passed all the bounds set by Your laws. However, I did not escape Your scourges. What mortal can?

For You were always near me, mercifully severe, and so sprinkling with bitterness all my unlawful pleasures, that I might seek elsewhere pleasures without bitterness, and that where I could find such delight, I might find only You. For You turn sorrow into a lesson for us (cf. Ps 94:20), so that You may heal and kill us (cf. Dt 32:39) lest we be separated from You.

Where was I, and how far was I banished from the delight of Your house, in that sixteenth year of the age of my flesh, when the fury of lust, licensed by the shameless practice of men, but ever prohibited by Your holy laws, presented the scepter to me and I completely embraced it?

In the meantime, my friends took no care to prevent my ruin by encouraging me to enter into lawful marriage. Their only care was that I should learn to make fine speeches and become a persuasive orator.

CHAPTER 3 — An Idle Year

MY studies were interrupted in that year. I had been called home from Madaura, the neighboring city to which I had been sent to study grammar and rhetoric. In the meantime the expenses for a further journey to Carthage were being raised, and that more by the determination than by the financial situation of my father, for he was a freedman of Tagaste with modest resources.

To whom am I relating these things? Not to You, O my God, but, in Your presence, to my own kind—to the human race, however small be the portion that shall ever chance upon these writings of mine. And to what purpose? That both I and they who read this may reflect from what profound *depths* we must *cry to You* (Ps 130:1). And what is more accessible to Your ears than a confessing heart and a life lived by faith?

Who did not at that time highly commend my father for laying out in my behalf, even beyond the strength of his means, what was necessary for me to carry on my studies at that great distance from home? Many citizens, far wealthier than he, did no such thing for their children. But in the meantime this same father had not the slightest concern about how I was maturing in Your eyes or whether I was chaste, provided that I was rich in eloquence, even though rather poor in regard to following Your Law, O God, Who are the one true and good Lord of Your field, my heart.

When, at sixteen years of age, I began to live idly at home with my parents since monetary difficulties forced me to leave school for a time, the briars of lust grew over my head, and there was no hand to root them out. Indeed, when my father saw me in the public baths now clearly growing toward manhood and imbued with a restless youthfulness, as if now he could finally look forward to grandchildren, he related the news to my mother with joy. He rejoiced with the drunkenness with which this world has forgotten its Creator and loves the creature instead of You, inebriated by the invisible wine of a will perverted and inclined to baseness.

However, in my mother's breast You had already begun to erect Your temple, laying there the foundation of Your holy habitation. At that time my father was only a catechumen, and that but recently. Upon hearing his news, she was seized with fear and trembling; she was concerned for me, because I was not yet baptized, and she feared that I might stray along those crooked ways where those walk who *turn their back to You rather than their face* (Jer 2:27).

Dare I say that You were silent, O my God, when it was I who was wandering still farther from You? But were You really silent? Whose but Yours were those words which, by means of my mother, Your faithful servant, You sang in my ears? Yet none of them so inspired my heart that I acted upon them.

It was my mother's wish—and she so privately admonished me with great solicitude—to keep myself pure with women, and above all to never defile anyone's wife. All this seemed to me to be merely a woman's admonition, which I should be ashamed to obey. But they were Your admonitions, and I knew it not; and I supposed You to be silent while she spoke, whereas through her You did speak to me. In her You were despised by me, by me her son, *the son of Your handmaid* (Ps 116:16), Your servant.

But I did not know this, and I rushed ahead with so much blindness that in the presence of my companions I was ashamed of being less filthy than they were. And when I heard them bragging of their wicked actions and boasting how much more beastly they were, I was determined to emulate their life, not merely for the pleasure of it, but in order that I might be praised for it.

What is more worthy of reproach than vice? Yet I became involved in ever greater depravity in order to avoid reproach.

But when I was not praised for doing what I considered equal to the most wicked deeds, I pretended to have done what I had not done, fearing that others might consider me more contemptible because I was more innocent, or more vile because I was more chaste.

Behold with what companions I traversed the streets of Babylon and how I wallowed in its mire, as if it were composed of spices and precious perfumes. And that I might cling more tenaciously to its very center, the invisible enemy trod me underfoot and seduced me, because I was willing to be seduced.

For even the mother of my flesh, who had *fled from the heart of Babylon* (Jer 51:6), though she continued to live in its outskirts, did not act on what she had heard about me from her husband with the same care that she had advised me about chastity. She saw that I was already afflicted with a disease that would become dangerous later on, but she did not insist that I restrict such urges to married life if they could not otherwise be overcome.

Her concern in this regard was that my hopes would be hindered by the impediment of a wife—

not those hopes of the world to come that my mother had in You, but the hopes of my proficiency in learning, upon which both my parents were too much intent: my father, because he had scarcely any thought of You and nothing but empty and vain hopes for me, and my mother, because she supposed that the usual studies would be no hindrance, but actually some help in my journey to You.

Thus I conjecture, recollecting as well as I can, the disposition of my parents. Therefore the reins were loosened to allow me to spend my time in play, beyond what a due severity would allow, which led to my being more dissolute in various inclinations. And in all of this, O my God, there were dark clouds preventing me from realizing the serenity of Your truth, *and my iniquity had come forth, as it were, from fatness.* (Ps 73:7)

CHAPTER 4 — A Senseless Theft

YOUR Law, O Lord, punishes theft, a Law written in the hearts of men, which even iniquity itself cannot blot out. For what thief is willing to have another steal from him? Even a thief who is rich will not forgive another stealing from him through want.

Yet I had a mind to commit theft, and I committed it, not for want or need, but because I loathed to be honest and longed to sin. I stole that of which I had plenty, and much better. Nor was I fond of enjoying the things that I stole, but only fond of the theft and the sin.

There was a pear tree near our vineyard, loaded with fruit, which was tempting for neither its beauty nor its taste. To shake off and carry away the fruit of this tree, some of us wicked youths went late at night, having, according to a vicious custom, prolonged our playing in the streets. And then we carried away great loads, not for eating, but to cast the pears to the hogs, after tasting just a few of them, the only pleasure derived being that we desired to do what we were not allowed to do.

Behold my heart, O my God, behold my heart, upon which You have had pity when it was in the depths of the bottomless pit. Behold, let my heart now tell You what it was I then sought, that I should be wicked without cause, and I had nothing to tempt me to evil but evil itself.

It was foul and I loved it; I loved to flirt with death. I also loved to be culpable—not the thing in which I was culpable, but the very culpability itself was what I loved. My soul was filthy, falling from Your intense love to utter ruin, as I craved not something disgraceful, but disgrace itself!

CHAPTER 5 — Reasons for Sin

THERE is an attractiveness in beautiful objects of gold, silver, and other minerals, and bodily touch affords pleasure that is very enjoyable. And in like manner the other senses find their suitable pleasures in their respective corporeal objects. Worldly honors and the power of commanding and excelling have the power to attract and are also the source of the desire for revenge.

However, in our pursuit of all these goals, we must never depart from You, O Lord, nor turn aside from Your Law. The life also that we live here has its own allurements by reason of a certain kind of beauty it possesses and the proportion that it has to all the rest of beautiful things here below. Likewise the friendship of men offers very sweet rewards by bringing many minds into unity.

In regard to all these and similar attractions, sin is committed when, by an excessive inclination to them which rank lowest among Your gifts, men forsake the best and highest, You, O Lord our God, and Your Truth, and Your Law. For these lowest things have indeed their delights, but not like my God Who made all things, *because in Him shall the just rejoice, and He is the delight of the upright of heart* (Ps 64:11).

Therefore, when we ask why any crime was committed, it is usually believed that there might have been a desire of acquiring some of these lowliest of goods, or a fear of losing them. For they are fair and beautiful, although in comparison with those higher goods and beatific joys, they are mean and contemptible.

A man has murdered another. Why? He was in love with this man's wife or his estate, or he did it to rob him to support his own lifestyle, or he was afraid of suffering a similar fate from him, or he had been injured and sought revenge. Would he commit murder without a reason, but merely for the sake of the thrill of the act of murder itself? Who would believe this?

An author has written in regard to an evil and exceedingly cruel man that he gratuitously chose to be wicked and cruel, attributing as his reason that he did not wish his hand or his will to become weak for lack of exercise. And what was his ulterior motive? That once he had taken control of the city through his wickedness, he might be enabled to obtain honors, riches, and power, and to be delivered from the fear of the laws, and from the difficulties he labored under through an impoverished estate, and from a guilty conscience. Therefore, even this man, Catiline, was not in love with his crimes, but with something else, for the sake of which he committed them.

CHAPTER 6 — The Good Sought in Sin

WHAT was it then that in my wretched folly I loved in you, O my theft, O wicked nocturnal exploit of my sixteenth year? You were not beautiful, since you were nothing but an act of theft. Or are you anything at all, that I should thus speak to you?

Those pears indeed that we stole were beautiful because they were the work of Your hands, O most beautiful of all beings, Creator of all, my good God, my sovereign good, and my true good. They were beautiful, but it was not after them that my poor soul lusted, for I had many better pears at home.

I took these particular pears only for the sake of stealing, for after I had taken them, my appetite being satisfied, I flung them away, enjoying nothing other than my iniquity in which I took such delight. For if any of that fruit entered into my mouth, nothing made it agreeable to me but the sin.

But now, O Lord my God, I am seeking to discover what it was that delighted me in that theft. And behold, I can find no beauty in it. I do not mean such beauty as is found in justice and prudence, or in the mind of man and his memory and senses and earthly life, nor such as is found in the stars, which are glorious and beautiful in their orbits, or in the earth and sea, full of embryonic life, generation following decay, nor even the flawed and shadowy beauty found in deceptive vices.

For pride causes us to feel superior, whereas You alone are the most high God above all things. What does ambition seek but honors and glory, whereas You alone are to be honored above all, and eternally glorious? The cruelty of the mighty has fear as its goal, but who is to be feared but God alone, and from His power what can be wrested or withdrawn, and when or where, or how, or by whom?

The caresses of the lascivious seek to be seen as indicative of love, whereas nothing has such charm as Your love, nor is anything so wholesomely loved as Your truth that infinitely exceeds all beauty and brightness. And curiosity pretends to indicate a desire for knowledge, whereas it is You Who most perfectly know all things.

Even ignorance itself and folly are often disguised as simplicity and innocence, but nothing can be found more truly simple than Yourself, and what is more innocent than You, since it is their own works that harm the wicked? Sloth also apparently has rest as its goal, but what sure rest can there be except in the Lord?

A life of luxury desires to be called satiety and abundance, but it is You who are the fullness and inexhaustible store of incorruptible sweetness. Prodigality hides itself under the guise of liberality, but the most exceedingly liberal bestower of all good things is no other than Yourself.

Avarice seeks to possess many things, yet You possess all things. Envy quarrels for the sake of excelling, but what is more excellent than You? Anger seeks revenge, and who executes vengeance as justly as You? Fear abhors what comes on strangely and suddenly to threaten the things that are loved, but nothing sudden or unusual can happen to You, and no one can take from You what You love. Or where is there any firm sense of security except with You?

Sadness pines away over the loss of delightful and desirable things, because it would not wish to have anything taken away, but nothing can be taken away from You.

Thus the soul prostitutes itself when it turns away from You and seeks outside of You pure and clean things that it cannot find except by returning to You. In a rather perverse way, all imitate You who depart far from You and rebel against You. Yet, even in this perverse way of imitating You, they show that You are the Creator of all nature, and therefore that there is no place where they can completely depart from You.

What was it then that I loved in that theft? Or in what way did I therein, though viciously and perversely, imitate my Lord? Was it that I took delight in breaking Your Law, at least through deceit, since I could not do so by power, and thus, being indeed a slave, sought to pretend a specious sort of liberty in doing with impunity, by a dark parody of omnipotence, that which was forbidden?

Behold, O Lord, Your slave as he flew from You and embraced a shadow. O corruption! O monster of life and depth of death! Was it possible that I loved that which was unlawful only because it was unlawful?

CHAPTER 7— Gratitude for Pardon of Sins

*W*HAT *shall I render to the Lord?* (Ps 116:12).
For my memory now recalls these things and
yet my soul is not in fear about them. May I love
You, O Lord, and give You thanks, and confess to
Your Name, because You have forgiven me such
great sins and wicked actions. It is owing to Your
grace and to Your mercy that You have dissolved
like ice the sins that I committed. I attribute also to
Your grace whatever other sins I have not committed. For what evil was there that I, who loved an
evil deed for its own sake, was not capable of doing?
And I confess that all my sins have been forgiven
me, both the evils I committed by my own will and
those that by Your grace I did not commit.

What man is there who, weighing his own weakness, dares to attribute his chastity or his innocence
to his own strength, and thus will love You less, as if
he owed less to Your mercy, by which You remit the
sins of those who seek You? Anyone who, having
been called by You, has heeded Your voice and has
avoided the things that he reads here in my record
and the confession of my guilt, let him not scorn
me. For I, being sick, received my cure from that
same Physician Who preserved that person from
being sick, or rather from being so sick. And, therefore, let him love You as much, and yes, even more,
because by that same hand by which he sees me
freed from such grievous sins, he sees himself having
been preserved from being involved in evils as great.

CHAPTER 8 — Partners in Crime

*W*HAT *fruit had I then, a wretched soul, in those
things of which I,* remembering them, *am now*

ashamed (Rom 6:21), especially in that theft, in which I loved the theft itself and nothing else? The theft itself was relatively insignificant, and therefore the more wretched was I, who loved it. And yet if I had been alone I would not have done it, for such I remember was my disposition at that time—if I had been alone I would certainly not have done it. Therefore, I dearly loved the company of those with whom I did it, and so I loved something besides the theft, though this something still amounts to nothing.

What in reality does all this mean? Who shall here teach me but the One Who enlightens my heart and discerns its shadows? What is this that comes now into my mind to search out and examine and consider? For if I had loved the pears that I stole, and only desired to enjoy them, I might, if this had been enough, have committed the sin by myself, and thus accomplished my goal of pleasure without inflaming the itch of my inordinate desire for the flattery of others. But since I had no delight in the fruit, my joy resulted from having the company of partners in my sin.

CHAPTER 9 — Dangerous Friendships

WHAT then was this feeling? Indeed, it was exceedingly base, and wretched was I who had it. But yet what was it? *Who can understand his sins?* (Ps 19:13). We laughed, as if our hearts were tickled by the fact that we were fooling those who little suspected that we were doing any such thing and would have been strongly opposed to it. Why then did I take delight in not doing it alone? Was it because no one easily laughs by himself?

However, laughter sometimes overcomes persons when they are all alone and something very ridiculous presents itself to their senses or imagination. But this I would never have done alone—I certainly would not.

Behold, the remembrance of my soul is before You, O my God. I would not have committed that theft alone, for it was not what I stole that delighted me, but the simple act of stealing, and in this I would not have found delight if I had done it alone.

O dangerous friendship! O seduction of the mind and unaccountable greediness for doing mischief simply in the spirit of fun and wantonness, in the desire for another's loss without any gain to myself or to satisfy a passion for revenge! Someone cries, "Let's go, let's do it," and we are ashamed of not being shameless.

CHAPTER 10 — Longing for God

WHO can untie this most tortuous and intricate mass of knots? It is foul; I refuse to look at it; I will turn away my eyes.

I want You, O Justice and Innocence, ever fair and beautiful to pure eyes and of insatiable satisfaction. With You is true rest and life undisturbed. He who enters into You *enters into the joy of his Master* (Mt 25:21), and he shall not fear, but shall be supremely joyous in his possession of the Supreme Good.

I had fallen away from You, O my God, and in my youth I strayed too far from Your loving care, and so became to myself a land of misery and want.

Book 3—Three Years at Carthage

Augustine goes to Carthage and remains there until his nineteenth year. After completing his course of studies, he is caught in the snare of licentious love. He professes a distaste for Scripture and is led astray by the Manichean heresy. His mother, Monica, is distraught and prays to God for his conversion. She experiences a vision from God.

CHAPTER 1 — Journey to Carthage

I CAME to Carthage, where a cauldron of insidious loves was roaring on every side of me. I was not yet in love, but I loved to be in love, and out of a more secret want I hated myself for wanting less. In love with loving, I sought for something to love, and I hated safety and a way without snares, because there was a famine within me for want of that interior food, which is no other than Yourself, O my God.

That famine did not cause a hunger in me, but I was without any appetite for incorruptible nourishment—not because I was full, but because the more empty I was, the more I loathed this kind of food. And for that reason my soul was sick and, being full of ulcers, broke out, miserably eager to be scratched by the touch of sensible things. Yet if such things had no soul, they would not be loved. For to love and to be loved was more sweet to me if I could enjoy the body of the person who loved me.

Thus I defiled the spring of friendship with the filth of concupiscence, and darkened its sparkling waters with clouds of a hellish lust. And yet, filthy and nasty as I was, with my excessive vanity I pretended to be elegant and well-bred. And I fell headlong into love, whose prisoner I desired to be.

O my God, my Mercy (Ps 59:18), with how much gall did You sprinkle those sweets that You allowed me, and how good You were to do so. For I was loved, and I secretly attained love's joyous bond. However, my joy was being fettered with those oppressing chains, in which I was to be scourged with the red-hot iron rods of jealousy and suspicion and fears and angers and quarrels.

CHAPTER 2 — Influence of the Theater

I WAS also much carried away with theatrical productions, which often mirrored my miseries and furnished fuel for my fire.

Why does a man take comfort in grieving over sad and tragic things that he himself would not be willing to suffer? And yet he is willing to suffer grief as a spectator, and this very grief affords him pleasure. What is this but a strange madness? For the less free a man is from such passions, the more is he affected by these things. However when a man suffers such things himself, it is usually called misery, but when he is grieved at others suffering them, it is styled pity.

But what kind of pity is that which is found in fictitious and theatrical representations? Here the spectator is not encouraged to aid a person in distress, but simply invited to grieve, and the more he is made to grieve, the more he applauds the author of these productions.

And if these calamities of men, either historically based or simply fictitious, are so acted as not to move the spectator to sadness, he leaves discontented and criticizes the performance; however, if he is moved to grief, he remains attentive and rejoices.

Do we then love tears and sorrows? Surely everyone rather desires joy. Or is it that while no man likes to be miserable, he is nevertheless willing to be compassionate? And as compassion cannot exist without sorrow, are sorrows then loved for this cause alone? And this proceeds from that vein of friendship.

But where does this go? Where does it flow? Why does it fall in a torrent of boiling pitch, into vast whirlpools of filthy lusts? Into these it is deliberately changed, and cast down from its heavenly serenity into something corrupt. Must compassion then be condemned? By no means. Sorrow then may sometimes be loved.

But beware of uncleanness, O my soul, under the protection of my God, *the God of our fathers, worthy to be praised and exalted above all forever* (Dn 3:52). Beware of uncleanness, O my soul, for I am not now without compassion. But then in the theaters I rejoiced together with lovers when they took sinful delight in each other, though it was only pretended in the play, and when they lost one another, I was grieved, as it were, out of pity.

In both emotions I took delight. But now I pity whoever rejoices in his own wickedness, rather than imagine that he will undergo a hardship because he is deprived of a pernicious pleasure and has lost that wretched happiness. This pity of mine is certainly a more authentic compassion, but here grief does not cause delight. For though he who grieves at another's misery is to be commended for his charitable act, yet, if he were truly merciful, he would prefer that there be no occasion for his grief. For unless you suppose that well-wishing can be ill-wishing (which indeed it cannot be), you cannot suppose that he who truly and sincerely pities another wants him to be miserable so that he may have compassion for him.

Some grief then is to be approved, but none ought to be loved. Hence You, O Lord God, Who love souls, are far more pure and incorruptible in Your mercy than we, because no grief can wound You. *And for such offices, who is qualified?* (2 Cor 2:16).

But I, a poor wretch, then loved to grieve, and sought for something to grieve at. Another man's disaster, one that was false and merely impersonated upon the stage, delighted me more and far more strongly allured me, which caused me more to shed tears. But was it any wonder that, as an unhappy sheep who had strayed from Your flock and was impatient with Your discipline, I became infected with hideous sores?

Hence my love of sorrow was not such as might sink deep into my soul, for I did not love to suffer such things myself that I was pleased to see enacted, but only those which, being heard and pretended, might, as it were, lightly scratch the surface. Nevertheless, as occurs from the scratching of infected fingernails, there followed an inflamed swelling and pus and filthy corruption. Such was my life, but could it be called life, O my God?

CHAPTER 3 — Manifold Wickedness

AND yet, Your mercy, ever faithful to me from afar, was now hovering over me. Iniquities in the meantime consumed me, as I pursued a sacrilegious curiosity for knowledge that led me, in forsaking You, to the treacherous depths below and the deceitful service of devils. To them I offered my wicked deeds in sacrifice, and as a result I was scourged by You.

I also dared during the celebration of Your solemnities, within the walls of Your church, to give way to concupiscence and even there to arrange an affair that could lead to the procuring of the fruits of death. For this You scourged me with grievous punishments, but nothing that was proportionate to my crime, O my exceedingly great Mercy, *my God, my Refuge* (Ps 46:1) from the terribly wicked companions among whom I wandered about with an outstretched neck, a runaway from You, loving my own ways and not Yours, in love with a vagabond freedom.

My studies, moreover, which were called honorable, were supposed to lead me to the practice of law, where I would excel and be praised according to my power to deceive people by my eloquence. So great is the blindness of men that they even glory in their blindness. And by this time I was the most renowned student in the school of rhetoric, and I was proudly joyful and swollen with self-conceit.

However, O Lord, as You well know, I was far more reserved and remote from the ways of those who are called "subverters." This cruel and diabolical name is, as it were, the badge of their gallantry. Among these I lived with a shameless shame, because I was not like them. I conversed with them, and was delighted sometimes with their friendship. However, I always abhorred their deeds, that is, their subvertings, as they call them, by which they shamelessly taunted bashful strangers, annoying them and making sport of them without cause, only to gratify their own malicious mirth.

Nothing surely resembles more the actions of devils than this way of acting. How justly, therefore, are they called "subverters." For they themselves are first subverted and wholly perverted by demons deriding and seducing them in this very fashion in which they themselves delight to mock and mislead others.

CHAPTER 4 — Cicero's Good Influence

IT WAS in such surroundings that I, in my youthful weakness, studied the texts on eloquence. I desired to surpass all others, out of a damnable and selfish motive of reaping the pleasures of human vanity.

Following the usual course of studies, I had now come upon a book of Cicero, whose language almost all admire, although not so his heart. This book contains his exhortation to philosophy, and is called *Hortensius*.

The reading of this book changed my disposition, for it turned my prayers to You, O Lord, and quite altered my inclinations and desires. All my vain hopes immediately appeared empty, and my heart longed with incredible ardor for the immortality of wisdom. I had begun to arise so that I might return to You.

I did not study that book to learn how to sharpen my tongue (a facility I seemed to be purchasing with my mother's income, for I was now nineteen years old, and my father had died two years before). It was not, as I say, to sharpen my tongue that I had recourse to that book, nor was it the style that had affected me, but the things that were said by the author.

How I was all afire, O my God, how I burned with a desire to fly up from these earthly things to You. But I did not know what You would do with me. For *with You is wisdom* (Jb 12:12). Now the love of wisdom in Greek is called philosophy and it was with such a desire that these writings inflamed me. Some there are who seduce by philosophy, disguising and coloring their errors with this great, pleasing, and honorable name: almost all who were such, in the author's time or before, are set down and described in that book.

There also is expressed that salutary admonition of Your Spirit, which was spoken through Your good and pious servant: *See to it that no one deceives you by philosophy and vain deceit, according to human traditions, according to the elements of the world and not according to Christ. For in Him dwells all the fullness of the Godhead bodily* (Col 2:8-9).

And I, at that time (for You know, O Light of my heart, that as yet I knew nothing of these words of the Apostle), was for this one reason so particularly pleased with that exhortation of Cicero that it strongly excited and enkindled and inflamed me, not to follow this or that particular sect, but to love, and seek, and pursue, and lay hold of and embrace wisdom itself, whatever it was.

In this intensely great ardor, only one thing displeased me—that I found not there the name of Christ. For this name according to Your mercy, O Lord, this name of my Savior, Your Son, my tender heart had piously imbibed with my mother's milk, and deeply retained. And whatsoever was without this name, no matter how learned or polished or truthful it might be, could not win me over completely.

CHAPTER 5 — Introduction to Holy Scripture

THEREFORE, I determined to turn my attention to the Holy Scriptures to see what they were. And behold, I encountered something in them not understood by the proud, nor made clear to children—lowly in its appearance, exalted in its sense and veiled with mysteries.

Nor was I someone who could enter into its thought or bend down my neck to its humble pace. For at the time when I first looked upon Holy Scripture, I did not have the thoughts that I now express. To me at that stage it then seemed unworthy to be compared to Ciceronian stateliness.

My swollen pride was unable to endure its humble style, nor could my sharpest wit penetrate into its depths. Yet, it contained a wealth of wisdom that would grow in little ones. But I disdained to be a little one, and, being puffed up with pride, appeared great to my own eyes.

CHAPTER 6 — Attracted by the Manichees

AND thus I fell in with men called Manichees who were bloated with pride, exceedingly carnal, and great talkers. In their mouths were the snares of Satan and a birdlime made up of a mixture of the syllables of Your name, and that of our Lord Jesus Christ, and of the Paraclete, the Holy Spirit, our Comforter. All these names were always in their mouths, but only as far as the sound and the noise of the tongue, their hearts being void of all that is true.

They repeatedly said to me, "Truth, truth," and many there were who repeated this to me, but the truth was nowhere in them. Indeed, they spoke false things, not only of You, Who are the Truth indeed, but also of these *elements of this world, Your creatures* (Col 2:20), concerning which the philosophers have spoken true things. Nevertheless, I ought to cease speaking of them for love of You, O my Father, supremely good, the Beauty of all things beautiful.

O Truth! O Truth! How deeply even then did my innermost soul sigh after You when, often and diversely and in many and large volumes, they spoke of You to me in empty words! And such were the dishes in which they served up to me, who hungered after You, the sun and moon, Your beautiful works indeed, but simply Your works and not Yourself. Nor are they Your highest works. For Your spiritual works have precedence over these material ones, though shining and celestial.

But I hungered and thirsted not for these higher works but for Yourself, O Truth, *with Whom there is no change, nor shadow of alteration* (Jas 1:17). Yet in those dishes they still presented me glittering fantasies. These falsehoods that through the eyes delude the mind are less worthy of love than the sun that at least is real to our eyes.

And yet, taking their words to reveal You, I fed upon them, though with no great appetite, for I experienced there no relish of You as You are in Yourself. These empty fictions revealed nothing of You, nor was I nourished by them, but was rather exhausted by experiencing them. Eating in a dream seems like eating when awake, but the person who is asleep is not strengthened by the food, for it is only a dream.

But these fictions had no resemblance at all to You, as You have now declared to me; for they were only corporeal phantoms, false bodies, better than which are these true bodies, whether heavenly or earthly, that we discern with our bodily sight. The sight of these is common to us with beasts and birds, and being thus seen they are more certain than when they are only represented to our imagination.

And again, we have a more certain imagination of them than when through them we picture others greater and infinite, which indeed have no being at all. Such were those empty things that I then fed on and yet was not nourished at all.

But You, O my Love, for whom I long, so that I may become strong, are neither those bodies that we see, though they be in the heavens, nor those that we do not see elsewhere. You have made them all, yet You do not count them among Your mightiest works.

How remote then are You from those fantasies of mine, those imaginings of bodies that have no being. And more certain than these fantasies are the representations of bodies that are real, and the bodies themselves are more certain than their representations, and yet You are not these bodies. Neither are You the soul, which is the life of bodies. And better and more certain is the life of bodies than the bodies. But You are the life of souls, the life of lives, having life in Yourself, and You are never changed, O Life of my soul.

Where were You then and how far distant from me? I was straying far from You, prevented from eating the very husks I fed to swine. Far better were the fables of the grammarians and poets than those snares.

For verses and poems and Medea in flight are certainly more to the purpose than the five elements variously colored to suit the five dens of darkness, which have no being at all and yet can slay those who believe them. I can convert verses and poems into real food for the mind. As for Medea's flying, I neither sang it to be believed nor believed it when I heard it sung; but those other things I did believe.

Alas! Alas! By what steps *was I led down into the abode of the dead* (Ps 31:18), laboring and restless in my quest of truth, while I sought You, O my God (for to You I now confess, Who did pity me even though I had not confessed You).

I sought You, not according to the understanding of the mind, in which You were pleased that I should surpass beasts, but according to the sense of the flesh. But You were more inward to me than my inward self, and higher than what was highest in me.

I blundered upon that shameless woman of the riddle of Solomon who was devoid of wisdom. She sat upon a stool at the door and called out to me, saying, "Come, eat willingly *the hidden bread,* and drink of the *sweet stolen water*" (Prv 9:17). She was able to seduce me because she found me dwelling externally through my carnal eyes, and ruminating within myself upon such things as I had devoured through them.

CHAPTER 7 — Disturbing Questions

FOR what lies beyond this and truly is I did not know. I was easily moved, by sharp wit, to assent to those foolish deceivers, who were asking me such questions as: "Whence is evil? Does God have bodily shape and hair and nails? Are they to be accounted just men who had many wives at once, and who killed men, and offered up living creatures in sacrifice?"

In my ignorance, I was disturbed by these questions, and in going away from truth, I thought I was going toward it, for I did not then know that evil is nothing but the privation of good, and that it is in reality nothing at all. For how could I have discerned this, when my eyes could only discern other bodies and my mind could only confront phantasms?

Again, I did not know that *God is a spirit* (Jn 4:24), without length and breadth of limbs, that he has no corporeal bulk. For all such bulk is less in a part than in the whole, and though you suppose it to be infinite, it is still less in some portion of it contained within a certain space than its infinitude. And so it is not wholly everywhere as the Spirit is, as God is. And I was altogether ignorant of what there was in us, according to which we were like God, and how we were rightly said in the Scriptures to be *made after the image of God* (Gn 1:27).

And I did not know true interior righteousness, which judges not by custom, but by the most righteous Law of an omnipotent God. By that Law were fashioned the customs of countries and times that were suitable for those places and periods, although the Law itself is still the same in all places and in all times. Thus were Abraham and Isaac and Jacob and Moses and David deemed to be just as well as all those others who have been praised by the mouth of God.

However, these same individuals have been considered ungodly by ignorant men who judge *according to human standards* (1 Cor 4:3) and measure all the ways of mankind by the short span of their own custom. They are like one who, being unacquainted with armor and not knowing for what part each piece was designed, would wish to cover his head with a greave and his feet with a helmet, and then complain that they did not fit; or like one who, on a day when business is forbidden in the afternoon, complains because he is not then allowed to sell although it was permitted in the morning; or like one who, seeing in any house some servant handling an object that perhaps another servant is not allowed to touch or something done behind the stable that is not permitted in the dining room, then takes offense that in one dwelling and the same family the same thing should not be allowed to everyone in every place.

Such are they who are angry when they hear that some things in that age were lawful to just men, which are not now allowed, and that God commanded one thing to them, another thing to us, for reasons suitable to the times, while both the one and the other were subject to the same justice. Yet they can clearly understand that in one and the same man, and on one day, and in one family, different things are fitting for different members, and that what is allowed in one hour is not allowed in another, and that what is permitted, or even commanded, to be done in one place is justly forbidden and punished if done in another.

Does that mean that justice varies and evolves? No, but the times over which this justice is in force are not constant, for times change. And men, whose life is short upon earth—being unable by their limited intelligence to connect and compare the causes of past ages and of other nations, of which they have no experience, to those with which they are familiar, whereas they can easily discern in one body or day or house what is suitable for each part, hour, room, or person—are offended in the one case, and well satisfied in the other.

At that time, I did not know these things, and I took no notice of them. On every side they were plainly visible to my eyes, and I did not see them. I composed verses and I was not allowed to place every foot wheresoever I wished, but rather various feet in different meters, and in any one verse not the same foot could be situated in every place; yet the art itself of poetry was not therefore different in different places, but at one and the same time it encompassed all these varieties.

And I did not see that justice, which good and holy men obeyed, did far more excellently and sublimely contain at one and the same time all those things that God commanded, and in itself never varied, though in various times it decreed and commanded what was proper to each time, and not all things at once. Hence, blind as I was, I censured those holy patriarchs, not only for using the present things as God had commanded and inspired them to do, but also for predicting things to come, according as God had revealed.

CHAPTER 8 — Natural Law and Positive Law

COULD it be wrong at any time or in any place *to love God with your whole heart, with your whole soul, and with your whole mind,* and *to love your neighbor as yourself* (Mt 22:37)? Clearly not! Therefore, those vicious actions that are against nature are in all places and at all times to be detested and punished, as were those of the Sodomites. And if all nations should commit such crimes, they would incur the same criminal guilt by God's Law, which has not made men to abuse one another in that manner. For that friendship which we ought to have with God is violated when that nature, of which he is the Author, is defiled by unnatural lust.

However, those deeds that are only sins against human customs are to be avoided according to the diversity of their several practices, so that a mutual covenant in any city or nation, ratified by custom or law, may not be violated at the pleasure of anyone, whether native or stranger. For the part is justly deemed offensive that does not act in conformity with its whole.

But when God, at any time, commands something contrary to any such custom or covenant, it must be done, even though it had never been done there before; or if it had been allowed to lapse, it must be restored; or if it had not been previously instituted, it is then to be enacted. For if the reigning monarch may command something that no one before him nor he himself had ever commanded, and if obedience in such cases is not against the common good of the state (nay, it would rather be against the common good if he were not obeyed, since there is a general agreement that human society is to obey its kings), how much more ought we without hesitation to obey God, the King of all creation, in whatever He commands? For, as among the powers of human society the higher power in regard to obedience is to be preferred to the lower, so must God be obeyed above all others.

This is also true in regard to crimes where there is a desire to hurt others, whether by calumny or injury. Such can be accomplished either out of revenge, as between enemies, or for some temporal interest (as by a highwayman to a traveler), or to avoid some perceived evil (as when done to one whom we fear), or through jealousy, as when one who is less fortunate envies one who is more so, or when one who is prosperous worries that a person he fears should grow to be his equal or is grieved that he is so already.

Finally, crimes may be committed merely to take pleasure in another's sufferings, as when persons are spectators at a match between gladiators, or delight in deriding and scoffing at others.

These are the major forms of iniquity, and they spring from lust for power and lust of the eyes and lust of the flesh—either from one of them, or from two, or from all three. Thus men live wickedly, ignoring the three and seven, the *ten-stringed instrument* (Ps 33:2), Your Decalogue, O God, Most High and Most Sweet.

But what lewd actions can reach You, Who cannot be corrupted or defiled? Or what crimes can touch You, who cannot be hurt? You rather seek vengeance for what men commit against themselves; for when they also sin against You, they do evil to their own souls, and their iniquity lies to itself.

They corrupt or pervert their own nature, which You have created and regulated, either by the immoderate use of things allowed or by lusting after things that are *not allowed because they are against nature* (Rom 1:26). Or they are guilty of raging against You in thought or word and kicking against the goad, or when they exceed the limits of human society as they dare to delight in private agreements or feuds, according to their likes or dislikes.

Such are the things that are done when You are forsaken, O Fountain of life, the true Creator and Ruler of the Universe, and when through pride some false element in some tiny part thereof is loved more than You. It is then through humble piety that we must return to You, after which You will cleanse us of our evil habits, show mercy to those who confess their sins, hear the groans of those who are fettered, and loosen the chains that we have made for ourselves—provided that we now no longer raise against You the horns of a false liberty through greed of having more, and so incur the loss of everything by loving our own personal good more than You, the Good of all.

CHAPTER 9 — Priority of God's Commands

AMONG these crimes of lewdness and malice and countless iniquities, there are sins that befall those who are making progress. Those whose judgment is sound blame these persons for falling short of the rule of perfection, and yet they also praise them for the hope they give of future progress, as the green blade has promise of corn.

There are also some things that are similar to shameful actions and crimes of violence, yet are not sinful because they offend neither You, our Lord God, nor human society—such as when things are procured suitable for one's needs in life according to the exigencies of the time and others are uncertain whether they may have been obtained out of a sense of greed, or when persons are punished by a lawful authority with the purpose of charitable correction, but to others it is uncertain whether such chastisement may have been administered out of malice.

Hence, many actions that to men might have appeared blameable have been approved by Your testimony, and many that have been praised by men are condemned in Your eyes, there being often a great difference between the outward appearance of a deed and the intention of the doer. Also one may not be certain whether or not there was a particular urgency for the deed at the time it was done.

When, therefore, You suddenly command some unusual and unexpected thing—although it be what You have previously prohibited, and although You conceal for the present the reason for Your command, and though it may be against the law of some human society—there is no doubt that what You command ought to be obeyed, since no human society is truly just unless it serves You.

But happy are they who know these Your commands. For all the extraordinary things that have been done by those who served You were either to exhibit something needful for the present or to foretell something to come.

CHAPTER 10 — Foolish Beliefs

NOT knowing these things, I regarded Your holy servants and Prophets with scorn. And in deriding them I myself deserved to be held in contempt by You. For I was brought by gradual degrees to such follies as to believe that, when a fig is plucked, both it and its mother tree weep with milky tears, and that if some "saint" should eat that fig (after it had been sinfully plucked by another and not by himself), he would digest it in his stomach, and from thence exhale angels. Indeed, by groaning in prayer and sighing, I believed that he would breathe forth particles of the deity, and that these portions of the sovereign and true God were imprisoned in that fruit till they were restored to liberty by the teeth and belly of some chosen saint.

In my wretched state I believed that more mercy ought to be shown to the fruits of the earth than to men for whom they were made. And if anyone, who was hungry and was not a Manichean, should have begged for any, I would have looked upon anyone who gave him a morsel as deserving capital punishment.

CHAPTER 11 — Dream of Conversion

THEN *You put forth Your hand from on high* (Ps 144:7), *and delivered my soul out of this profound darkness* (Ps 86:13), while my mother, Your faithful one, was weeping for me unto You, much more than mothers weep at the bodily death of their children. For she looked upon me as dead, by the faith and the spirit that she had from You, and You were pleased graciously to hear her, O Lord. You did hear her and despised not her tears when, flowing down, they watered the ground under her eyes in every place where she prayed, and You were pleased to hear her.

Where but from You was that dream with which You comforted her, so that she allowed me to again live with her and share the same table in the house with her, which previously she had refused to do because she detested the blasphemies of my errors?

In that dream she saw herself standing upon a certain wooden bar, and a beautiful young man coming toward her, cheerful and smiling upon her, whereas she was sorrowful and spent with grief. He asked her the cause of her sorrow and of her daily tears, with the intention, as often happens, not of being informed, but of informing her. She answered that she bewailed my perdition.

He bade her to be at ease and to look and see that where she was I was also. She looked and perceived me standing by her upon the same log.

How can I explain this except by the fact that Your ears were open to the cry of her heart, O omnipotent Good, You Who have as much care for each one of us as if You had no other person under Your care, and Who show as much care for all as for each single one.

When she related this vision to me, I tried to distort its meaning as indicating that she rather should not despair of being one day what I then was. She instantly without any hesitation replied: "No, not so, for was it not said to me, 'Where he is, there also are you,' but 'Where you are, there he is also.' "

I confess to You, O Lord, as much as I remember (and I have often spoken about it), that this Your answer, given by my mother who was not disturbed by my false though plausible interpretation, and who so readily discerned the truth (which I before she spoke had not seen), struck me at the time far more forcefully than her dream that brought such joy to that pious woman—a joy that was to come so long afterward but was foretold to her so long beforehand for the comfort of her present state of uneasiness.

For there were yet to follow almost nine years during which I still lay wallowing in *that mire of the deep* (Ps 69:3) and in the darkness of error, often attempting to rise and falling back into a worse state, while that chaste, devout, and sober widow, similar in every respect to those You love, more cheerful indeed now in her hopes, yet in no way relaxing in her sighs and tears, ceased not in all the hours of her prayers to grieve over me before You. And her prayers were admitted into Your presence, and yet You allowed me to become still more involved and reinvolved in that darkness.

CHAPTER 12 — Son of Many Tears

MEANWHILE, You gave my mother another answer, which I remember. Allow me to pass over many details at I hasten to those that press me more to confess to You, and of course there are many others also that I have forgotten. You gave her, then, yet another answer through one of Your priests, a certain bishop brought up in Your Church and well-read in Your books. Asked by her to agree to confer with me, to refute my errors, to show me how my beliefs were evil and to teach me what was good (an office he willingly performed when he met with persons fitted to receive it), he refused—and that was a very prudent decision on his part, as I have come to understand.

The bishop replied that I was as yet unteachable, because I was puffed up with the novelty of that heresy, and even more because, as she had also told him, I had already puzzled many inexperienced persons with some captious questions. "Let him alone," he said. "Simply pray to our Lord for him. He will at length, by reading, discover his error and how great is its impiety."

At the same time the bishop told her how his mother, being deceived, had given him to the Manichees when he was still very young, and that he had not only read but also copied out almost all their books, and had by himself come to realize, without anyone disputing with him or convincing him, how much that sect was to be abhorred, and for that reason he had forsaken it.

When he told her this, she still was not satisfied, and continued to persist, entreating him with many tears to see me and talk with me. He then became somewhat annoyed with her persistent entreaty and said to her, "Go on your way and continue in your life of prayer, for it cannot be that a son of such tears should perish." As she many times afterward told me, she received those words as if they had sounded forth from Heaven.

Book 4—Augustine the Manichee

Augustine describes the events of his life during a period of nine years following his nineteenth year. He follows the Manichean sect and writes a treatise on the "Fair and Fitting" after suffering much grief at the death of a friend. He also begins the study of the liberal arts and the Aristotelian categories.

CHAPTER 1 — Seduced by Falsehood

FOR the space of nine years, from my nineteenth to my twenty-eighth year, we were seduced and did seduce others, being deceived and deceiving others in various inordinate desires, openly by what they call the liberal sciences, secretly by the false name of religion—proud in the one, superstitious in the other, vain in both.

By the former, I sought the emptiness of popular glory, down to the applause of the theater, competitive contests for crowns of hay, worthless stage plays, and the intemperance of lusts. By the latter, I sought in that false religion to be purged from these defilements by carrying food to those who are called the "elect" and the "saints," so that in the workroom of their stomachs they might mold it into angels and gods by whom we were to be delivered. Such things I followed and practiced with my friends, who were deceived with me and by me.

Let the proud, and those who, for the sake of their salvation, have not yet been cast down and broken by You, my God, *laugh at me* (Ps 25:2) if they please, but in Your praise I still wish to confess my shame to You. Grant me, I beseech You, and enable me, with my present memory, to once again traverse the circuitous course of my former error and to offer to You *a sacrifice of jubilation* (Ps 27:6).

For what am I to myself without You but a guide to a precipice? Or what am I when things go well with me but one sucking Your milk and enjoying You, the food that does not perish? Or what is any man, since he is nothing but a man? Let the strong and the mighty laugh at us; we who are weak and needy will confess to You.

CHAPTER 2 — Faithful Cohabitation

IN THOSE years I taught rhetoric and sold to others the secrets of gaining victories through loquacious speech, while I myself was overcome by cupidity.

It was my wish, O Lord, as You know, to have good scholars, in the usual sense of calling them good, and without deceit I taught them how to be deceitful, not that they would use them to condemn an innocent man, but sometimes in defense of the guilty.

And You, O God, beheld me from afar, staggering as it were in a slippery place, and sending out, amid much smoke, signs of my glittering faith, which in that teaching I exhibited toward those *who were in love with vanity, and sought after lying* (Ps 4:3), being no better myself.

In those years I lived with a woman who was not joined to me by lawful marriage, but chosen by the wandering heat of imprudent passion. Yet I had only this one, and I was faithful to her, so that I might experience by myself the distance there is between the true purpose of the matrimonial contract, made for the sake of offspring, and the covenant of a lustful love, where children are born unwanted, though when once born they force us to love them.

I remember, also, that when I had determined to compete for a prize in poetry, a certain soothsayer asked me what I would give him to insure my victory. Since I detested and regarded as abominable such foul mysteries, I answered, "Even if the crown were made of imperishable gold, I would not permit a fly to be sacrificed to give me the victory." For it was his intention to sacrifice some living creature, and he pretended that by such acts of honor he would secure the help of demons.

However, I did not reject this evil because of my chaste love for You, O God of my heart, for I did not know how to love You, since I could think only of bodily brightness, which I mistook for You. And does not a soul that gives way to such fictions *commit fornication against You* (Ps 73:27), and trust in false things, *and feed the winds* (Hos 12:2)?

But although I would not allow any sacrifice to be offered to the devils for me, still I sacrificed myself to them by my superstition. And what else is it "to feed the winds" but to feed those wicked spirits, that is, by going astray to become the subject of their sport and their derision?

CHAPTER 3 — Addicted to Judicial Astrology

NEVERTHELESS I had no scruples about consulting those planet-gazers, who were called "mathematicians," because they offered no sacrifice nor addressed any prayers to any spirit in their divinations. Even so, they are properly condemned by true Christian piety. For it is good to confess to You, O Lord, and to say, *Have mercy on me, heal my soul, for I have sinned against You* (Ps 41:5). It is also good not to abuse Your mercy by seeking the opportunity to sin again, but to remember that saying of our Lord: *Behold you are cured. Sin no more, lest something worse befall you* (Jn 5:14).

However, these men seek to destroy those wholesome precepts when they say, "From Heaven is the inevitable cause of your sin," and, "Venus has done this," or "Saturn," or "Mars." In other words, they wanted man, who is flesh and blood and corrupted by pride, to be guiltless, and they wished to cast the blame upon the Creator and Ruler of the heavens and the stars. And who is this but You, our God, all sweetness and the source of righteousness, Who *render to everyone according to his works* (Mt 16:27), and *do not despise a contrite and humble heart* (Ps 51:19)?

There was at that time a clever man, most skillful in the medical arts and renowned in that profession, who as proconsul had with his own hand set that victorious garland of competition on my sick head, but not in the capacity of physician, for You alone can cure diseases, *Who resist the proud, but give grace to the humble* (1 Pt 5:5). Yet even by this old man You did not fail to offer me Your helping hand, nor refrain from healing my soul.

For I became better acquainted with him and was an assiduous and attentive hearer of his discourses, which, without ornament of words, were agreeable because they were couched in lively and earnest phrases. When he understood by my talk that I was addicted to the books of the horoscope-casters, he advised me in a kind and fatherly manner to throw them away and not idly to bestow upon that empty study the care and labor necessary for more useful things.

This physician told me that he himself in his younger days had studied astrology and had even intended to make a profession of it for his livelihood, and that, if he could understand Hippocrates, he certainly was not incapable of understanding also that kind of learning. But he had abandoned it to take up the study of medicine for no other reason than that he had plainly discovered the falsity of that pretended science, and, being a serious man, he had refused to make a living by deluding people.

"But you," he said, "have the profession of rhetoric for your livelihood, and yet you follow that fraud, not out of necessity, but of your own free choice. Therefore, much more should you believe me, since I labored to attain perfection in it with the purpose of earning my living by it."

When I asked him why so many things were correctly foretold, he answered, as clearly as he could, that this was to be attributed to the power of chance, which is diffused throughout the whole order of nature. If a man dips haphazardly into the pages of a poet, who was recounting and intending quite different things, the reader often discovers a verse that is wonderfully applicable to the business at hand. Therefore it should not be considered a thing of wonder if by some higher instinct, out of the soul of man—whose workings are unknown—something should be said that is relevant to the affairs and the actions of the inquirer.

All this You brought to my knowledge from or through that man, and You marked in my memory what I would afterward investigate by myself. Yet at that time, neither he, nor my dearest friend Nebridius, a very good and prudent young man who laughed at all sort of divination, could persuade me to lay aside these things. I was more impressed by the authority of those writers, and I had not yet discovered unassailable proof, such as I was looking for, which might show me unambiguously that the correct predictions of these astrologers were the result of chance, and not a product of an art or a knowledge derived from star-gazing.

CHAPTER 4 — Death of a Dear Friend

IN THOSE years, when I first began to teach in my native town, I had a friend whom common pursuits had made exceedingly dear to me: one of the same age, and equally flourishing in the bloom of his youth. We had grown up together as children, gone to school together, and played together. However, at that time he was not so great a friend as he would be afterward, nor indeed was he so afterward, according to the rule of true friendship; for that friendship only is true by which such as adhere to You are fastened together by You, by the *Charity poured forth in our hearts by the Holy Spirit Who has been given to us* (Rom 5:5).

Even so, that friendship was exceedingly sweet, and strengthened by the eager pursuit of similar studies. I had also perverted him from the true faith, of which he had only an imperfect knowledge, and turned him toward those superstitious and pernicious fables for which my mother was weeping over me. This young man was going astray with me, and my soul could not endure being without him.

But you pursue closely upon the heels of those who are fleeing from You, at once both the avenging

God and the Fountain of mercy, Who by wonderful ways convert us to Yourself. You took that young man out of this life when he had scarcely completed one year in that friendship, sweeter to me beyond all the sweetness of that life of mine.

Who will recount all Your praises that he has experienced in himself alone? What did You do at that time, O my God, and how unsearchable was the abyss of Your judgments? For he became ill with a burning fever, and having for a long time lain unconscious in a mortal sweat so that his recovery was despaired of, he was baptized while unconscious.

Meanwhile, I did not care what they did, presuming that his soul would rather retain what he had received from me than what was done to his body without his knowledge. But it proved far otherwise, for he revived and recovered. And presently, as soon as I could speak with him (which was as soon as he could speak, for I did not leave him, and our intimacy was too great to prohibit me), I began to mock, expecting that he would also mock the Baptism he had received when he was quite out of his senses, though by this time he had been informed that he had received it.

However, he looked at me with great horror as an enemy, and with a wonderful and unexpected liberty he admonished me that if I wanted to continue as his friend, I should speak no more to him in that manner. Astonished and troubled, I thought it best to defer giving vent to the emotions of my heart until he had recovered his strength and was in a more proper condition for me to deal with him as I wanted. But he, happily, was snatched out of the hands of my madness, so that with You he might be reserved for my eternal comfort. Within a few days, when I was absent, he was again seized by fever and died.

Great was the grief with which my heart was darkened, and whatever I looked upon was death to my mind. My own country became a torture to me, and my father's house caused me to experience a strange unhappiness. Whatever I had shared with my friend had turned into a frightful torment for me, now that I was without him. My eyes longed for him everywhere, but nowhere could they see him. I hated all things, because they had him not, nor could they now say to me, "Here he comes," as they used to do when he returned after an absence.

Thus I became a great riddle to myself, and I asked my soul why it was depressed and why it disturbed me so (cf. Ps 42:6). And it knew not what to answer me. And if I said to my soul, *"Hope in God"* (Ps 42:6), it had good reason not to obey me, for the dear man it had lost was far better and more real than the phantom deity in which I bade it to hope. Weeping was then the only thing that was sweet to me, and it had succeeded my friend in the dearest place of my affection.

CHAPTER 5 — The Sweetness of Mourning

NOW, O Lord, those things are long since past, and time has soothed my wounds. May I learn from You, Who are the Truth, and apply the ear of my heart to Your mouth that You may tell me why weeping is sweet to those who are in misery? Have You, though You are present everywhere, cast away our misery at a distance from You, and do You remain in Yourself, while we are tossed about in trials? And yet, if we were not to bemoan ourselves in Your ears, no spark of hope would remain.

How is it that a sweet fruit is gathered from the bitterness of life, from groaning and weeping and sighing and bemoaning ourselves? Is this sweetness born from the hope that You will hear us? This would be true in the case of prayers, where there is a desire of obtaining You; but is it so in the grief for a thing lost, and in the mourning with which I was then overwhelmed?

For I had no hopes of his returning to life, neither did I petition for this by my tears; but I only grieved and lamented because I was miserable and had lost my joy. Or is weeping indeed in itself a bitter thing, and does it give us pleasure because of the loathing we have for the thing we delighted in before, and which we now abhor?

CHAPTER 6 — Horror of Death

BUT why do I speak of these things? This is not the time to ask questions, but to confess to You. I was miserable, and every soul is miserable that is tied down by love of perishable things, that is torn to pieces when it is separated from them, and then feels that misery by which it was also miserable before it lost them. It was so with me at that time, and I wept most bitterly, and in that bitterness I found my repose.

Thus was I miserable, and yet I loved that life, miserable as it was, more dearly than my friend. For though I wished to change my life, yet I was more unwilling to lose it than I was to lose him. And I know not whether I would have been willing to lose it even for him, as it is related about Orestes and Pylades, if it be not a fable, that they strove to die for each other, or at least together, because to them it was worse than death not to live together.

But for my part, there was, I know not why, quite a contrary disposition in me at that time; for I loathed life exceedingly, and yet feared to die. I believe that the more I loved my friend, the more I hated and feared death as a most cruel enemy that had taken him away from me, and I thought that it would suddenly devour all other men because it had that power over him. Such, I remember, was my disposition at that time.

Behold my heart, O my God, behold and see within me that I remember this, O my Hope, You Who cleanse me from the impurity of such affections, *directing my eyes to You, and plucking my feet out of the snare* (Ps 25:15). For I marveled that the rest of mortals could live, because he was dead whom I had loved as if he were never to die. I was astounded still more that I myself, who was a second self to him, could live when he was gone.

Well did someone say of his friend that he was one-half of his soul. I considered that my soul and his were but one soul in two bodies, and hence I loathed life, unwilling to live simply as a half. Therefore, perhaps I was afraid to die, lest he whom I had loved so much would die completely.

CHAPTER 7 — Departure for Carthage

OH MADNESS that knows not how to love human beings the way they should be loved! What a foolish man I was then, to so immoderately take to heart our human lot!

Therefore, I grew angry and sighed and wept and was distraught, bereft of both rest and counsel. For I carried about with me my soul that was all wounded and bleeding, unwilling any longer to be borne by me, but I could find no place to lay it down.

It could take no delight in pleasant groves, nor in plays and music, nor in fragrant odors, nor in elegant banquets, nor in the pleasures of the chamber and the bed, nor in fine books and poems. All things seemed loathsome to me, even the very light itself. And whatever was not he I found loathsome and hateful, except sighs and tears, for in these alone I found a little rest.

But when my soul was removed from these, I was weighed down by a grievous load of wretchedness. I knew that it was by You, O Lord, that it should be lifted up and lightened, but I had neither the will nor the strength, especially because You were not anything solid or stable to me when I considered You. For it was not You but an empty phantasm, and my own error was my god.

If I endeavored to place my soul there so that it might rest, it came tumbling down unimpeded through the empty air and fell back upon me, and I still remained to myself an unhappy place where I could neither be, nor from which I could escape. For where could my heart fly to, away from my heart? Where could I flee from myself? And where would I not follow myself?

However, I fled from my own country, for my eyes missed him less where they were not used to seeing him, and from Tagaste I came to Carthage.

CHAPTER 8 — Consolation from New Friends

TIME takes no vacation, nor does it roll idly by through our senses, but it works wondrous things in the soul. Behold, it came and passed day after day, and in coming and passing it imprinted in me other images and other remembrances, and by degrees they renewed in me my former delights.

My grief gave way to them. However, it was succeeded not indeed by other sorrows, but by the causes of other sorrows. For that former great grief so easily and so deeply had wounded me only because I had poured out my soul upon the sand by loving one who was to die, as if he would never die.

What now most of all healed and restored me was the solace of other friends with whom I loved something else instead of You. This was that grand fable and long-spun lie which through the ears corrupted our itching minds by its adulterous incitations, nor did this fable die when any of my friends died.

There were other things also in my friends that more completely captivated my attention: to chat together and to laugh together and to do mutual friendly services for one another; to read pleasant books together; to jest together, and then to be grave together; to dissent from one another sometimes without ill will, as a man would do from himself, and by this disagreeing in some few things to season, as it were, and better relish our agreements in many others.

Still other things were: to teach one another something or to learn something from one another; to wish uneasily for the return of one another when absent and to welcome one another with joy upon a return home.

These and similar signs proceeding from the heart of those who mutually love one another, through the countenance, through the tongue, through the eyes, and through a thousand agreeable ways, were so many fires to forge our souls together, and out of many to make but one.

CHAPTER 9 — Human and Divine Love

THIS it is that we love in friends, and such deep love that a man's conscience accuses itself if he loves not one who returns his love, or if he does not love in return the man who loves him first, seeking nothing from him in the carnal way, but only signs of his good will.

This is the explanation for that mourning when a friend dies, and that darkness of sorrow, and a heart lamenting at its sweetness being turned to bitterness, and, at the loss of life of the dying, the death of the living.

Blessed is he who loves You, O Lord, and his friend in You, and his enemy for Your sake. For he alone never loses anyone dear to him, to whom all are dear only in Him Whom he never loses. And Who is this but our God, the God Who *made heaven and earth* (Gn 1:1) and fills all things with His presence, because it is by filling them that He made them.

No one loses You, but he who leaves You. And where does he who leaves You go, or where does he flee? While running away from You in Your love, he will encounter You in Your wrath. Wherever he goes, he will find Your Law in his punishment. For *Your Law is Truth* (Ps 119:142), and Truth is Yourself.

CHAPTER 10 — The Fleeting Character of
Earthly Things

O GOD of hosts, convert us, and show us Your face and we shall be saved (Ps 80:4). Wherever the soul of man turns, it beholds sorrow, excepting only those times when it turns to You, even though it fastens upon beautiful things outside of You, and outside itself. These beautiful things, moreover, could have no being, if they were not from You.

All things have their rising and their setting; and in their rising they begin, as it were, to be, and they grow that they may be perfected; once perfected, they fade away and they perish, for all things grow old, and all die. So, then, when they rise and tend toward being, the more speedily they advance to be, the more haste they make ceasing to be; such is their law.

More than this You have not given them because they are but parts of things that exist not all at once; but by one passing away and another coming on they make up the universe of which they are parts. Our speech is in like manner compounded of a succession of significant sounds. The whole sentence cannot be completed unless each word gives way when it has sounded its part and makes room for another to succeed it.

For all these things let my soul praise You, O God, the Creator of all things, but do not allow it to cleave to them with the glue of love through the senses of the body. These things proceed on the way they were going so that they may cease to exist, and they leave the soul wounded with pestilent desires because it would still love to possess them and longs to repose in them, but they abide not and run away.

And who can follow them with any bodily sense when they are gone, or hold them fast while they are at hand?

The sense of the flesh is slow because it is only the sense of the flesh, and such are its limitations. It is sufficient for the ends for which it was made, but it is not able to detain and hold fast things that never stand still but are always running from their appointed beginning to their appointed end. For in Your Word, by which they are created, they hear their decree, "From here, and no further than there."

CHAPTER 11 — Desire for God Alone

BE NOT foolish, O my soul, nor let the ear of your heart be deafened with the clamor of your vanity. Hearken also: the Word Himself calls you to return, and with Him there is a place of undisturbed rest, where love is never forsaken unless it first forsakes that place. Behold, those things all pass away so that others may succeed them and this lower universe may thus be completed in all its parts.

"But do I anywhere depart?" asks the Word of God. There establish your dwelling, O my soul, entrust there everything you have, after having been wearied out with delusions. Entrust to truth all that you have gained from truth and you shall lose nothing; and what has been corrupted in you shall flourish again, and all your diseases shall be healed, and these inconstant perishable things of yours shall be reformed and renewed, and fixed around you. Neither shall they bring you down where they naturally tend, but they shall stand with you and remain with you before that God Who stands firm and abides forever.

Why be perverted, O my soul, and follow the inclinations of your flesh? Let it now be converted and follow you. Whatever you perceive by it exists only in part, and you know not the whole of which these are parts, and yet they delight you. But if the sense of your flesh were capable to comprehend the whole and had not itself also been justly confined for your punishment to the prospect only of some small part, you would have wished for a speedy passing away of all that which for the present exists, so that you might receive more pleasure from the whole.

For by the same bodily sense you hear all that which we speak, and yet you would not have any one syllable to stand still, but to fly away, so that others may succeed it and you may hear the whole. It always is so with things that make up one whole, for all those things of which that whole is made appear totally different when viewed individually. All of them together would delight more than each part, if they could be perceived altogether. But far better than all these things is He who made them all, and He is our God. And He never passes away because there is nothing that can succeed Him.

CHAPTER 12 — Loving Things in God

IF MATERIAL things please you, take occasion from them to praise God, and turn your love from them toward Him Who made them, lest in these things that please you, you displease Him.

If souls please you, let them be loved in God, because they also are subject to change, but being fixed in Him they are firmly established; without Him, they would perish and pass away. In Him then let them be loved, and take along with you to Him as many of them as you can. Say to them, "Him let us love, Him let us love; He it is Who made all these things, and He is not far off. For He did not make them and then go away from them, but they are from Him and in Him. Behold, there He is, wherever truth is relished. He is in the most inward part of the heart, but the heart has strayed from Him."

Sinners, return to your heart (Is 46:8) and cling to Him Who made you. Stand with Him and you will stand indeed; rest in Him and you will be at rest. Where are you going, and along what rough ways? Where are you going? The good that you love comes from Him, but what is it in comparison with Him? It is good and sweet, but it will justly be made bitter because anything He has made is unjustly loved when He Himself is forsaken for it.

To what purpose would you stubbornly continue to tread *those hard and toilsome ways* (Wis 3:7)? Rest is not there where you seek it. Seek what you are seeking, but it is not to be found where you are seeking it. You seek for a happy life in the land of death, but it is not there. For how can there be a happy life where there is no *life?*

Our Life Himself came down to us and bore our death, and He slew death out of the abundance of His Life. He thundered forth and called out to us that we should return to Him, to that secret place from whence He at first came forth to us into the Virgin's womb, where He espoused to Himself our human nature, our mortal flesh, but which would not be mortal forever.

And thence *like a bridegroom coming out of his bridal chamber, He rejoiced as a giant to run the way* (Ps 19:6). For He was not slow-paced, but He ran all the way, calling aloud by words, by deeds, by His death, His life, His descending, His ascending, calling out to us to return to Him. And He withdrew Himself from our eyes, so that *we might return into our hearts* (Is 46:8) and find Him there.

He has gone away, and yet behold He is here. He did not stay long with us, and yet He has not left us. For He has gone to that place which He never left *because the world was made by Him, and He was in this world* (Jn 1:10), and *He came into this world to save sinners* (1 Tm 1:15). To Him my soul now confesses, that He may heal it because *it has sinned against Him* (Ps 41:5). *O you sons of men, how long will you be so dull of heart?* (Ps 4:3).

Is it possible that after Life has come down to you, you will not ascend and live? But where shall you then ascend when you have set up yourselves on high and *set your mouth against the heavens* (Ps 73:9)? You must descend if you wish to ascend, ascend to God. For you fell by ascending against Him.

Tell these things to the souls you love, that they may weep in this valley of tears, and so you may carry them with you to God. For it is by His Spirit that you tell them these things, if you speak inflamed with the fire of charity.

CHAPTER 13 — The Beauty in Things

THESE things I did not then know, and I was in love with the beauty of earthly things. I was sinking into the very depths and I said to my friends, "Do we love anything but what is beautiful? What then is beautiful? And what is beauty? What is it that attracts us and attaches us to the things we love? For if there were not in them a gracefulness and beauty, they would not attract us."

And I observed and perceived that in the bodies themselves some derived their beauty from being whole, while others derived their beauty from being aptly suited to another, as a part of the body is to the whole, or a shoe to the foot, and the like. And these speculations gushed forth in my mind out of my inmost heart and I wrote the work called *On the Beautiful and Fitting*—in two or three books I believe. How many there were, O my God, You know, for I have forgotten. I do not have them; they have been lost, I know not how.

CHAPTER 14 — Seeking a Worldly Reputation

WHAT was it that moved me, O Lord my God, to dedicate these books to Hierius, an orator of Rome? I had never seen him, but I loved the man for the eminence he had achieved because of his learning, which was much renowned. I had heard of some of his sayings, and I was pleased with them. But I was pleased even more because others were pleased with them, and they highly praised him, admiring that, even though he was a Syrian by birth and first trained in Greek eloquence, he had become so great a master also in Latin and was most learned in all things pertaining to the study of wisdom.

If a man is praised, and though absent is loved, does this love then enter into the heart of the hearer from the mouth of the praiser? No, certainly, but from one lover another is enkindled with love. Hence is love conceived for a person who is praised, when the one who praises him is supposed to commend him with a sincere heart, that is, when one both loves him and praises him.

In this manner did I love men at that time, according to the judgment of men, and not according to Your judgment, O my God, You Who deceive no man. But why then was I not affected by the praise given to some famous charioteer or huntsman who is highly regarded by the people, but with a far different and more serious affection, and in a way that I myself also would have been glad to have been praised? I would not have been willing to be praised or loved, as actors are, though I also praised them and loved them, but I would rather have chosen to be unknown than to be known in that manner.

Where are distributed the weights of such various and different loves in the same soul? How is it, since we are both men, that I love in another man that which I hate in myself, for unless I hated it, I would not detest and spurn it? May we not say the same of an actor who shares our nature as we would of a good horse that is loved by a man, who yet would not, if he could, be the thing he loves? Do I then love in a man what I hate to be, though I am a man?

Man himself is a great deep, *of whose very hairs, O Lord, You keep an account* (Mt 10:30), and they are not lessened in Your sight. And yet his hairs are more easily numbered than his affections and the motions of his heart.

That orator was the sort of man whom I so loved that I would have wished myself to be like him. I went astray through pride, and *was carried about with every wind* (Eph 4:14), and yet was steered by You, though most secretly. But how do I know and so confidently confess to You that I loved him more because of the love of those who praised him than on account of the things themselves for which he was praised? If the same men, instead of praising him, had disparaged him and related those same things of him with contempt and scorn, I would not have been so captivated by him. Yet certainly the facts about him would not have been otherwise, nor would the man himself have been different, but there would only have been a different affection in those who related them.

See where a weak soul lies wounded that is not yet fixed upon the solidity of truth. As the gales of tongues blow from the breasts of fallible men, so is the soul carried and turned and whirled about, and its light is beclouded and it sees not the truth. And yet, behold, it stands before us.

To me it was a matter of great importance if my style and my studies were known to such a man. And if he approved them I would be even more inflamed, but if he disapproved them, it would have wounded my vain heart that was void and empty of Your solidity. And yet the subject of the "beautiful" and the "fit," concerning which I had written to him, I turned over with delight in my mind and admired, contemplating it by myself where I had no one to praise it with me.

CHAPTER 15 — Misguided Search for Truth

BUT I did not as yet see that the hinge of so great a matter lies in Your own art, O Almighty One, You *Who alone do wondrous things* (Ps 72:18; 136:4). My mind wandered through corporeal forms, and I defined and distinguished "the beautiful" as "that which is so of itself," but "the fitting" as "that which is becoming because it is adapted to some other thing."

I supported this belief by corporeal examples. Then I turned my attention to the nature of the mind, but my false notion of spiritual beings did not let me discern the truth. And yet the very power of truth flashed upon my eyes, and I turned away my throbbing mind from incorporeal things to lineaments and colors and swelling magnitudes. And because I could not see these things in my mind, I thought I could not perceive my mind.

Furthermore, since in virtue I loved peace, and in vice I hated discord, I noted a certain unity in the one and a division in the other. I imagined unity to consist in the rational mind, the nature of truth, and the sovereign good; but in that division, I believed in my folly, there was some substance of irrational life and the nature of the sovereign evil that I took to be not only a substance, but also true life, and yet not to have its being from You, O my God, *from Whom are all things* (1 Cor 8:6).

The one, such as a sexless soul, I called a monad. The other, such as wrath in crimes of malice and acts of impurity, I called a dyad. However, I really did not know what I said. For I did not then know, nor had I learned that evil is no substance at all, and that the soul itself is not the supreme and unchangeable good.

Just as we have crimes of violence, when the soul's disposition for violent action is aroused, resulting in insolent and turbulent behavior, and we have shameful sins, when that propensity of the soul to indulge in carnal pleasures is intemperate, so also errors and false opinions defile life if the rational soul itself is corrupted.

So was it then with me, for I did not know that my mind was to be enlightened with another light in order to be a partaker of the truth because it is not itself the very nature of truth. *For You light my lamp, O Lord; O my God, You enlighten my darkness* (Ps 18:29); and *of Your fullness we have all received* (Jn 1:16); for *You are the true Light that enlightens every man who comes into the world* (Jn 1:9), for in You *there is no change or shadow of alteration* (Jas 1:17).

I pressed toward You but was driven back from You, that I might taste death because *You resist the proud* (1 Pt 5:5). And what could be prouder than for me to affirm with strange madness that I myself was naturally what You are. And whereas I was mutable, which was plain to me since I desired to be wise, so that from being worse I might become better, I chose rather to believe You also to be mutable than not to think that I was the same thing that You are.

Therefore I was rejected by You, and You resisted my insolent pride. I could only imagine corporeal forms, and being flesh I accused the flesh. Like *a wind that goes,* I still did not *return to You* (Ps 78:39), but going on I passed to things that have no being, neither in You, nor in me, nor in the body. Nor were they created for me by Your truth, but were fabricated from bodily things by my vanity.

I spoke to the little ones, Your faithful, my fellow citizens, from whom I lived in exile without knowing it, and I asked them, talkative and foolish as I was, "Why then can a soul err, since it was made by God?" But I was unwilling to hear anyone say to me, "Why then does God err?" And I preferred to argue that Your immutable substance had been necessitated to err, rather than to confess that my nature, which is mutable, had, by its free will, gone astray and was reaping error as its punishment.

I was about twenty-six or twenty-seven years of age when I wrote those books, revolving within myself the corporeal fancies that continually buzzed about the ears of my heart. These ears, O sweet Truth, I turned to Your interior melody, meditating on the "beautiful" and the "fitting," and longing to stand firm and hear You and *to rejoice at the voice of the Bridegroom* (Jn 3:29).

I could not do so because I was stopped by the voice of my error, and the weight of my pride caused me to sink down to the depths. *You did not give joy and gladness to my hearing, nor did my bones rejoice* that had not yet been *humbled* (Ps 51:10).

CHAPTER 16 — The Writings of Aristotle

WHAT did it profit me that, when I was scarcely twenty years old, there came into my hands a book by Aristotle entitled *The Ten Categories*? I regarded this work as almost something profound and divine because my master, who taught rhetoric at Carthage, and others who were accounted learned, spoke of it with cheeks almost bursting with pride.

What did it profit me that I read it alone by myself and understood it? When I had conferred about it with others, who said they had considerable difficulty in understanding those things, even with the help of learned teachers who not only expounded them in words, but also, to better explain them, drawing many figures in the sand, I did not conclude that they could give me any better account of these than what I knew by my own private reading.

The book seemed to me to speak plainly enough of substances, such as man is, and of the accidents existing in these substances, such as the figure of a man, what sort of a man he is, his stature, how tall he is, his kindred, whose brother he is, where he lives, when he was born, whether he sits or stands or whether he has his shoes on or is armed, whether he acts or is acted upon, and whatsoever else is found in these nine categories whereof I have given these examples, or in the chief category of substance.

What did all this profit me, when indeed it did me harm? I believed that whatever had a being was encompassed in those ten categories, and I endeavored also to conceive You, O my God (Who are without any composition and unchangeable), as if You also were subject to Your greatness, to Your beauty, so that they inhered in You as in their subject, as do bodily accidents. However, Your very being is Your greatness and Your beauty.

On the other hand, a body is not great or beautiful because it is a body, for even if it were less great or less beautiful, it would nevertheless still be a body. What I imagined of You was falsity, and not the truth. It was the fiction of my error, not the solid foundation of Your blessedness. For You have commanded, and so it came to pass unto me that *the earth should bring forth thorns and thistles for me,* and that *with the sweat of my brow* I should *earn my bread* (Gn 3:18).

And what did it profit me that I read and understood all the books on the so-called liberal arts, while I myself was still a wretched slave to my wicked lusts? I enjoyed the books, but I did not know the basis of all that was true and certain in them. I had my back turned to the light, and my face turned toward the things reflected in the light. Therefore my face itself, with which I saw the things that were enlightened, was not itself illuminated.

Whatever was taught concerning the art of speaking and of reasoning, whatever concerning the dimensions of figures, and on music and numbers, I understood with no great difficulty and without any teacher. You know this to be true, O Lord my God; for both quickness of apprehension and sharpness of wit for learning are Your gifts; and yet I did not offer sacrifice to You in gratitude for that gift.

Therefore, it was not to my profit, but rather to my harm, that I desired to have so great a part of my substance in my own hands. *I did not keep my strength for You* (Gn 3:18) but went away from You into a far country, that I might waste it upon the harlots of wicked desires.

Of what profit were good gifts to me when I did not make good use of them? I did not perceive that those subjects were not understood even by the studious and intelligent without great difficulty until I endeavored to explain them to such people and came to realize that those who ranked highest were the ones who were not too slow in following me as I taught them.

But yet, what did this profit me, who was thinking all this while that You, O Lord my God, the Truth, were simply an immense brilliant body, and I myself a small piece from that body? Oh excessive perversity! But so it was with me. Nor am I, who was not ashamed then to profess my blasphemies to men and to rail against You, ashamed now to confess to You Your mercies toward me and to call upon You.

What then did my intelligence profit me, who was so quick to comprehend those sciences and without any teacher's help to understand so many complicated books, when I so foully and sacrilegiously erred in the doctrine of piety? Conversely, what disadvantage was a much slower learning capacity to Your little ones, who never strayed far from You, when they were safely feathered in the nest of Your Church and nourished their wings of charity with the food of sound faith?

O Lord our God, *let us hope under the shadow of Your wings* (Ps 63:8). Protect us and bear us up. You shall bear us up when we are little, and *even to our old age You shall bear us up* (Is 46:4). When You are our strength, it is strength indeed, but when it is our own, then our strength is merely weakness. Our good always exists only with You, and because we turned away from You we became perverted.

Let us now return to You, O Lord, that we may not be overturned. For with You our good exists without decay, and that good is Yourself. Nor need we fear lest at our return there should not be a place to receive us, for though we indeed fell by departing from it, yet in our absence our home did not fall, which is Your eternity.

Book 5—Augustine the Catechumen

Having attained his twenty-ninth year, Augustine meets Faustus, a Manichean leader, who unwittingly shakes his confidence in Manicheism. He journeys to Rome and Milan, hears Saint Ambrose, and becomes a catechumen in the Catholic Church once again.

CHAPTER 1 — A Prayer

RECEIVE, O Lord, the sacrifice of my confessions, which I offer to You through the medium of my tongue, which You have formed and aroused to confess to Your Name. Heal all my bones, that they may say, *O Lord, who is like You?* (Ps 35:10).

He who confesses to You does not teach You what is done within him, for no heart is so closed as to shut out Your eye, nor does the hardness of men repel Your hand. You dissolve it at any time that You wish, either through Your mercy or through Your punishment. For *there is no one who can hide himself from Your searing heat* (Ps 19:7).

But let my soul praise You, so that it may show its love for You, and let it confess Your mercies to You, so that it may praise You. Your whole creation never ceases or keeps silent from singing Your praises.

The spirit of every man praises You by his voice turned toward You, and all living creatures and corporeal things also do so through the mouth of those who contemplate them. In this way, our soul may ascend toward You from its weariness, by the steps of the things that You have made, and may pass on to You Who have most wonderfully fashioned them. For with You is refreshment and true strength.

CHAPTER 2 — God's Omnipresence

L ET the restless and the wicked go their way and
flee from You. You will still see them and pierce
their shadows. Behold, everything around them is
beautiful, but they themselves are ugly. Yet how have
they been able to hurt You, or in what way have they
disgraced Your Kingdom, which from the highest
heavens to the lowest abyss is ever just and perfect?
Where did they flee when *they fled from Your face* (Ps
139:7)? Or where are they that You do not find
them?

But they fled away, so that they might not see
You, Who always see them, and so with eyes blinded
they stumbled against You, Who never depart *from
any of the things You have made* (Wis 11:24). Unjust
as they were, they stumbled against You and they
met with a just punishment: withdrawing themselves
from Your mercy, stumbling upon Your righteousness, and falling before Your severity. For such people do not know that You are everywhere, for no
place can enclose You, and that You alone are present even to those who go far from You.

Let them be converted then, and seek You, for
though they have forsaken You, their Creator, yet
You have not forsaken Your creatures. Let them return, and lo, You are there in their heart, in the
heart of those who confess to You and who cast
themselves upon You, and upon Your breast bewail
their rugged ways. And You will gently wipe away
their tears, so that they may weep the more and find
their comfort in weeping. For You, O Lord, and not
any man that is flesh and blood, but You, O Lord,
Who made them, alone can refresh and comfort
them. And where was I when I was seeking You?

You were there before me, but I had strayed away even from myself and could not find myself. How much less could I find You?

CHAPTER 3 —Faustus, the Snare of the Devil

I WILL now lay open in the presence of my God the twenty-ninth year of my age. There had just come to Carthage a certain bishop of the Manichees, named Faustus, a great *snare of the devil* (1 Tm 3:7), and many were caught in that snare by the lure of his persuasive speech.

Though I admired the language, I was still able to separate it from the truth of the things that I was eager to learn. I was not so much interested in the kind of language as in the scholarly fare that was set before me by this Faustus, who was greatly renowned. Reports had represented him to me as someone who was well versed in all worthwhile studies and especially skilled in the liberal arts.

Since I had read and remembered much of what was taught by the philosophers, I had compared some of them with those lengthy fables of the Manichees. Of the two, the teachings of the philosophers seemed to me to be the more probable, even though what was said came from men who could only *make judgments about the world, though they did not discover the Lord therein* (Wis 13:9).

You are great, O Lord, and You look upon the lowly, but those that are high You know from afar (Ps 138:6). Neither do *You draw near to* any but *the contrite in heart* (Ps 34:19), nor are You found by the proud, even if in their skill they can number the stars and the sands and measure out the celestial regions and discover the courses of the planets.

For with the mind and the understanding that You have given them, they search into these matters. They have discovered many things, and foretold the eclipses of the sun and moon long beforehand—what day, what hour, and whether partial or total—and their calculations were found to be accurate. Everything has come to pass as they predicted, and they have left in writing rules that they have discovered by their study that are read to this day. By them men still foretell what year, what month of the year, what day of the month, what hour of the day, and for what part of its light the sun or moon shall be eclipsed, and their predictions come true.

The unknowing admire these things and stand amazed, while those who know them rejoice and exult. In their wicked pride they depart from You and hide Your light from themselves. They can foresee the eclipse of the sun long before it happens, and yet cannot see their own present eclipse, for they do not religiously reflect whence they have this understanding by which they search out these things.

If they find that You have made them, they do not give themselves to You so that You may keep what You have made. Nor do they sacrifice to You what they themselves have wrought. They refuse to forsake their proud imaginations, which are like *birds of the air*, or their curiosity, with which they wander in the secret paths of the deep like *fishes of the sea*, or their carnal lusts, which are like *beasts of the field* (Ps 8:8), so that You, *O God,* Who are *a consuming fire* (Dt 4:24), may consume their dead cares and recreate them to immortality.

They did not know the way, Your Word, by which You have made all the things they number and themselves who number them, the senses by which they see the things they number, and the understanding by which they know how to number. *To Your wisdom there is no measure* (Ps 147:5). Your only-begotten *Son has become for us wisdom, and justice, and sanctification* (1 Cor 1:30), and He was numbered among us *and paid tribute to Caesar* (Mt 22:26). They did not know the way by which they were to go down from themselves to Him, and through Him ascend to Him. They knew not this way, and yet they fancy themselves to be high and bright like the stars, whereas they have fallen down to the earth, and *their senseless minds have been darkened* (Rom 1:21).

They say many true things concerning the creature, but they do not piously seek the Truth, the Maker of the creature, and so do not find Him, or if they find Him and acknowledge that He is God, *they do not glorify Him as God, or give thanks, but become vain in their reasoning, professing themselves to be wise* (Rom 1:21), by attributing to themselves what is Yours, and strive by a most perverse blindness to attribute also to You what is their own, that is, imputing lies to You Who are the Truth. *They have changed the glory of the incorruptible God into an image made into the likeness of corruptible man, and of birds and four-footed beasts and creeping things* (Rom 1:23), *and they change Your truth into a lie, and they worship and serve the creature rather than the Creator* (Rom 1:25).

Yet many true things did I retain in my memory that they had spoken concerning Your creation, and reason confirmed these things to me from calculations, the order of time, and the visible testimony of the stars. I compared them with the words of Mani, who in his exuberant madness had written much on these subjects, but I could discover therein no explanation of solstices, equinoxes, and the eclipses, nor any of the things I had learned in the books on natural philosophy. I was commanded to believe his theories, but they did not agree with the conclusions that my calculations and my eyes had discovered, and indeed were far different from them.

CHAPTER 4 — The Happiness of Knowing God

O LORD, *God of truth* (Ps 31:6), is then everyone pleasing to You who knows these things? Rather, unhappy is the man who knows all these things but does not know You, and happy is the one who knows You, although he does not know such things. Moreover, whosoever knows both You and them is not happier for knowing them, but only happy for knowing You, provided that *knowing You he glorifies You as God, gives You thanks, and becomes not vain in his own reasonings* (Rom 1:21).

For someone who possesses a tree and gives You thanks for its use, even though he does not know how tall it is or how wide its branches spread, is far superior to one who measures it and numbers all its branches but does not own it and does not know or love its Maker. Even so is the man of faith, to whom the whole world of riches belongs, and who *has nothing yet possesses all things* (2 Cor 6:10), by adhering to You Who are the Lord of all things, even though he is not aware of such bits of knowledge as the circles of the Great Bear. Yet it would be folly to doubt his superiority to the one who measures the heavens and numbers the stars and weighs the elements, yet neglects You, Who *have ordered all things in measure, number, and weight* (Wis 11:20).

CHAPTER 5 — The Rashness of Mani

WHO then asked this person named Mani to write also upon these things, without the knowledge of which piety might well be acquired? For You have said to man, *Behold, the fear of the Lord is wisdom* (Jb 28:28). About this he might still be ignorant, though he had known perfectly ever so many facts. However, not knowing these things and yet most impudently taking it upon himself to teach them, he plainly could not have any knowledge of piety. For it is an act of vanity to profess these worldly things even when known, but an act of piety to confess to You.

However, having gone astray, Mani spoke much about these worldly subjects, and as a result he was scorned by those who were truly learned in them, highlighting the true nature of his opinions on more difficult subjects. And since he did not want to be regarded as someone of no account, he endeavored to persuade men that the Holy Spirit, the Comforter and Enricher of Your faithful, with full authority personally resided in him.

Therefore, when he was found to have erred concerning the heavens, the stars, and the motions of the sun and moon, though these things do not belong to the sphere of religion, it was plain enough that his pretensions were sacrilegious in that he said things, of which he not only was ignorant but which indeed were false, with such an extravagant vanity and pride as to attempt to attribute them to himself as to a Divine Person.

When I hear this or that Christian brother who does not know these things and mistakes one thing for another, I regard the man with patience and overlook his error. I cannot see that it does him any harm, provided that he believes nothing unworthy of You, O Lord, the Creator of all things, even though perhaps he is ignorant of the position and nature of corporeal creation.

However, it would do him harm if he believes this to belong to the very essence of religious doctrine and he continues stubbornly to affirm what he does not know.

Even this weakness in a faith that is in its formative stage is tolerated because of charity, that tender mother, until the new man grows up *into a perfect man, so as not to be carried about by every wind of doctrine* (Eph 4:13-14). But as for him who presumed to make himself the teacher, author, leader, and chief of those whom he persuaded in such a way as to make them believe that those who followed him were following not any man, but Your Holy Spirit, who would not judge that such great madness should be detested and utterly rejected, once he had been convicted of having made false statements?

However, I had not yet clearly ascertained whether the variations of the longer and shorter days and nights, and of the night itself and the day, and the eclipses, and similar things I had read in other books, might not also be explained according to his words. For if they could, it would become indeed uncertain to me whether they were so or not, but because of his reputed sanctity, I might have based my belief on his authority.

CHAPTER 6 — The Coming of Faustus

FOR almost all those nine years in which with an unsettled mind I had listened to these men, I had longingly awaited the coming of this Faustus. The others whom I had met were unable to resolve my doubts, but they promised me that by his coming and conferring with me, not only those but any more difficult questions would be easily cleared up. When he came, therefore, I found him to be a man who was pleasant and agreeable in his discourse and proclaiming the very same things that the others were accustomed to say, but much more gracefully.

Yet how could this most courteous cupbearer assuage my thirst? My ears were already clogged with such things. Neither did they now seem any better to me because they were more elegantly delivered, nor, therefore, true because elegant, nor the soul, therefore, wiser because the countenance was agreeable and the utterance graceful. Those who had promised him to me were not good judges of things, since they regarded him as prudent and wise because his speech delighted them.

On the other hand, I have also met with another kind of man, the type who even regards truth itself with suspicion and refuses to accept it even when it is presented in refined and ordered language. But You had then already taught me, O my God, by wonderful and secret ways, and I therefore believe that You had taught it to me because it is true, and You alone are the teacher of truth wheresoever and whensoever it is revealed to us.

You had already taught me that nothing should be regarded as true because it is eloquently delivered, nor automatically be considered false because it is couched in ill-arranged words. Nor again is something untrue because it is elegantly delivered or true when presented in simple language. Rather I learned that wisdom and folly, both of which may be served up in plain or beautiful language, are like wholesome and harmful meats that may be served in fine or plain dishes.

Therefore, the great desire with which I had so long awaited this man was indeed gratified by the touching and lively manner of his discourse, and by his words so well-adapted to his subject and ever ready to adorn his ideas. I was delighted, as were many others with me, and more than many others I praised and extolled him. However, it annoyed me that because of all his hearers, I could not approach him alone and communicate to him in personal conversation the questions that troubled me.

As soon as I had an opportunity, I sought his attention in the company of my friends at a time when it was not improper to discuss matters together. I presented some matters that perplexed me, and I quickly found that the man was a stranger to all the liberal arts, aside from grammar—and even of this latter he had only an ordinary knowledge.

But because he had read some of Tully's orations and a few books of Seneca and some of the poets, and as many of the books of his own sect as had been written in an orderly manner and in good Latin, and daily exercised his talent in speaking, he had acquired that eloquence which became more agreeable and more persuasive because it was guided by a good mind and a certain natural gracefulness.

Did it not thus occur as I recall it, O Lord my God, the Judge of my conscience? My heart and my remembrance are in Your sight, and through the hidden mystery of Your Providence You were then instructing me and beginning to set my ugly errors before my face, so that I might see and detest them.

CHAPTER 7 — The Ignorance of Faustus

AFTER it had become clear to me that Faustus was ignorant of those arts in which I had thought he excelled, I began to despair of receiving from him any solution of the doubts that perplexed me. A man who was ignorant of these things might, nevertheless, retain the truths of religion if he were not a Manichee.

For their books are full of lengthy fables of the heavens and the stars and the sun and moon, and now I no longer thought that he could clearly explain to me (which was what I wanted) whether, by comparing the calculations that I had read in other books with what Mani had written, better reasons or as good reasons for those things could be found in the Manichean system.

When I proposed them for consideration and discussion, Faustus modestly excused himself and shrank from undertaking the task, for he was aware of his ignorance of these things, and he was not ashamed to acknowledge it. He was not like the talkative ones I had endured who undertook to teach me these things and actually said nothing.

Although his heart was not rightly disposed toward You, he was not a careless or imprudent individual. Not altogether unaware of his own ignorance, he was not willing rashly to engage himself in a controversy from which he could neither retreat nor withdraw gracefully. This characteristic endeared him to me even more. For the modesty of a candid mind is something more beautiful than the knowledge of those things that I desired to learn. And I found him to be thus in all the more difficult and more subtle questions.

The zeal that I had shown for the writings of Mani had now considerably abated. Despairing of their other teachers, when he, renowned among them, appeared ignorant of many things that perplexed me, I began to turn my conversation with him to those studies with which he was much more familiar—subjects that I, being then master of rhetoric, taught the youth of Carthage—and to read with him such books as he desired to hear or I thought would be suitable to his intelligence.

However, all my efforts to make further progress in that sect collapsed as a result of my acquaintance with this man. Not that I quite forsook them, but not finding anything better, I determined to remain content in the meantime with what I had stumbled upon until I could discover something more worthy of my consideration.

Thus, this Faustus, who had been to many the *snare of death* (Ps 18:6), neither willingly nor knowingly began to loosen that snare in which I was caught. For Your hands, O my God, in the secret of Your Providence, never let go of my soul, while my mother continued day and night to offer to You on my behalf her tears and the sacrifice of a bleeding heart. And You dealt with me by wonderful and secret ways. It was Your work, O my God, for *with the Lord shall the steps of man be directed, and he shall like well his way* (Ps 37:23). What other cause can procure our salvation but Your hand, remaking what You have made?

CHAPTER 8 — Journey to Rome

IT WAS, therefore, through Your action that I was persuaded to go to Rome to teach there what I was teaching at Carthage. And how I came to be persuaded to do this, I will not neglect to confess to You, because in these things also Your deepest designs and Your ever-present mercy deserve to be considered and proclaimed.

My reason for going to Rome was not the prospect of greater profits and greater honors that were promised by my friends who persuaded me to accept the post, though such things at that time played some part in swaying my mind. But the principal and almost the only reason was that I heard that the youth there studied more quietly and were kept under more orderly discipline. Students in one school were not allowed at will and insolently to rush into the school of another teacher, nor were they admitted at all without a teacher's permission.

In contrast, the freedom that the students are allowed at Carthage is shameful and intolerable. They shamelessly break into other schools and, with an attitude approaching madness, disturb the order that each teacher has established for the proficiency of his students. They commit many outrages with strange blindness that would be punishable by law, were they not patronized by custom. This custom allows them to be more miserable, in that they now do as lawful what by Your eternal Law could never be sanctioned. And they think that their acts escape punishment, when indeed their blindness with which they commit these foul deeds is itself a great punishment, and the punishment they suffer from so doing is incomparably worse.

Those manners, therefore, that I as a student refused to emulate, I was now forced to endure from others, and so I determined to go to a place where all who were knowledgeable assured me that no such things were done. But You, *my hope and my portion in the land of the living* (Ps 142:6), so that I might change my earthly dwelling for the welfare of my soul, both administered a spur to drive me from Carthage and proposed allurements to draw me to Rome.

You made use of men who loved this dying life, some doing mad things, others promising vain allurements. And to enable me to eventually straighten out my life, You secretly used both their and my own perversity. For both they who disturbed my peace were blind with a disgraceful frenzy, and they who invited me elsewhere had a relish for earthly things. And I myself, who here loathed my true misery, coveted an unreal happiness there.

But the true reason why I went from this place to the other, You knew, O my God, and told neither me nor my mother, who grievously lamented my departure and even followed me to the seacoast. Realizing that she intended to stick close to me, and that she had resolved either to bring me back or to go with me, I deceived her and pretended that I had a friend whom I could not leave until he had a fair wind to set sail.

Thus I told a lie to my mother—to such a wonderful mother—and got away. And this sin also You have mercifully forgiven me, saving me from the waters of the sea, full as I was of execrable filth, to bring me to the healing waters of Your grace. This was the water that would wash me clean and dry up the floods flowing from my mother's eyes, tears with which she daily watered the ground beneath her face, pouring them forth to You on my behalf.

When she still refused to return without me, I persuaded her with much difficulty to remain for that night in a place near our ship where there was an oratory of Blessed Cyprian. That same night I stole away, but she remained there praying and weeping. And what was it that with so many tears she begged of You, but that You would not allow me to sail away? However, in the depth of Your counsel and hearing what was at the heart of her desires, You did not grant her request, so that You might fulfill that for which she was at all times praying.

The wind blew and swelled our sails and carried us out of sight of the shore, where she in the morning was overwhelmed with grief, and with her complaints and sighs filled Your ears. However, You disregarded them, while through my desires You were hurrying me where these desires might have an end. Thus my mother's carnal affection for me was punished by a just scourge and sorrow. For, as mothers do, and much more than most other mothers, she loved to have me with her. She did not know how much joy You would bring her by allowing me to depart from her.

She knew it not, and therefore she wept and lamented, and in these her sufferings showed the heritage of Eve in her, seeking with sorrow what in sorrow she had borne. However, after having ac-

cused me of deceit and cruelty, she turned herself to
You to pray for me, and went about her accustomed
affairs, and I arrived at Rome.

CHAPTER 9 — A Mother's Prayers

A T ROME, I was smitten with the scourge of
bodily illness, and was going down to hell, carrying with me all the sins I had committed against
You, against myself, and against my neighbors,
many and grievous, besides the bond of original sin,
by which *we all die in Adam* (1 Cor 15:22). For as
yet You *had forgiven nothing unto me in Christ* (Eph
4:32), nor *had He in His flesh taken away that enmity*
(Eph 2:16) with You which I had incurred by my
sins. For how should He take away my sins on that
cross of a phantom which was all that I had believed
Him to be?

As false then as the death of His flesh seemed to
me, so true was the death of my soul, and as true as
the death of His flesh indeed was, so false was the
life of my soul, which believed it not. Thus, with my
fever increasing within me, I was about to depart
and to perish forever. Where could I have gone, if I
had died at that time, but *into that fire and torment*
(Mt 25:41), which my deeds had deserved according to Your truthful ordinance?

My mother knew nothing of this, and yet, though
absent, was praying for me. And You Who are present everywhere did hear her where she was, and had
pity on me where I was, so that I recovered the
health of my body, though as yet very unhealthy in
my sacrilegious heart. Nor did I even desire Your
Baptism in that great danger. My spiritual state was
much better when, as a boy, I had earnestly re-

quested it of my mother's piety, as I have before related and confessed. But now I had matured shamefully and, fool that I was, I scorned the prescriptions of Your medicine.

However, You did not allow me to die a double death, nor such a wound to pierce my mother's heart as could never have been cured. I cannot sufficiently express the affection she had for me, and with how much greater pain she had suffered in observing my spiritual decline than she had suffered before at my carnal birth.

I see not, therefore, how she would ever have been cured if my death in such a fallen spiritual state had pierced the very depths of her love. And what would then have been the result of her so many and so frequent prayers, addressed to no one but You? Or could You, *O God of mercy* (2 Cor 1:3), *despise the contrite and humbled heart* (Ps 51:19) of so chaste and prudent a widow, generous in giving frequent alms, faithful in her help to Your holy ones, never failing even one day to attend the sacrifice at Your altar, coming to Your church without fail twice a day, morning and evening, not for vain gossiping and idle talk, but so that she might hear You in Your admonitions and You might hear her in her prayers?

Could You, by Whose grace she was such, despise and reject her tears with which she did not beg of You gold or silver, or any fading and perishable good, but the salvation of her son's soul? Never, O Lord! But You were present and heard her, and You granted her request, according to the plan that You had designed.

Far was it from You that You should deceive her in those visions and answers of Yours, some of which I have mentioned while omitting others, which she retained in her faithful heart, and in her prayers ever represented to You as Your personal guarantees. For *because Your mercy endures forever* (Ps 118:1), You deign, by Your promises, to make Yourself a debtor to those whose debts You remit.

CHAPTER 10 — In the Company of False Saints

YOU did, therefore, restore my health from that sickness and *saved the son of Your handmaid* (Ps 86:16) in the body, that You might afterward give me a better and more lasting health. At Rome, I again associated with those deceived and deceiving "saints": not only with their hearers, of which number there was one in whose house I had been ill and recovered, but also with those whom they call the elect. For it still seemed to me that it was not we who sinned, but I know not what other nature sinned in us.

It pleased my pride to be free from guilt, and, when I had committed any evil, not to confess that I had done it, that so *You might heal my soul that had sinned against You* (Ps 41:5). I loved to excuse myself, and to accuse I know not what that was in me, and yet was not I. But in truth, it was wholly I.

My impiety had divided me against myself. And my sin was so much the more incurable because I did not consider myself to be the sinner. My iniquity was most execrable, in that I would rather have You, O omnipotent God, to be overcome in me for my damnation than myself to be overcome by You for my salvation.

You had not then as yet *set a watch before my mouth and a door of caution about my lips, that my heart might not incline after evil words to make excuses in sin with men that work iniquity* (Ps 141:3-4), and therefore I was still in touch with their elect. Yet, despairing of making any further progress in that false doctrine, I began to be more remiss and negligent even in the opinions that I retained and with which I decided to be content till I could find something better.

I also began to think that the philosophers, whom they call the Academics, were wiser than the rest, because they held that we ought to doubt all things and contended that nothing of truth could be comprehended by man. This was what I understood their sentiments to be, as they are commonly represented, not comprehending as yet their true meaning.

I freely and openly discouraged my host from that excessive confidence which I found he had in the fables with which the Manichean books are filled. Yet I lived in closer friendship with them than with other men who were not of that sect. Though I did not defend their doctrine with my former earnestness, yet my close association with them (for there are many sheltered at Rome) made me more remiss in seeking elsewhere.

I especially despaired to find in Your Church, O Lord of Heaven and earth, Creator of all things visible and invisible, the truth from which they had turned me aside. And it seemed to me very unseemly to believe that You have the figure of human flesh and are circumscribed by the bodily lineaments of our limbs.

When I wanted to think of my God, I could fancy nothing but corporeal extension (for I conceded that whatever did not have such extension was nothing). This was the greatest and almost the only cause of my inevitable error.

From this I also imagined that there was some such substance of evil with its corporeal bulk, dark and deformed, and this either gross, which they called earth, or thin and subtle (as the body of the air is), which they conceive to be a malignant mind insinuating itself through that earth. And because the least degree of piety obliged me to believe that a good God would create no evil nature, I therefore imagined two opposite substances, the one good, the other evil, both infinite, yet the evil lesser, the good larger, and from this pernicious beginning followed the rest of my sacrilegious opinions.

When at any time my mind made an effort to return to the Catholic Faith, I was driven back again, because the Catholic Faith was not what I thought it was. It seemed to me to be more reverent to believe You, my God, to Whom I now confess Your mercies to me, to be infinite on all other sides, though I was forced to acknowledge You finite on one side on which the substance of evil was set against You, rather than to think You to be on every side confined within the form of a human body.

Again, I thought I did better to believe that You had not created any evil than to believe that such a nature of evil as I supposed it to be was from You, which my ignorance took to be a certain substance, and that corporeal, for I knew not how to conceive of mind otherwise than as a subtle body that was nevertheless diffused through space.

As for our Savior, Your only-begotten Son, I thought that He was sent forth for our salvation as a stream from the most lucid mass of Your substance, believing nothing else of Him than what in my vanity I was able to fancy. I supposed Him then to be of such a nature that it could not be born of the Virgin Mary without being mingled with flesh. And I could not imagine how this nature which I myself had envisioned could be mingled and not defiled.

Therefore, I was afraid to believe Him born in the flesh, lest I should be obliged to think Him defiled by the flesh. Now Your spiritual ones, if they read these my confessions, will gently and lovingly laugh at my folly. But such was the way I reasoned at that time.

CHAPTER 11 — Struggle To Be Free

FURTHERMORE, I did not think that those things which the Manichees criticized in Your Scriptures could be defended. But sometimes I had a desire to discuss every particular with some person well read in those books and to see what he could say. Already, the discourse of a certain Elpidius, who had disputed in public with those same Manichees, had begun to influence me even at Carthage, when he confronted them with certain things from the Scriptures that were not easy to refute.

Their answers seemed to me very weak. And they did not often give these answers in public, but usually only in private to us, saying that the Scriptures of the New Testament were falsified by I know not whom, who wished to insert the Jewish law into the Christian Faith. However, they were not able to produce any other uncorrupted copies.

But those two "bodily masses" chiefly held me down, captive and almost suffocated as I conceived only of corporeal things, under whose weight I lay gasping for the air of Your Truth. But still I was unable to breathe it in its unadulterated purity.

CHAPTER 12 — Teaching Rhetoric at Rome

I HAD then begun diligently to exercise the profession of teaching rhetoric, for which I had come to Rome. I first gathered some in my house to whom and through whom I had begun to be known. And then I was informed of some offenses that had been committed at Rome and that I had not suffered in Africa.

I had been assured that there was no rowdiness of wicked youths here as there was in Africa. "However," they said, "many youths, to avoid paying their teacher, conspire together and go off to another teacher"—deserters of their word, despising honesty for the love of money. My heart hated these also, though not with a perfect hate: for perhaps I hated them more because of what I should suffer from them than for the wrong they did to all.

Yet, certainly such as these are very base. They fornicate against You by loving the ephemeral mockeries of temporal things, and filthy lucre, which defiles the hand that grasps it, and by embracing this fleeting world and slighting You, Who always remain and call after them and are ready to pardon the adulterous soul of man when it returns to You.

Now, indeed, I hate such wicked and crooked persons, yet I love them as capable of amendment, trusting that they may prefer the doctrine they learn to money, and before their learning may prefer You, O God, Who are the Truth and Abundance of all assured good, and most pure peace. But at that time, I rather disliked them for my own sake than wished them to become good for Your sake.

CHAPTER 13 — Ambrose of Milan

WHEN, therefore, a request was sent from Milan to Rome to the prefect of the city to provide a professor of rhetoric for that city and to send him at public expense, I applied for the position through those same persons who were intoxicated with Manichean vanities (which I was going to be delivered from, though neither they nor I knew anything of that). Symmachus, who was then prefect, sent me, after testing my ability upon some subject of oratory.

And thus I came to Milan, to Ambrose the bishop, known as one of the most excellent men of the whole world, Your devout servant, whose discourses plentifully dispensed to Your people there the fat of Your wheat, the joy of Your oil, and the sober intoxication of Your wine. To him was I unknowingly brought by You, that by him I might knowingly be brought to You. That man of God received me with a father's affection, and he welcomed my coming with a bishop's kindness.

I began to love him, not at first as a teacher of truth, which I had no hopes of finding in Your Church, but as a man who was kind to me. And I eagerly listened to him when he preached to the people, not with a right intention, but, as it were, to see whether his eloquence was equal to his fame, or whether it was greater or less than was reported. I listened most attentively to his words, but with regard to his subject matter I was a careless and scornful onlooker.

I found myself delighted with the sweetness of his discourse; it was more learned than that of Faustus, yet in manner less cheerful and enchanting. But as to the matter, there was no comparison: for the one wandered through the delusions of Manicheism, the other taught most soundly the doctrine of salvation. *But salvation is far from sinners* (Ps 119:155), and such was I then as I stood before him. Yet, I was insensibly drawn nearer, although I did not realize it.

CHAPTER 14 — Breaking Away from the Manichees

WHILE I took no pains to learn what he said, but only to hear how he said it (for this vain care still remained in me, while I despaired of man's finding his way to You), there came into my mind, together with the words that I valued, the things that I slighted. For I could not separate them. And while I opened my heart to catch the eloquence of his words, there also entered the truth of what he said, though only by degrees.

First it began to appear to me that the things he said might be defended. And so I began to think that the Catholic Faith, for which I had previously supposed that nothing could be said in answer to the objections of the Manichees, might be plausibly maintained, especially after I had heard one or more of the obscure places of the Old Testament explained, and frequently so "in a figure," whereas when I understood them "literally," *the letter killed me* (2 Cor 3:6).

When, therefore, very many passages of those books had been explained in a spiritual sense, I blamed my own despair, in that I had thought no reply could be made to those who rejected and derided the Law and the Prophets. Neither did I think that I should now adopt the Catholic way merely because it could find learned defenders who were able to give adequate and not absurd answers to objections, nor yet did I think that what I held was to be condemned because both sides could be defended. While the Catholic cause did not appear to be vanquished, neither did it as yet seem victorious.

I began then diligently to consider if I could upon any certain grounds convict the Manichees of error. And could I but once have conceived a spiritual substance, I would quickly have demolished and cast out of my soul the whole structure of their system. But this I could not do.

Yet, concerning the system of this corporeal world and every part of nature that our bodily senses can perceive, the more I considered it, the more I was convinced by comparing them together that the philosophers had come nearer the truth than the Manichees. Therefore, after the manner of the Academicians (as they are commonly represented), doubting of all things and wavering between all things, I resolved once and for all to leave the Manichees, thinking that I ought not even for that time of my doubt to remain any longer in that sect to which I already preferred some of the philosophers.

Nevertheless, I refused absolutely to commit the cure of my sick soul to these philosophers because they were without the saving name of Christ. Upon this I determined to continue as a catechumen in the Catholic Church, which had been recommended to me by my parents until something certain should appear by which I might steer my course.

Book 6—Gravitating Toward Faith

At thirty years of age, Augustine, under the influence of Saint Ambrose, gradually abandons his errors. He realizes that he has blamed the Catholic Church wrongly and determines to amend his life.

CHAPTER 1 — Despair of Finding the Truth

O GOD, *my hope from my youth* (Ps 71:5), where were You then, or where did You withdraw Yourself? Was it not You Who had made me and distinguished me from the four-footed beasts and the birds of the air? You had made me wiser than they, and *I was walking in darkness* (Ps 81:5) and upon slippery paths, and was seeking You abroad in things outside of me, but I did not find You, *the God of my heart* (Ps 73:26). I had now sunk to the bottom of the sea, and I became despondent and despaired of finding the truth.

But now my mother had come to me, following me over land and sea, courageous through her piety, and in all perils relying on You. For when the sailors were in danger at sea, she comforted even them (whereas the sailors are usually the ones who comfort inexperienced passengers), and she assured them of a safe arrival, because You had promised this to her in a vision.

She found me in grave danger of renouncing, through despair, the prospect of ever finding the truth. And when I told her that I was no longer a Manichee, though not yet a Catholic Christian, she expressed no extraordinary joy as if I had told her something that was unexpected. For she had already been assured with regard to that aspect of my misery in which she had wept over me as dead, yet cried to

You that I might be raised by You, and she had carried me forth upon the bier of her thoughts, in order that You might say to the son of the widow, *Young man, I say to you, arise* (Lk 7:14), and he would return to life and begin to speak, and You would restore him to his mother.

Therefore, her heart did not pound with exultant joy when she heard that what she daily begged of You with her tears was accomplished to this extent, that although I had not yet attained the truth, I was already delivered from error. Being certain that in due time You Who had promised her the whole would give the rest, she calmly answered me with a heart full of confidence that she believed that Christ would allow her to see me a faithful Catholic before she departed from this life.

This was all she said to me, but to You, O Fountain of mercies, she redoubled her prayers and tears that You would hasten Your aid and *enlighten my darkness* (Ps 18:29). She would run more zealously to the church and hang on the words of Ambrose as a *fountain of living water springing up into life everlasting* (Jn 4:14). For she loved that man as *an angel of God* (Gal 4:14), because she knew that through him, in the meantime, I had been brought to that doubtful state of wavering in which I then was. She confidently anticipated that my disease had now passed the crisis stage, as the physicians call it, and that with his help I would pass from sickness to health.

CHAPTER 2 — Monica's Submission to the Church

THEREFORE, when according to the custom of Africa she had brought porridge and bread and wine to the tombs of the Saints, she was stopped by the doorkeeper. As soon as she heard that the bishop had prohibited these things, she so piously and obediently embraced his will that I admired the ease with which she so suddenly rather condemned her former practice than disputed the present prohibition. For her spirit was not a slave of intemperance, and she was not like so many men and women whom the love of wine provokes to hate the truth and who loathe a lesson of sobriety, as men steeped in drink loathe a glass of water.

When she had brought her basket with the usual festive food, of which she first tasted and then distributed the rest, she would put aside only one small cup of wine, tempered with water, for her sober palate, to take a little as courtesy required. And if there were many memorials of the dead that were thought to deserve this kind of honor, she carried about the one same cup to serve her for them all. But now, not only was it much diluted with water, but also hot from being carried about. By small portions she divided that watered-down wine between herself and her companions, for it was devotion she sought there, not pleasure.

When, therefore, she learned that this illustrious preacher and pious prelate had commanded that no such custom should be practiced, even by those who would do it soberly, lest an occasion should be given to drunkards to become intoxicated, and because these things much resembled the superstitious ancestor worship of the heathens, she most willingly abstained from them.

And instead of a basket filled with the fruits of the earth, she had learned to offer at the chapels of the martyrs a heart full of more purified prayers and to give what she could to the poor, and there to celebrate the Communion of the Lord's Body, by the imitation of Whose Passion the martyrs had been immolated and crowned.

However, it seems to me, O Lord my God, and it is the thought of my heart in Your sight, that my mother perhaps would not so easily have yielded to the breaking of that custom, if it had been forbidden by another man whom she did not love as much as Ambrose. For she loved him very much for the sake of my salvation, and he in turn also loved her for her most religious assiduity, by which, filled with good works and *fervent in spirit* (Acts 18:25), she frequented the church.

Therefore, many times when he saw me he would break forth in her praises, congratulating me that I had such a mother, not knowing what a son she had in me. For I doubted all things, and thought that the *way of life* (Acts 2:28) could not be discovered.

CHAPTER 3 — Focusing on Ambrose

I HAD not yet sighed in prayer to obtain assistance from You, but my mind was intent on research and restless to dispute. As for Ambrose himself, I looked upon him as a man happy according to worldly standards because he was so much honored by important people. Only his celibacy appeared to me to be painful.

However, as to what hopes he entertained, what struggles he had against the temptations he faced because of his very excellence, what comfort he felt in his adversities, and what sweet joys he tasted in the inward mouth of his heart in ruminating upon Your bread—these I had no notion of, nor had experienced.

Nor did he know my doubts, nor the depth of my danger. For I was unable to ask of him what I wished and as I wished, being shut off from his ears and voice by so many people to whose infirmities he ministered. And the time that he was not with them, which was little indeed, was taken up in refreshing either his body with necessary food or his mind by reading.

When he was reading, his eyes moved over the pages and his heart sought understanding, but his voice and tongue were silent. Often when we were present (for no one was refused entrance, nor was it the custom to give him notice of anyone's coming), we saw him reading in this manner in silence, and never otherwise. And after sitting down in long silence (for who would dare to be troublesome to one so intent?) we departed. We supposed that for the short time that he had for refreshing his mind, free from the noise of other men's business, he was loath to be disturbed.

Perhaps also for this reason, he did not read aloud, lest his hearer, being attentive to the reading, might desire enlightenment where the author seemed obscure, or it might be necessary to discuss some of the more difficult questions, so that, his time being thus spent, he would be hindered from reading as many volumes as he desired. Then again, perhaps his chief reason for reading in silence might have been to save his voice, which was easily weakened. But whatever he had in mind, that man certainly had nothing in view but what was good.

In reality then, I had little opportunity to ask the things I desired to draw from the heart of this, Your saintly oracle, unless the question could be answered briefly. Moreover, my perplexities required one perfectly disengaged, to whom they might be fully represented, and I could never find him so much at leisure.

However, I heard him among the people every Sunday as he was *rightly expounding the Word of truth* (2 Tm 2:15) to the people, and I was more and more convinced that all these knots of artificial calumnies, which my deceivers had tied so tightly to impugn the Divine Books, could be unraveled.

And when I also discovered that *man created by You in Your own image* (Gn 1:26) was not understood by Your spiritual children (whom by grace You have caused to be born again of their Catholic mother) in such manner as to believe or imagine You to be bound by the form of a human body (though as yet I could not even faintly apprehend what a spiritual substance could be), I was both glad and ashamed to find that for so many years I had been barking not at that which was indeed the Catholic Faith, but at the fictions of carnal concepts.

I had been so rash and wicked all that time as to be more ready to accuse and condemn that which I should have tried to learn by inquiry. For You, O Most High Who are most near, most hidden, and most present, Who are not composed of several members or parts, some greater and some less, but are everywhere whole, and yet within no place at all, are not indeed this corporeal form. And yet You have made man in Your image, and behold, from head to foot he is contained in space.

CHAPTER 4 — Suspended in Doubt

WHEN, therefore, I was unable to see how this Your image could subsist, I should have knocked and inquired in what manner this was to be believed, instead of insultingly opposing it, as if it were believed in the way I imagined. Hence, the doubt as to what I should now hold for certain gnawed the more sharply at my heart in proportion to my greater shame for having been so long deluded and deceived with the promise of certitude, and for having all the while with childish error and heat babbled endlessly about so many uncertainties, as if they had been things most certain.

That they were absolutely false, I did not fully know till afterward, but I was now sure that they were uncertain, and that I had formerly taken them for certain, when with blind contentions I accused Your Catholic Church. Though I had not yet fully discovered that she taught the truth, neither had I found that she taught the things with which I so vehemently had charged her.

Therefore, I was in the process of being confounded and converted. I rejoiced, O my God, that Your only Church, the body of Your only Son, in which when a child I had received the name of Christ, held no such childish fopperies, and that her sound doctrine did not shut You up, the Creator of all things, within a space, however high and large, yet terminated on every side by the figure of a human body.

I rejoiced also that those ancient writings of the Law and the Prophets were not now offered to me to be read with that eye to which they formerly seemed absurd, when I charged Your Saints with such sentiments that were not really theirs. And I often heard with pleasure Your servant Ambrose in his sermons to the people repeating and most diligently recommending as a rule that *the letter kills, but the Spirit gives life* (2 Cor 3:6).

And drawing aside the mystical veil, he opened the spiritual sense of many things that taken literally seemed to teach something that was wrong and he said nothing that could give me offense, though he said things the truth of which was still unknown to me. For I withheld my heart from giving any assent, fearing a precipice, and my suspense was even more pernicious.

I wanted to have the same certitude of things that are invisible as I had that seven and three make ten. I was not so mad as to think that even this could not be certainly known, but I desired to have all other things equally demonstrable, whether material, which were not present to my senses, or spiritual, of which I knew not how to think otherwise than in a corporeal manner.

I could have been cured by believing, and so my mental eyesight, being purified, might in some manner have been directed toward Your truth which is everlasting and knows no shadow of deficiency. But as it often happens that the man who has fallen into the hands of a bad physician is also afraid to commit himself to a good one, so it was with the sickness of my soul, which could not be healed except by believing. And for fear of believing things that were false, I refused to be cured, resisting the hands of You Who have made up the medicines of faith and distributed them for the diseases of the whole world, giving them so great an authority.

CHAPTER 5 — Beginning To Believe

I WAS led from this time to prefer the Catholic doctrine, which required belief in what was not yet demonstrated (either because it was a matter that could be demonstrated but perhaps not to everyone, or because it was indemonstrable). I found that the Church was more honest in this and less pretentious than the Manichees by whom believing was ridiculed, and certain knowledge was rashly promised, and many incredible and absurd things that could never be demonstrated were imposed as things to be believed.

Then, little by little, You, O Lord, touching and quieting my heart with a most gentle and merciful hand, thoroughly persuaded me by the consideration of the numberless things I believed although I had never seen them nor been present when they took place. This is true of so many things in human history, so many accounts of places and cities that I had never seen, so many things about friends, so many things about physicians, so many things about a variety of other men. Unless we accepted these things, we could accomplish nothing in this life.

In particular, how firmly I believed I had been born of some designated parents, a thing I could not possibly know except by believing those from whom I had heard it. By all this You thoroughly persuaded me that they were not to be blamed who believed Your books, to which You have given such great authority almost throughout all nations, but that they were to be blamed who did not believe them.

Nor were there any to be heard who said to me, "How do you know that these books were delivered to mankind by the Spirit of the one true and most truthful God?" This truth was of all the most credible, since no contentiousness of malicious questionings in the many conflicting systems that I had read in the philosophers could ever extort from me a disbelief of Your existence, whatever Your nature might be. Nor could they make me believe that the government of human affairs was not in Your hands.

My faith in these things was at times stronger and at other times weaker, yet I always believed in Your existence and Your providence over us, though I did not know what to think of Your substance or what was the way that led toward You or back to You.

Therefore, since we were too weak to find out Your truth by pure reason and thus stood in need of the authority of the Sacred Scriptures, I had begun to believe that You would by no means have given such complete authority throughout the whole world to those Scriptures if it had not been Your Will that through them we should believe in You and seek You. For after I had heard satisfactorily explained many of the apparent absurdities that had formerly offended me in Scripture, I attributed my difficulty to the sublimity of its mysteries. Its authority appeared to me so much the more venerable and worthy of a religious assent, in that it could easily be read by all, and yet preserved the dignity of its mystery in its more profound meaning.

Scripture makes itself accessible to all by the plainness of its words and the lowliness of its style, and yet captures the close attention of those who are not *light of heart* (Sir 19:4). Thus it receives all in its friendly arms, and through narrow passages introduces a few to You, although there would be far fewer if it either were not so transcendent in its authority or did not attract such multitudes into the bosom of its holy humility.

These were my thoughts and You were with me, I sighed and You did hear me, I wavered and You did guide me, I walked in the way of the world and You did not forsake me.

CHAPTER 6 — Confession of Wickedness

I LONGED for honors, riches, and marriage, and You laughed at me. In pursuing these desires, I underwent most bitter anxieties, and You were the more merciful to me, the less You permitted anything to be sweet to me that was not Yourself. Behold my heart, O Lord, for You have willed that I should now remember this and confess it to You. Let my soul now cleave fast to You, which You have rescued from the sticky birdlime of death.

How miserable I was! And You were still piercing the sensible part of my wound, so that leaving all other things I might be converted to You, *Who are over all things* (Rom 9:5), and without Whom all things would be nothing at all, and that in being converted I would be healed.

How miserable I was then, and You did everything possible to make me feel my misery on that day when, having prepared a panegyric in praise of the emperor, I was to tell many lies and yet be applauded by those who knew them to be lies. My heart was anxious for the success of the undertaking, and it burned in a fever of consuming thoughts.

As I passed through a certain street in Milan, I there took notice of a poor beggar, who, I believe, had gotten all the drink he wanted, and he was joking and full of mirth. I sighed and spoke to my friends who were with me of the many sorrows of our follies, for with all our endeavors (such as I was then laboring under, pricked by the goad of restless desires, and dragging after me the heavy load of my own unhappiness, which grew heavier by my dragging it), we desired nothing else but to attain a secure joy, which this poor beggar had achieved before us, a joy that perhaps we would never attain. For what he had already procured at the price of a few pennies obtained by begging, namely, the pleasure of a temporal happiness, I was still toiling for through many winding and difficult paths.

It is true that his was not genuine joy, but that which my ambition was pursuing was much more false. And certainly he was cheerful and I was perplexed; he was secure and I was in fear. If anyone would have asked me whether I would rather rejoice or be in fear, I would have answered that I would rather rejoice, but if he would have asked me again, whether I would rather choose to be like the beggar in his condition or in my own, I would have preferred my own, notwithstanding all my cares and fears. But I would have spoken perversely, for how could that be true?

Nor would I have preferred myself to him because I was more learned, since I did not rejoice in this, but only sought thereby to please men. I was not concerned about teaching them, but merely wanted to please them. Therefore, You most justly stood against me and *broke my bones* (Ps 42:11) with the rod of Your discipline.

Let them, therefore, depart from my soul who say to it, "Everything depends on the reason for a person's joy. That beggar found joy in drinking wine; you sought joy in getting glory." What glory was this, O Lord, that did not have its source in You? For as his was no true joy, so neither was this true glory, and it upset my mind even more. That very night he would sleep off his drunkenness, but I had slept and risen again with mine, and was to sleep and rise again with it for many days.

Yes, it does make a difference upon what grounds a man's joy is based. I know this, for the joy of a hope rooted in faith is incomparably beyond such vanity. And there was a difference also between him and me. He was the happier of the two of us—not only in being full of mirth while I was racked with cares, but that he, by wishing blessings upon people, had obtained some wine, and I by telling lies was hunting after empty praise.

This was the essence of my talks with my friends, and I thus often observed that things were not right with me. When I grieved about this, I immediately doubled my load. And if I met with any prosperity, I was loath to take any notice of it because, before I could take hold of it, it would fly away.

CHAPTER 7 — Alypius

THOSE of us who were living together as friends lamented about these things, but I communicated my thoughts chiefly to Alypius and Nebridius. Alypius had been born in my native town—his parents belonged to the leading families in that place—and he was younger than I. He had been my pupil, both when I first set up school in our town and afterward at Carthage. He loved me greatly because he thought me to be good and learned, and I also loved him for his great inclination to virtue, which was remarkable for one of his tender years.

However, the whirlpool of Carthaginian customs, where all sorts of vain shows are hotly followed, had carried him away to an insane love for the circus. When he was miserably wrapped up with these sports, I was teaching rhetoric at Carthage in a public school. However, because of some disagreement between me and his father, he at that time was not one of my students. I had found out that he was passionately fond of the circus, and I was deeply grieved that one who gave such great promise would be lost, or rather, to my thinking, was lost already.

I did not think that I had any means of admonishing him or reclaiming him by any restraint, either by showing him the benevolence of a friend or exercising the authority of a teacher, for I imagined that he shared his father's thoughts about me. In fact, however, he was not so disposed. Hence, disregarding his father's wishes in this matter, he began to greet me kindly and to come sometimes into my lecture room to listen for a while and then depart. Yet I had refrained from speaking to him and trying to prevent the loss of so good a mind as the result of a blind and headstrong love for such vain sports.

But You, O Lord, Who rule over all things You have created, had not forgotten him who was one day to be numbered among Your sons as a bishop of Your Church. And so that his reformation in this matter might evidently be Your work, You brought it about through me without my knowledge.

One day, when I was sitting in my usual place and my students were about me, he came in, greeted me, sat down, and gave his attention to what was being discussed. Now it happened that in expounding on the subject, to make it both more agreeable and more plain, I borrowed a comparison from the shows of the circus, not without biting mockery of those who had become slaves to that particular insanity.

You know, O God, that I had no thought at that time of curing Alypius of that sickness. But he instantly applied it to himself and thought I spoke it purely for his sake. Another would have taken it as a reason to be angry with me, but he, being a well-disposed youth, made it an occasion of being angry with himself, and of loving me more dearly.

You said long ago, and inserted in Your holy Books the saying, *Rebuke a wise man, and he will love You* (Prv 9:8). However, I had not yet rebuked him, but You, Who make use of all, whether they know it or know it not—according to the order that You know, and that order is just—from my heart and tongue did form "burning coals," with which You were pleased to set on fire that promising mind, which was then languishing, and so cure it.

May the man be silent in Your praises who considers not Your mercies, which I from the bottom of my soul confess to You. For Alypius, after those words, immediately burst out of that deep pit into which he had willingly plunged, having been blinded by wretched pleasure. Shaking his soul with a resolute self-restraint, all the filth of the circus fell off from him, and he returned there no more. After this, he prevailed upon his unwilling father to allow him to be my student, and the father yielded and consented to his request.

Therefore Alypius, beginning to attend my lectures again, became involved with me in the same superstition, being much taken with the ostentatious continence of the Manichees, which he supposed to be true and sincere. However, it was a senseless and deceitful continence, ensnaring precious souls unable as yet to reach the height of virtue, but easily deceived by a superficial appearance of that which was but a shadowy and counterfeit virtue.

CHAPTER 8 — Alypius in the Amphitheater

NOT forsaking the worldly career that his parents had planned for him, Alypius had gone before me to Rome to study law, and there again he was carried away incredibly with an insatiable passion for gladiatorial shows. Although he was at first very much averse to them and detested such spectacles, some of his friends and fellow students, meeting him by chance in the streets after dinner, with a playful violence dragged him in spite of his vehement refusal and resistance to the amphitheater upon a day when those cruel and deadly sports were taking place.

All the while he was saying, "If you drag my body along with you there and settle it there, can you force me also to turn my mind or my eyes upon those shows? I shall be absent, therefore, though present in body, and so shall overcome both you and them." Despite hearing this, they nevertheless drew him along with them, wishing perhaps to discover whether he had power to do as he said.

When they arrived and had gotten such seats as they could, the whole place was seething with savage delight. But Alypius, shutting the doors of his eyes, forbade his mind to even think about such wicked sights. Would that he could have stopped his ears too! For at the moment when someone fell during the fight, struck by a mighty roar of the entire crowd, he was overcome by curiosity. Wishing only to see what was the matter, and, whatever it was, to despise it and ignore it, he opened his eyes and was immediately smitten with a more grievous wound in the soul than the gladiator whom he desired to behold had suffered in his body.

He fell more miserably than the one whose fall had occasioned this roar, which, entering his ears, had unlocked his eyes, and through them had given a mortal wound to his soul. For his soul was more bold than strong, and the weaker, because it had relied on itself when it should have relied only on You.

No sooner did he see that blood than he also drank in the savage cruelty of it. Nor did he turn away his eyes, but fixed them upon it. He drank in that frenzy, and knew it not, and became delighted with the wickedness of the fight and was made drunk with that gory pastime. He was no longer the same man, but was one of the crowd he had joined, and a true associate of those who had brought him there.

Need I say more? He looked on, shouted, and was inflamed. He carried away with him a madness that would spur him on to return again, not only with those who had dragged him there before, but he would come first, drawing others after him. Yet, from hence also, with a most strong and merciful hand, You delivered him, and taught him to rely no more on himself, but to trust in You. However, this took place long afterward.

CHAPTER 9 — Alypius in the Marketplace

FOR a time this was laid up in his memory to be a medicine for the future. So also was that which happened to him when he studied and followed my courses at Carthage. At noon in the Forum he was meditating upon the scholastic exercise that he was afterward to recite, as is customary among students, when You allowed him to be apprehended as a thief by the officers of the marketplace. I believe this was permitted by You, my God, for no other reason but that he who was hereafter to be so great a man might begin to learn by this, that in judging cases, one may not condemn another with rash credulity.

As he was at that time walking alone with his tablets and pen in his hand before the court of justice, another young man, who was one of the students and the real thief, secretly concealing a hatchet, went in, without Alypius noticing it, to the leaden rails that are over the silversmiths' shops and began to cut off the lead. The silversmiths underneath, hearing the noise of the hatchet, began to make a stir, and sent men to apprehend anyone they should find. The thief, overhearing their voices, ran away, leaving the hatchet behind for fear of being caught with it.

Alypius, who had not seen him enter, had noticed his coming out and how hurriedly he had left. Wishing to know the reason, Alypius entered the place. Finding the hatchet, he stood there examining it and wondering what had happened, when suddenly those who had been sent came in and found him holding in his hand the hatchet, the noise of which had brought them there. They apprehended him, and dragged him along, and, calling together the shopkeepers of the neighborhood, they boasted that now they had caught the true thief in the act. From there they led him to face the judge.

But his lesson was not prolonged beyond this point. For You, O Lord, immediately came in to vindicate his innocence, of which You were the only witness. As they were leading him along either to prison or to punishment, an architect, who was the caretaker of the public buildings, met them. They were glad to meet him, for he used to suspect some of them of stealing such things as were lost in the marketplace, and he would now see at long last who it was who had committed all these thefts.

However, it happened that this man had often seen Alypius at the house of a certain senator whom he used to visit. Recognizing him, he took him by the hand aside from the crowd and asked him the cause of so great a misfortune. Having heard the whole story, he then bade the crowd, who were shouting violent threats, to go along with him.

And so they came to the house of the young man who had done the deed. At the door they met a servant boy who was so young that he could be relied upon to tell the whole truth without suspecting that any harm could come to his master, for he had accompanied the thief to the marketplace. Alypius, recognizing him, indicated this to the architect. The latter, immediately showing him the hatchet, asked him if he knew whose it was. The boy quickly answered, "It is ours." And upon being questioned further, he revealed the rest of the story.

Thus the crime was traced to that house, and the mob, which had begun to hurl taunts at Alypius, was confounded. And Alypius, who was to be a dispenser of Your Word and an examiner of many causes in Your Church, departed a wiser and more experienced man.

CHAPTER 10 — The Three Friends

I WAS reunited with Alypius in Rome. He stuck close to me with a very strong bond of friendship and went with me to Milan. He did this so that he would not be separated from me and might there practice to some extent the law he had studied, more to please his parents than to satisfy himself. There he had already sat three times as an assessor, admired by the rest for his integrity, while for his part he much more wondered at those who valued money above honesty. His disposition in this regard was also tried not only by the allure of avarice but also by the temptation of fear. He was assessor at Rome to the director of the Italian treasury.

There was at that time a senator, a man of great power, to whose favors many had become indebted and whose severity was dreaded by many more. Now, seeking special privileges because of his power, he wanted to be permitted to do what was forbidden by the laws, but Alypius withstood him. A reward was promised him, but he scorned it. He was assaulted with threats, but he despised them.

All admired such an extraordinary spirit that neither wished as his friend nor feared as his enemy a man who was so powerful and renowned for countless ways of doing good or evil to many. The judge himself, whose counselor Alypius was, though he also was opposed to the granting of the favor, did not openly declare his opposition. Rather, shifting the onus upon Alypius, he said that Alypius would not allow him to consent to it. In truth, had the judge approved it, Alypius would have resigned.

Only in one respect was he ever tempted to take advantage of his position, when in his zeal for study he gave some thought to procuring books for himself at a lower rate. However, after taking into account the principles of justice, he chose to follow the more honorable course, valuing more the equity that forbade this than the power that permitted it. This was indeed a matter of little significance, *but he who is faithful in a very little thing is faithful also in the greater* (Lk 16:10). Neither can that by any means be vain which has proceeded from the mouth of Your truth: *If in the case of wicked mammon you have not proved faithful, who will entrust you with what is true? And if in the case of what belongs to another you have not proved faithful, who will give you what is your own?* (Lk 16:11-12).

Such was the man who was then closely united to me, and in his plans he wavered no less than myself as to what course of life we ought to take.

There was also Nebridius, who had left his native country near Carthage, and Carthage itself, where he most frequently lived, leaving his father's fine estate and country house, and also his mother, who would not follow him. He had come to Milan for no other reason than to live with me in a most ardent search after truth and wisdom. He joined his sighs with ours and was equally perplexed, being a most fervent seeker after a happy life and a most earnest inquisitor into the most difficult questions.

And so there were together three famished mouths, bewailing to one another their wants, and waiting for You *that You might give them their food in due season* (Ps 145:15). In all that bitterness which, by Your merciful approval, attended our worldly pursuits, when we considered to what end we underwent those sufferings, we discovered nothing but darkness.

Then, with a sigh, we would turn away and ask: "How long shall these things last?" These words we often repeated, and yet, having said so, we did not cease our worldly pursuits, because we could not discern anything certain that, having left these, we might embrace in their place.

CHAPTER 11 — Pondering the Future

I CONTINUED to reflect excessively when I considered and called to mind the length of time that had elapsed since my nineteenth year, when I first began to be inflamed with the desire for wisdom, and determined that, upon finding it, I would relinquish all empty hopes of vain desires and deceitful follies. And now here I was, thirty years old, still stuck in the same mire, greedy and enjoying present things, which fled away and debased my soul.

Meanwhile I would say to myself: "Tomorrow I shall find it out; behold it will clearly appear and I shall accept it; and lo, Faustus will come and explain everything. O you great men, you Academicians! Can nothing be known with certainty for regulating the conduct of life? Rather, let us seek with greater diligence, and not yield to despair. Behold those things that seemed absurd in ecclesiastical books are not truly absurd, but may be understood in a rational way. I will continue to hold the religious beliefs that my parents taught me as a child, until the clear truth be discovered.

"But where or when shall we seek this truth? Ambrose has no leisure time, and we have no time to read. Where shall we find such books? With what, or when, can we procure them? From whom shall we borrow them? Let us set some time apart, allotting certain hours of the day for the welfare of the soul.

"Great hope has been given to us, for the Catholic Faith does not teach what we imagined and foolishly charged it with. Its learned men look upon it as blasphemy to believe that God is confined within the figure of a human body. Why do we fear to 'knock' so that the rest may 'be opened' to us? My students take up the morning hours, but what do we do with the rest of our time? Why not do this?

"But when then shall we court our influential friends, whose favor we depend upon? What time must we take to prepare the books we sell to our students? What time will we have to restore our strength by relaxing our mind from absorbing cares?

"Let all such unimportant matters be forgotten! Laying aside these vain and empty things, let us apply ourselves to the search for truth alone. This life is wretched, and the hour of our death is uncertain. If it should come upon us suddenly, in what state shall we depart hence? And where shall we learn what we have here neglected? And shall we not be punished for this neglect? But what if death put an end to all care, together with sensibility? This then also must be examined.

"But God forbid it should be so. Surely it is no vain, no empty matter, that the excellent dignity of the authority of the Christian Faith should have spread all over the world. Never would God have done such great things for us if the death of the body were to put an end also to the life of the soul. Why then do we delay forsaking the hopes of this world to give ourselves up wholly to seek after God and the blessed life?

"But consider for a moment. Even these things are pleasant; they have in them no small sweetness. We must not part with them too hastily, for it would be shameful to return to them again. Yet it is not so difficult to obtain some honorable position. And what more should we then wish for? We have a large number of powerful friends if nothing else is offered and we are unwilling to wait for something better. A governorship may be given to us. I may marry a wife of comfortable means, so that our expenses will not be excessive. Such will be the limit of my ambition. Many great men who have been most worthy of imitation have been married, and yet have given themselves up to the study of wisdom."

While I was saying these things, and these shifting winds in turn drove my heart to and fro, time passed on, and still I delayed *being converted to the Lord God.* I put off *from day to day to live* (Sir 5:8) in You, but I did not put off daily dying in myself. I hoped for a happy life but was afraid I would find it where You abode, and while fleeing from it, I sought after it.

I thought that I would be exceedingly miserable if I were to be deprived of the embraces of a woman. I did not think that the medicine of Your mercy could cure this infirmity because I had not tried it. I believed that continence depended on one's own strength, which I knew I did not possess. I was foolish not to know that it is written: *No one can be continent, except You give it* (Wis 8:21). You indeed would have given it if with inward sighs I assailed Your ears and with a firm faith cast my care upon You.

CHAPTER 12 — Decision To Marry

ALYPIUS was indeed greatly opposed to the idea of my taking a wife, repeatedly asserting that we could in no way, with any secure leisure, live together in the love of wisdom, as we had long desired, if I were to marry. In this regard he was even then living a most chaste life, and it was truly remarkable how, in the beginning of his youth having experienced those pleasures, he did not remain stuck in the mire, but rather was sorry for what he had done, and despising those enjoyments lived ever after most continently.

However, I opposed him, pointing to the examples of those who, being married, had studied wisdom and pleased God, and had faithfully kept and loved their friends. But I could hardly compare to those men in their greatness of soul. Bound by the disease of the flesh with its poisonous pleasure, I continued to drag my chains after me, being afraid to be loosed from them. And, as if my wound had been struck, I rejected the words of him who so well advised me, as I would reject a hand that would set me free.

Moreover, the serpent also spoke through me to Alypius, and by my tongue wove and spread in his way his pleasurable snares to entangle those virtuous feet that were then at liberty. He was unable to understand how I, for whom he had such great esteem, could remain stuck so fast in the birdlime of that pleasure as to declare, in our frequent discussions, that I could not possibly lead a celibate life.

To defend myself when I saw his confusion, I would tell him that there was a vast difference between his short stolen pleasures, of which he had now scarcely any remembrance and which he might easily now despise, and the delights of my habitual experience, and that, if the honorable name of marriage were added, he could have no reason to wonder at my choice of that kind of life.

On hearing this he also began to wish to enter the married state, not that he was overcome with a desire for that pleasure, but out of curiosity. He said he wanted to know what that was, without which my very life that pleased him so much would seem to me not life but a punishment.

His mind that was free from that chain wondered at my slavery, and from this wondering proceeded to a desire of trying, ready to go to the trial itself, and from there perhaps to fall into that slavery which he wondered at. He was willing to make *a covenant with death* (Is 28:15); and *he who loves danger shall fall into it* (Sir 3:25).

Whatever honor there may be in the office of married persons ruling a family and educating children, neither he nor I had given it much thought. But it was my habit of satisfying an insatiable concupiscence that chiefly and most vehemently tortured me, who was its captive. And it was his curiosity about me that drew him on toward the same bondage. So were we until You, the Most High, not forsaking our dust, but commiserating with us in our misery, came to our rescue in marvelous and secret ways.

CHAPTER 13 — Promised in Marriage

EARNEST efforts were made to hasten my entry into the married state. The girl to whom I proposed was promised to me. My mother was the driving force behind this, for she believed that once I was married, I might be cleansed by the saving waters of Baptism. She was pleased to see that I was daily better disposed for it, and took notice that her prayers and Your promises began to be fulfilled by my faith. Yet when both by my entreaty and by her own inclinations she daily begged You with loud cries of her heart to show her in a vision something concerning my future marriage, You never did grant her request.

My mother saw some vain and fantastic things, the product of her own human mind that was greatly overwrought by her anxiety in this matter. She related them to me, not with the confidence she usually had when You had shown her anything, but rather disparaging them. She said that she was able to discern, in a mysterious and indescribable way, the difference between Your revelations and her own dreams. Yet the matter was pressed forward and a maiden was asked for, though legally she would not be of marriageable age for almost two years. However, because I liked her, I was willing to wait.

CHAPTER 14 — Ten Friends with One Resolve

MANY of my friends and I had often pondered and debated together on the vexatious troubles of a worldly life that we all detested, and we now had almost resolved to live a life in solitude apart from the world. In our plan for this life of retirement, everyone would bring in what he possessed and deposit it in a common fund. Thus, in unadulterated friendship, no one would claim anything as his own, but the whole would belong to everyone and everything would belong to all.

There were about ten of us who were ready to join this society, some of whom were very rich, especially Romanianus, our fellow townsman and a close friend from my childhood, who had come to the emperor's court to resolve some troublesome concerns of his. He was most enthusiastic about our plan, and since he had a much greater estate than any of the rest, his opinion had a greater weight.

We had agreed that two of us yearly, like magistrates, should take care of all necessary matters, leaving the rest undisturbed. When we began to consider whether the wives, which some of us already had and I proposed to have, would permit it, this whole project, which had been so carefully conceived, fell to pieces in our hands, broken and cast aside.

Then we returned again to sighing and groaning and turned our steps to follow the broad and beaten paths of this world, for *many thoughts were in our hearts, but Your counsel stands forever* (Prv 19:21). From this Your counsel You then derided our projects, and made way for Your own, ready *to give us food in due season, and to open Your hand, and to fill our souls with Your blessing* (Ps 145:15-16).

CHAPTER 15 — A New Liaison

MEANWHILE my sins were multiplied. The woman with whom I had lived so long in concubinage was torn from my side as an obstacle to my marriage, leaving my heart, which had clung to her, torn and wounded and bleeding. She returned to Africa, making a vow to You never to know any other man, and leaving with me the natural son I had by her.

But I, in my unhappiness, unable to follow a woman's example, and impatient of delay (for it would be two years before I was to have her to whom I proposed), because I was not a lover of marriage but a slave of lust, procured myself another woman, though not as a wife. And so I desired to sustain and keep up, entire or even augmented, the slavery of an enduring habit, that disease of my soul, until I would reach the realm of matrimony.

Nor was that wound of mine healed, which had been made by the cutting away of my former concubine. After the inflammation and acute pains, it putrefied and ached with a pain more cold, as it were, yet more desperate.

CHAPTER 16 — A Would-Be Follower of Epicurus

TO You be praise, and to You be glory, O Fountain of mercies! I became more miserable, and You drew nearer to me. And now continually Your right hand was ready to draw me out of the mire and to wash me clean, and I knew it not. Nor was there anything that restrained me from sinking still deeper into the pit of carnal pleasures except the fear of death and of Your judgment to come, which throughout all the variety of my opinions never quite left my mind.

I often discussed with my friends Alypius and Nebridius about the ends of good and evil, and that, to my mind, Epicurus above all men had carried away the prize, were it not that I believed the soul survived after death, and was treated according to its merits, which Epicurus did not believe.

And I asked: "If we were immortal and lived in the perpetual enjoyment of the pleasures of the body without any fear of losing them, would this not be enough to make us happy, or what else would we want?" For I did not know how great was my misery when, having plunged so deeply and in my blindness, I could not raise my thoughts to the light of virtue and sovereign beauty that are to be embraced for their own sake. These the eye of the flesh does not see, but they are seen in the innermost soul.

Nor did I, in my wretchedness, consider the source from which I was able to converse with pleasure with my friends about these things, filthy as they were. Nor did I even then, with the notions I then had, think that I could be happy without friends, even though I were to have an unending abundance of carnal delights. And yet, I loved these friends for their own sake and felt that I was loved by them in the same manner.

Oh crooked ways! Woe to my foolhardy soul that vainly hoped to find something better after it had departed from You! It turned and turned itself again upon its back and sides and belly, but all positions were hard and uncomfortable, for You alone are its rest. Behold, You are with us, and You deliver us from our miserable errors. You direct us on Your path and encourage us, saying: "Run on! *I will carry you, and I will bring you to the end of your race* (Is 46:4), *and even there I will continue to carry you*" (Jer 39:17).

Book 7—From Error to Truth

Augustine gradually abandons his errors concerning the nature of God and the origin of evil. He also begins a more careful study of the Sacred Scriptures and attains at last to a true knowledge of God, though not yet rightly understanding the mystery of the Incarnation of Jesus Christ.

CHAPTER 1 — Striving To Know God

MY WICKED youth was now dead and gone, and I was entering into the state of manhood. The older I grew, the more defiled I was by vanity. I could conceive of no substance except those I usually beheld with my own eyes. I did not indeed imagine You, O my God, in the shape of a human body, for, from the time I had absorbed anything of wisdom, I always abhorred that, and I rejoiced to find that the faith of our spiritual mother, Your Catholic Church, also abhorred it.

But then I was at a loss to know what other idea I was to form of You. Being a man—and such a man!—I endeavored to conceive and apprehend You, the supreme and the only true God. From the bottom of my heart I believed You to be incorruptible and inviolable and immutable because, though I knew not how nor where, I plainly saw and knew with absolute certainty that that which can be corrupted is inferior to that which cannot. What could not be hurt I unhesitatingly preferred to what could be hurt, and the perfectly immutable to what could suffer change. My heart strongly cried out against all my illusions.

With this one blow, I strove to drive away from the eyes of my mind the swarm of unclean images that hovered before me. And scarcely had they been

removed, when in the twinkling of an eye they gathered again before me, rushing into my sight and
overclouding it. Therefore, although I did not represent You to myself in the form of a human body, I
was still forced to imagine You as some kind of corporeal being, either infused into the world through
earthly space or else endlessly diffused beyond it.

I much preferred this same incorruptible and inviolable and immutable being to that which is corruptible or violable or mutable, because whatsoever
I conceived without such spatial characteristics
seemed to me to be nothing, yes, not to exist at all,
not even so much as a void. For if a body is taken
out of a place and the place remains void without
any body at all in it, either earthly or watery or airy
or heavenly, there yet remains an empty place like a
spacious nothing.

I, therefore, being dull of heart, without even a
clear concept of my own self, thought all that to be
nothing which was not extended through some
space, nor spread out, nor condensed, nor swollen,
or did not or could not contain such things. Such
forms over which my eyes were accustomed to
range were the images my heart followed after. Nor
did I reflect that the concept of the mind, by which
I formed these images, was not of this sort, and yet
it would not form them if it were not something
great.

In this manner also I imagined You, O Life of my
life, to be extended through infinite space and to
penetrate on every side the whole mass of the world
and to be diffused beyond the world on all sides to
an immensity without limit, so that the earth had
You, and the heavens had You, and all things had

You, and they were bounded in You, but You were bounded nowhere.

The body of the air that is above the earth does not hinder the light of the sun from passing through it. The sun penetrates it in such a manner as not to break or divide it, but to fill the whole. Similarly, I thought that not only the bodies of the heavens and air and sea, but of the earth also, were penetrable by You, and in all their smallest as well as greatest parts penetrable to receive Your presence everywhere by a secret inspiration both within and without, governing all things that You have created.

Thus was my belief, and I was unable to conceive anything else, for it was false. Therefore, a greater part of the earth would have a greater part of You, and a lesser would have a lesser part, and in such a manner would all things be filled with You, so that the body of an elephant would hold much more of You than the body of a sparrow because it is larger and occupies a greater place. Thus You would be present by parts of Yourself to the parts of the world—by bigger pieces to the greater parts of the world, and by lesser pieces to the lesser parts. Clearly it is not so. But as yet You had not *enlightened my darkness* (Ps 18:29).

CHAPTER 2 — The Argument of Nebridius

THAT was enough for me, O Lord, to combat those deceived deceivers and mute chatterers, for it was not Your Word that sounded from their mouths. That argument was enough, I say, which long ago, even from the time of our stay at Carthage, Nebridius used to propound, strongly affecting us who heard it: "That nation of darkness, which the Manichees are wont to set up against You as a hostile mass—what could it have done to You if You had refused to fight with it?"

If they answered that it would have done You some harm, it would imply that You were subject to injury and corruption. But if they should say that it could not have caused You harm, no reason could be given for Your fighting, and fighting in such a manner that some part or member of Your being, or an offspring from Your own substance, would be mingled with the inimical powers and those natures that were not created by You. Thus it would be so greatly corrupted by them and changed for the worse as to have fallen from blessedness to misery and to need some help by which it could be freed and purified.

They would assert that this part of Your substance is the soul, which, in its enslaved, defiled and corrupted state, would be relieved by Your Word, which is free, pure, and sound, without any defect. And yet, this Word itself would also be subject to corruption because it was of one and the same substance. Therefore, if they affirmed that You, whatever You are—that is, Your substance by which You are—are incorruptible, then all those things were false and abominable. But if they affirmed that You are corruptible, the mere concept of this would prove to be false and abominable.

This argument, therefore, was sufficient against those who merited to be vomited from my burdened breast, because they had no way to wriggle out of this dilemma without committing a horrid sacrilege of the heart and tongue by thinking and saying such things of You.

CHAPTER 3 — The Cause of Evil

A LTHOUGH I thus maintained and firmly believed You our Lord, the true God (Who have
made not only our souls but our bodies also, and
not only our souls and bodies, but all persons and
all things), to be incapable of being defiled or altered, or in any part changed, I did not as yet apprehend, clearly and without difficulty, the cause of
evil. Whatever this cause of evil might be, I saw that
in seeking it, I was not to look for such a thing as
might oblige me to believe the immutable God to be
liable to suffer change, lest I myself should become
the evil that I sought for.

Hence, I sought it, free from anxiety, certain that
what the Manichees said was not true. I fled from
them with my whole heart, for I saw that while seeking the origin of evil, they were themselves filled with
evil because they chose rather to think that Your
substance suffered evil than that their own did evil.

I strained hard to see and discern what I often
heard, that our free will was the cause of our committing evil, and that it was *Your just judgment* (Ps
119:137) that we suffer evil, but I could not clearly
see it. I endeavored to draw forth my mind's vision
out of the deep pit, but I sank back again, and as
often as I tried, I sank back over and over again.
What raised me up toward Your light was that I
knew that I had a will, as surely as I had a life.

When I willed or did not will anything, I was
most certain that it was I alone who willed or did
not will. And I saw directly that therein lay the cause
of my sin. But that which I did against my will, I saw
that I rather suffered than committed, and I judged
it to be not a fault but a punishment. Considering

You to be just, I readily confessed that I was not unjustly punished in this manner.

But again I argued: "Who made me? Was it not
my God, Who is not only good, but goodness itself?
Whence, therefore, have I this will to evil and repugnance to good, so that there is an occasion for my
being justly punished? Who has put this in me and
engrafted in me this root of bitterness, when all of
me was made by my most sweet God? If the devil is
the author, whence comes the devil himself? But if
he also, by his perverse will, from a good angel was
made a devil, whence came in him this evil will, by
which he became a devil, since the whole angel was
made good by the most excellent Creator?"

By these thoughts I was plunged back again and
stifled. Yet I had not sunk into that hell of error
(where no one will confess to You) as to believe that
You suffer evil, rather than that man commits it.

CHAPTER 4 — The Supreme Good

I NOW strove to find out all the rest, as one who
had already discovered that what is incorruptible
is better than the corruptible, and for that reason I
confessed You, whatever You were, to be incorruptible. Never was any soul able, or will it ever be able,
to conceive anything that is better than You, the
supreme and most excellent Good. Since, therefore,
that which is incorruptible is most truly and most
certainly preferred to that which is corruptible, as I
also then preferred it, then if You were not incorruptible, my thoughts could have conceived something better than my God.

Therefore, where I saw that the incorruptible is to
be preferred to the corruptible, there ought I to seek

You, and from then on perceive whence evil comes, that is, whence comes corruption itself, by which Your substance can by no means be violated.

In no way at all does corruption defile our God— by no will, by no necessity, by no unforeseen accident—*because He is God* (Ps 100:3), and whatever He wills for Himself is good, and He is that same good. But to be corrupted is not good.

Neither are You forced to anything against Your will, for Your will is not greater than Your power. If it were greater, You would be greater than Yourself, for the will and power of God is God Himself. And what can be unforeseen to You, Who know all things, and since no nature exists without Your knowledge? It hardly seems necessary to say so much to show that the substance that is God is incorruptible, since if it were corruptible, it would not be God.

CHAPTER 5 — The Fact of Evil

I SOUGHT to discover the source of evil, but I did so in an evil way and I failed to see the evil in my very search. In the picture depicted in my mind I placed the entire creation, both as to the things that we can see (such as earth and sea and air and the stars and trees and all mortal creatures) and whatever in it remains unseen (such as the firmament of heaven, and all the angels and its spiritual inhabitants).

In this picture also, as if they had been bodies, my imagination appointed their several places. And I framed one great mass, distinguished by various kinds of bodies of Your creation, which either were true bodies, or which I myself feigned in place of spirits. This mass I imagined to be huge, not as it was, a thing I could not know, but according to my fancy, vastly extended on all sides, but yet finite.

But You, O Lord, I conceived as encompassing on all sides and penetrating this vast mass, yet in every way infinite: as if the sea were everywhere, alone infinite through boundless space on all sides, and had within it sponge of great but finite magnitude, and this sponge were in every part full of the boundless sea. In this way I conceived Your finite creature to be full of You, O Infinite One. And I said:

"Behold God, and behold all the things that God has created, and God is good, and most excellently and incomparably better than any of these things. Yet being good He has created good things, and behold how He encompasses and fills all things.

"Where then is evil and whence, and how has it crept in here? What is its root, and what is its seed? Or is it nothing at all? Why then do we fear and fly from that which does not exist? Or if we vainly fear it, then surely this fear itself is an evil by which our heart is pricked and tortured without cause, and so much the greater is this evil, the more we are wanting a reason for fear, and yet do fear.

"Therefore, either there exists an evil that we fear, or our very fear is an evil. Whence then is it, since God, a good God, made all these things good? Truly He, the greater and sovereign Good, made these lesser goods, yet both the Maker and the things made by Him are all good. From whence then is evil? Or was there some evil matter out of which He made these things, and which He formed and put in order, yet so as to leave something in it that He did not convert to good?

"But then why this? Was He not able to convert and change it entirely, so as to leave no evil in it, since He can do all things? Finally, why would He make anything at all out of it, and not rather use that same omnipotence to reduce it to nothing? Or could it ever exist against His will? Or if it was eternal, why did He for endless ages allow it to exist in that manner, and after so long a time choose to make something of it?

"If He now suddenly willed to do something, He, the Almighty, should rather have employed Himself in annihilating that evil matter, that He alone might be the whole, true, supreme, and infinite Good. Or if it were not good for Him Who is good not to fashion and create something good, He might have indeed taken away and annihilated that evil matter and made another that was good, out of which He might produce all things. For He would not be omnipotent if He could not make anything good without the help of a matter that He Himself had not made."

Such things as these I turned over in my wretched heart, burdened with corroding cares from the fear of dying without having discovered the truth. Yet the faith of Your *Christ, our Lord and Savior* (2 Pt 2:20), professed in the Catholic Church, was strongly fixed in my heart. In many ways indeed I was as yet unformed, and I did not always adhere to the rule of sound doctrine. Yet my mind did not forsake it, but rather more and more imbibed it with each passing day.

CHAPTER 6 — Firminus

I HAD also now cast away from me the lying divinations and the wicked ravings of the astrologers.

In gratitude for this also may Your mercies, O my God, confess to You from the depths of my soul. For it was You who brought it about—You most certainly. Who else can recall us from the death of every error but the life that cannot die and the wisdom that enlightens the needy minds while itself needing no light, by which the whole world is governed, down to the flying leaves of the trees?

It was You Who provided a remedy for my obstinacy, by which I had before resisted both Vindicianus, a sharp old man, and Nebridius, a youth of wonderful talents. The former strongly affirmed and the latter said repeatedly although doubtfully that there was no such art by which man could foresee things to come, but that such conjectures often resembled games of chance. So many things were spoken that several would afterward come to pass, not because these men had any foreknowledge, but because, by talking so much, they happened to stumble upon them.

Therefore, You provided for me a friend who was not a slothful consulter of the astrologers, nor one well versed in that science, but, as I said, a curious consulter. Furthermore, he knew something that he had been told by his father, but how far it went to overthrow his belief in that art, he did not know. This man, then, Firminus by name, an eloquent person with a liberal education, consulted me as an intimate friend concerning some of his affairs to which his worldly hopes aspired. He desired to know what I thought might be their possibility of success according to his so-called constellations.

I, who had begun to lean to Nebridius' opinion, did not refuse to express my thoughts according to what came to my doubting mind, but in general I told him that I was now almost sure that those things were ridiculous and vain. He then proceeded to tell me how his father had been a most curious searcher into those books and had a friend no less attached to them than himself. Joining in the same studies and conferring together, they had followed those follies with so much ardor as to observe the moments of the births even of dumb animals whenever any such were bred in their houses, and they recorded the positions of the heavens at those times, in order to make, as it were, experiments in that art.

He added he had heard from his father that when his mother was pregnant with Firminus himself, a certain maidservant of his friend was also pregnant, a fact that could hardly not be observed by her master, who was so solicitous as to examine even the times when his dogs gave birth. And so it happened that as they most exactly recorded—the one, the days, hours, and minutes of his wife, the other, those of his servant—both infants were delivered at the same instant. So they were forced to set down the same constellations, down to the minutest points—the one for his son, the other for his servant.

As soon as the women went into labor, the two men gave mutual notice, and had messengers ready to send word to each other as soon as the child was born, taking care to be informed of it at that very instant. And he said that the messengers who were sent met at a point exactly midway between both houses, so that neither of them was able to notice any difference in the position of the stars or in the moment of time. Yet, Firminus, born of high estate in his parents' home, prospered in the ways of the

world, increased in wealth, and advanced in ranks of
honor, while the slave, having the yoke of his condition in no way eased, continued to serve his masters,
as I was told by Firminus who had known him.

Having heard this and believed it as coming from
such a man, all my former reluctance was now quite
overcome. First of all, I tried to disengage Firminus
himself from his curiosity. I told him that from the
inspection of his constellations, if I were to foretell
the truth, I should have found in them that his parents were of the first rank, his family noble in its
own city, his birth high, his education honorable,
and his learning liberal. But if afterward the servant
should consult me concerning the same constellations, which were likewise his, to tell him the truth
also, I should have discovered in them a most abject
family, a servile condition, and all other things far
differing and quite opposite to the former.

Thus, from the same inspection of the stars, I
would conclude two opposite things, if I wanted to
state the truth; or if I came to identical conclusions,
I would have to say what was false. I thus became
certain that any true statement made from the observation of such constellations was the result of
guesswork and not skill, and that any false statement
was not from any unskillfulness in the art, but from
faulty guesswork.

I took occasion from this for further consideration
of these things. Lest any of these vain men whose
living was earned by this trade (whom I now much
desired to attack and render ridiculous) should reply
that what Firminus had related to me, or his father
to him, was false, I reflected on those who are born
twins. Most of the time they come so quickly into

the world, one after the other, that the small interval of time (whatever effect they pretend it may have in nature) cannot be registered by human observation or expressed in any figures, out of which the astrologer is to make his prognostication.

His predictions, therefore, will not be true, because from the inspection of the same tables, he should foretell identical futures for Esau and Jacob, but the same things did not happen to them. Or, if he should speak truly, he must not say the same of both, though their horoscope be the same. Therefore, it must be by chance and not by art that he speaks the truth.

For, O Lord, the most just Ruler of the universe, while neither those who consult nor those who are consulted know anything of it, by a sacred instinct You so order matters that he who consults should hear what it is fit he should hear, according to the hidden merits of souls, from the abyss of Your just judgment. To You let no man say, *What is this?* or *To what end is this?* (Sir 39:21). Let him not say it, let him not say it, for he is simply a man.

CHAPTER 7 — The Origin of Evil

YOU had, O my Helper, now freed me from those bonds, and I was still seeking the origin of evil and could find no way to account for it. Yet You did not allow me by any of those waves of thought to be carried away from the Faith, by which I believed both You to exist and Your substance to be immutable, and that You had compassion for us and that there was a judgment to come, and that in Christ Your Son our Lord, and in the Holy Scriptures, which the authority of the Catholic Church recommends to us, You have appointed a way for man's salvation unto the life that is to come after this death.

These points, therefore, being safe and strongly settled in my mind, I inquired anxiously about the origin of evil. What pangs did my heart then suffer in this labor! What groans did it send forth, O my God! Your ears were attentive to my cries, though I knew it not. And when in silence I earnestly sought an answer, the secret sufferings of my soul were loud cries for Your mercy.

You knew what I suffered, but no man was aware of it. Very little was that which passed from my heart to my tongue, and so to the ears of my most intimate friends. Did the torment of my soul, which neither my time nor my tongue was sufficient to express, resound in their ears? But all was heard by You, which *I roared out from the groaning of my heart. And my desire was before You, and the light of my eyes was not with me* (Ps 38:9-11).

For that was within, but I was without, nor was it in that place. I was only intent upon things contained in places, but I found there no place of rest, nor did they receive me so that I could say, "It is enough, it is well." Nor did they let me return to where it might be well for me.

I was superior to them but inferior to You, for You were the true joy to me Your subject and You had made subject to me the things that You have created inferior to me.

This was the true mean and the middle region of my salvation, that I should remain according to Your image, and, by serving You, should have command of my bodily inclinations. But when I proudly rose up against You and *ran against* the Lord *with the thick neck of my shield* (Jb 15:26), even these lowest of things rose above me and pressed me down, and nowhere could I find any respite or relief. These bodies offered themselves in crowds on all sides to my eyes, and their images to my thoughts.

These waylaid me and opposed my return to You, as if to say, "Where are you going, so unworthy and filthy as you are?" And these had grown out of my wound because *You have humbled the proud as one who is slain* (Ps 89:11), and by the swelling of my pride I was separated from You, and so puffed up was my face that it closed my eyes.

CHAPTER 8 — The Lord's Mercy

*B*UT *You, O Lord, remain forever and You will not be angry with us forever* (Ps 85:6). For You have had compassion upon our dust and ashes, and it seemed good in Your sight to reform my deformities. Therefore with secret goads You stirred me up so that I might be uneasy until You would be clearly manifest to me in my inner sight. And my swelling pride abated through the hidden touch of Your healing hand, and the troubled and darkened sight of my mind was healed from day to day by the healing salve of sorrow.

CHAPTER 9 — The Books of the Platonists

*I*T was first Your desire to show me how *You resist the proud and give grace to the humble* (1 Pt 5:5), and how mercifully You pointed out to men the way of humility, in that Your Word was made flesh and dwelt among us. So You provided me, by means of a man much puffed up with the conceit of his own knowledge, some books of the Platonists that had been translated from Greek into Latin.

In these I read, not indeed in the same words, but offering the same thought, confirmed with a great many reasons, that *in the beginning was the Word, and the Word was with God, and the Word was God. He was in the beginning with God. All things were made through Him, and without Him was made nothing that has been made. In Him was life, and the life was the light of men. And the light shines in darkness, and the darkness grasped it not* (Jn 1:1-5).

I also read there that the soul of man, though *it bears testimony to the light, yet is not itself the light,* but the Word of God is that light. For God is the *true light that enlightens every man who comes into the world.* And therein I read that *He was in the world, and the world was made through Him, and the world knew Him not.* However, I did not find there the revelation that *He came unto His own, and His own received Him not, but to as many as received Him, He gave power of becoming sons of God, to those who believe in His Name* (Jn 1:8-12).

Again, I read there that *God the Word was born not of flesh, nor of blood, nor of the will of man, nor of the will of the flesh, but of God,* but not that *this Word was made flesh and dwelt among us* (Jn 1:13-14). For I discovered in those books, frequently repeated and in many ways expressed, that the Son is *in the form of the Father, and thinks it no robbery to be equal with God* (Phil 2:6), because He by nature is God.

However, *that He emptied Himself, taking the form of a slave, being made like unto men, and appearing in the form of a man, He humbled Himself, becoming obedient unto death, even to the death of the Cross. Where-*

fore *God has exalted Him from the dead, and given Him a name that is above every name, so that at the Name of Jesus every knee should bend, of those in heaven, on earth, and under the earth, and every tongue should confess that the Lord Jesus Christ is in the glory of God the Father* (Phil 2:7-11)—all this these books do not say.

That Your only-begotten Son before all times remains unchangeably coeternal with You, and that of *His fullness souls receive* (Jn 1:16), so that they may be blessed, and that they may be renewed by the participation of His self-subsisting wisdom so that they may be wise—these truths are to be found there. But that *in due time He died for the wicked* (Rom 5:6), and that *You did not spare Your only Son, but delivered Him up for us all* (Rom 8:32), is not found there.

For *You have hidden these things from the wise, and have revealed them to little ones, so that they who labor and are burdened might come to Him and that He might refresh them, because He is meek and humble of heart* (Mt 11:25-29). And *the meek He guides in judgment, and to the mild He teaches His ways, seeing our humility and our labor, and forgiving all our sins* (Ps 24:9, 18).

But those who are raised, as it were, upon the heights of more lofty knowledge do not hear Him when He says: *Learn from Me, for I am meek and humble of heart, and you will find rest for your souls* (Mt 11:28). *And if they know God, they do not glorify Him as God or give Him thanks, but become vain in their reasonings, and their foolish heart is darkened, and, professing to be wise, they become fools* (Rom 1:21-22).

And, therefore, I also read there that *the glory of Your incorruptibleness was changed into idols* and a variety of forms, *into the likeness of the image of a corruptible man, and of birds, and of four-footed beasts, and of creeping things* (Rom 1:23), namely, into that Egyptian food by which Esau lost his birthright. For Your firstborn people worshiped the head of a four-footed beast instead of You, *turning back their hearts toward Egypt* (Acts 7:39) and bowing down their soul, Your Image, *before the image of a calf that eats grass* (Ps 106:20). These things I found in those books, but did not feed upon them. For You were pleased, O Lord, to take away from Jacob the reproach of being the younger, so that *the elder might serve the younger* (Rom 9:12), and the Gentiles You called into Your inheritance.

I had come to You from the Gentiles, and was intent upon the gold that You were pleased to will that Your people should carry away from Egypt, for it was Yours wherever it was. You did say to the Athenians through Your Apostle that *in You we live, and move, and have our being, as some of their own writers have said* (Acts 17:28). In truth those books came from the Gentiles. However, I had no regard for the idols of the Egyptians, which they served with Your gold, *who changed the truth of God into a lie, and worshiped and served the creature rather than the Creator* (Rom 1:25).

CHAPTER 10 — No Room for Doubt

BEING thus admonished to return to myself, I entered into my inmost self with You as my guide, and this I was able to do because *You were my Helper* (Ps 30:11). I entered in, and saw with the eye of my soul, such as it was, above the same eye of my soul, above my mind, the Light unchangeable. It was not the common light of day that is visible to all flesh, nor some greater light of the same kind, as if the light of day were to be much more clear and bright and with its greatness fill the whole universe.

It was not such a light as this, but quite another thing, very different from all others. Neither was it above my mind, as oil is above water, or heaven above earth. But it was superior, because it made me, and I was inferior, because I was made by it. He who knows the truth knows this light, and he who knows it knows eternity. It is Love that knows it.

O eternal Truth and true Love and beloved Eternity! You are my God, and for You do I sigh night and day. When I first began to know You, You lifted me up so that I might see that there was something to be seen, but I was not as yet able to see it. You drove back the weakness of my sight, shining upon me most powerfully, and I shook with love and fear.

I found that I was very far from You, in the "land of unlikeness," as if I heard Your voice from on high: "I am the food of grown men; grow up and you shall feed upon Me. You shall not convert Me into you, like your bodily food, but you shall be changed into Me." I knew that *it was because of iniquity that You have corrected man and have made my soul to waste away like a spider* (Ps 39:12).

Then I said, "Is the truth then nothing, because it is not spread out through any space finite or infinite?" And You cried out to me from afar, "Yes, in very truth, *I AM WHO AM*" (Ex 3:14). And I heard as the heart hears, and there was no room left for doubt. I could more easily doubt that I was alive than that Truth is not, which is *clearly seen, being understood by the things that are made* (Rom 1:20).

CHAPTER 11 — The Being of Creatures

THEN I looked into the other things that are below You, and I saw that they neither altogether had being nor altogether lacked being. They had being indeed, because they are from You, and they were lacking in being because they are not what You are, for that truly exists which remains unchangeable. *But it is good for me to adhere to God* (Ps 73:28), for if I do not abide in Him, neither can I abide in myself. But He a*bides in Himself and makes all things new* (Wis 7:27). *You are the Lord my God, for You have no need of my goods* (Ps 16:2).

CHAPTER 12 — Evil, Deprivation of Good

IT became clear to me that those things also are good that are subject to corruption. If they were the supreme good, they could not be corrupted, but they could not be subject to corruption unless they were good. If they were the supreme good, they would be incorruptible, and if they were not good at all, there would be nothing in them that could be corrupted, for corruption injures, which it would not do if it did not diminish goodness.

Therefore, either corruption injures not at all, which cannot be said, or, as is certain, all things that are corrupted are deprived of some good. But if they are deprived of all good, they will no longer exist at all. If they continue to be and still cannot be corrupted, they will be better than they were before because they will subsist incorruptibly.

What can be more monstrously absurd than to say that things become better when they have lost all that was good in them. Therefore, if they are deprived of all good, they will be nothing at all. Hence as long as they exist, they are good, and thus all things that exist are good.

Clearly, evil, the origin of which I have sought for so long, is not a substance, for if it were a substance it would be good. It would either be an incorruptible substance, a great good indeed, or it would be a corruptible substance, which if it were not good could not be corrupted.

Thus I saw, and it was very clear to me, that You have made all things good, and that there is no substance at all that You did not make. And because You have not made all things equal, it therefore follows that all things are good individually and all things together are very good because You, our God, have made all things very good.

CHAPTER 13 — Universal Good

TO You there is nothing evil at all, and not only to You, but also to Your whole creation, because there is nothing outside of You that can break in and corrupt the order You have established in it. However, in the parts thereof, there are some things that, because they are unsuitable to some other things, are considered evil. Yet these same things are suitable to other things and consequently good, and in themselves are good. And all these things that are not suitable to one another are most suitable to this lower part of nature we call the earth, which has its sky around it, cloudy indeed and stormy, yet suitable for it.

Far be it from me to say: "I wish these things were not so." If I should see these things by themselves, I might wish for better things, yet even if there were no other things I *still ought for these alone*

to praise You, because from the earth You show forth
Your gifts worthy of praise: dragons and all deeps, fire,
hail, snow, ice, and stormy winds that fulfill Your word,
mountains and all hills: fruitful trees and all cedars,
beasts and all cattle, serpents and feathered fowls, kings
of the earth and all people, princes and all judges of the
earth, young men and maidens, old men and young, let
them all praise Your Name (Ps 148:7-12).

From the heavens also let Your praises be sung.
Let all the Angels praise You, our God on high, and all
Your powers, the sun and moon, all the stars and light,
the heavens of heavens, and the waters that are above
the heavens, let them praise Your Name (Ps 148:
1-5).

I now could not wish for any better things when I
thought of all of them together, and although by a
sound judgment I looked upon those higher things
as better than these below, yet I was no less convinced that both together were better than the
higher alone.

CHAPTER 14 — False Images of God

THERE is no soundness in those who are displeased with anything of Your creation, as in
me there was none when many things displeased
me that You had made. And because my soul did
not dare to be displeased with my God, it refused
to admit as Yours whatever displeased it. Hence, I
had adopted the theory of two opposing substances,
but I found no satisfaction there, and talked non-
sense.

Turning from that belief, I fashioned for myself a
god extended through infinite spaces of all places,
and took him for You, and him I placed in my heart.

Thus once more my soul became the temple of an idol of its own making, abominable in Your sight. But after You had applied Your cure to my head, although I did not realize it, and had shut my eyes so *that they might not see vanity* (Ps 119:37), I lost a little of my old self and my frenzy was stilled. I awakened in You, and saw that You are infinite, although in quite a different manner, but this knowledge was not derived from the flesh.

CHAPTER 15 — All Things Are in God

I LOOKED back upon other things, and I saw that they owe their being to You, and that in You they all have their bounds, although not in such a way as to be circumscribed by You as by a place, but because You hold them all in Your hand by Your Truth. All things are true, insofar as they have a being, nor is there any falsity, except when something is thought to be but is not. And I saw that all things are not only suitable to their proper places, but also to their proper times.

I also saw that You, Who alone are eternal, did not begin to work after innumerable ages had passed, because all ages, both those that have passed and those that still await, neither come nor depart except through You, working and abiding.

CHAPTER 16 — The Essence of Iniquity

I SAW and experienced that it was nothing unusual that bread that tastes sweet to a sound palate is loathsome to the sick, and that light that is pleasing to healthy eyes is painful to sore ones. Your righteousness displeases the wicked; how much more is this true of a viper or a worm, which nevertheless You have created good and befitting their rank in the lower parts of Your creation. With the lower regions sinners themselves fit in, and the more so as they are more unlike You, but they fit in with the higher regions in proportion to their becoming more like You.

I sought to discover what iniquity was, and I found that it is not a substance but the perversity of the will turned away from You, O God, the sovereign substance, and toward the lowest things, casting out its innermost parts and swelling outwardly.

CHAPTER 17 — Attaining a Knowledge of God

I WAS astounded that I now loved You, and not a phantom instead of You. Yet I did not stand still to enjoy my God. I was strongly drawn to You by Your beauty, and then again torn away from You by my own weight, and I fell down groaning among these lower things. This weight was my carnal habit.

Even so I did not lose the remembrance of You. I did not have the least doubt that there was One most worthy to be adhered to, but I was not yet in a state in which I could adhere to Him. *For the corruptible body is a load upon the soul, and the earthly habitation presses down the mind that muses on many things* (Wis 9:15). Yet I was now most certain that *Your invisible things from Your creation of the world are clearly seen, being understood by the things that are made, even Your eternal Power and Godhead* (Rom 1:20).

Seeking to learn why it was that I approved of the beauty of bodies, whether heavenly or earthly, and what helped me to make the correct judgment about mutable things and say: "This ought be so and that should not be so"—seeking, I say, why it was that I made a particular judgment when I did so, I had found that there was above my changeable mind the unchangeable, true and eternal truth.

Thus I ascended gradually from bodies to the soul, which feels through the body, then to its inward faculty, to which the bodily senses bring their information concerning external objects, as far as beasts are able. Then I moved onward, again to the reasoning faculty, to which is referred what is received through the senses, so that it may be judged.

My rational faculty in me, perceiving itself to be changeable, raised itself up to its own understanding and led away its thought from its habits. It withdrew from the crowd of contradictory phantasms so that it might thus find by what light it was illumined, when it cried out that without the slightest doubt the unchangeable is to be preferred to the changeable. From there on it had a notion of the unchangeable, for unless it had some knowledge of it, how could it so certainly have preferred it to that which is changeable?

And so, in the twinkle of a trembling glance, my mind reached THAT WHICH IS. Then it was that I perceived *Your invisible things understood by the things that are made* (Rom 1:20). But I could not fix my gaze upon them. In my weakness I was beaten back and I returned to my former habits. I carried nothing away with me but a loving memory and a longing after that, the scent of which I had, as it were, perceived, but was not yet able to feed upon.

CHAPTER 18 — The Way, the Truth, and the Life

I SOUGHT for the way of acquiring strength sufficient to enjoy You, but I did not find it until I embraced the *Mediator between God and man, the Man Christ Jesus* (1 Tm 2:5), *Who is above all, God blessed forever* (Rom 9:5), calling unto me, and saying, *I am the Way, the Truth, and the Life* (Jn 14:6). He mingled with our flesh the food [i.e., the Divine Nature] I was unable to take. For *the Word was made Flesh* (Jn 1:14), that Your wisdom, by which You have created all things, might become milk for our infancy.

I did not then as yet approach my Lord Jesus Christ as I ought, humbly embracing my humble Savior. Nor did I know the lesson that He came to teach me by His weakness. For Your Word, the eternal Truth, Who is supereminent above the most eminent parts of Your creation, raises up to Himself those who are subject to Him. But in these lower regions He has made for Himself out of our clay a lowly dwelling by which He might protect from themselves those who would become His subjects, and bring them over to Himself.

In this way He would heal their swollen pride and nourish their love, so that they might not go farther by self-confidence, but rather become weak in their own eyes, seeing before their feet the Divinity made weak by taking on our "human nature," and when wearied might cast themselves down upon It, while It arises and raises them up.

CHAPTER 19—The Incarnation of Jesus Christ

BUT I imagined quite another thing at that time, regarding my Lord Jesus Christ only as a Man of excellent wisdom Who could in no way be equaled. Above all, because He had been miraculously born of a Virgin, to give us an example of despising temporal things for the attainment of immortality, He seemed to have attained to that great authority of lordship by the divine care He had for us.

However, I could not in the least comprehend the meaning of the mystery in the words, *The Word was made Flesh* (Jn 1:14). I only knew from what was written of His eating, drinking, sleeping, walking, rejoicing, grieving, and discoursing that this flesh was not united to Your Word without a human soul and mind. Everyone who knows that Your Word is unchangeable must know this, as I then knew it, and without any question believed.

For now to move by the will the parts of the body, at other times not to move them, sometimes to be affected one way, at other times another, now by outward signs to express wise judgments and then to be silent—all these are proper to the mutability of soul and mind. And if they had been falsely written of Him, all the rest might in like manner be untrue, nor would there remain in those writings any saving faith for mankind.

But since the Scriptures are written truthfully, I acknowledged the whole Man in Christ and not only the body of a man, nor with the body a principle of life without the mind, but a true Man. I thought that He was to be preferred before all others, not from being the person of Truth, but from some great excellence of His human nature and a more perfect participation in Wisdom.

However, Alypius imagined that Catholics believed God to be clothed with flesh in such manner as not to acknowledge in Christ, besides the God-head and human flesh, any soul or mind of a man. And because he was fully persuaded that the deeds recorded of Him could not be performed except by a living and rational creature, this made him slower in embracing the Christian Faith. But afterward, finding that this was the condemned error of the Apollinarian heretics, he rejoiced in and more readily accepted the Catholic Faith.

As for myself, I confess it was not until sometime afterward that I learned to distinguish in the expression "The Word was made Flesh" between the error of Photinus and Catholic doctrine. Indeed, the refutation of heretics makes the tenets of the Church and its sound doctrine stand out more brilliantly. *For there must be heresies so that they who are approved may be made manifest among the weak* (1 Cor 11:19).

CHAPTER 20 — Paving the Way for Scripture

NOW that I had read the books of the Platonists, and being thereby advised to seek after an incorporeal truth, I beheld *Your invisible things, understood by the things that are made* (Rom 1:20). Though encountering roadblocks in my search, I had a perception of that which, by reason of my soul's darkness, I could not more fully contemplate.

I had at this point become convinced that You exist and that You are infinite, yet without any extension of Yourself either through finite or infinite space, and that You are truly One Who always is the very same, in no part and by no movement changeable, and that all other things are from You, by this one most certain argument: because they have being.

Of all these things I was assured, and yet I was too weak to find my joy in You. I babbled endlessly as if I were an expert, whereas, if I had not sought out the way to You, which is in Christ our Savior, instead of being an expert, I would have perished. For I had begun to wish to seem wise, not caring about any resulting punishment and failing to bewail my misery, and I was puffed up with knowledge.

Where was that edifying charity built upon the foundation of humility, which is Christ Jesus? Or when would those books teach this to me? I believe it was Your will that I should come across these writings before I studied Your Scriptures, so that it might be imprinted in my memory how I had been affected by them.

Thus afterward, when I had been humbled by Your books, and my wounds had been dressed by Your healing hands, I might well discern and distinguish the difference between presumption and confession, between those who saw the place to which they should go but did not see the *way* to it, and that way itself that leads not only to the vision of that blessed country but to dwelling therein.

If I had first been instructed in Your Sacred Scriptures, and if, in the familiar use of them, You had become sweet to me, and if I had afterward happened to come across those other writings, they might have torn me away from the foundation of piety. Or if I had continued to remain steadfast in the wholesome sentiments I had imbibed from the Scriptures, I might have thought that those other books read by themselves alone might have produced the same sentiments.

CHAPTER 21 — The Epistles of Paul

THEREFORE, with great eagerness I betook
myself to the venerable writings of Your Spirit,
and above all to the Apostle Paul. And those difficulties disappeared wherein his discourse had formerly seemed to me to contradict itself and not to
agree with the testimonies of the Law and the
Prophets. Now his writings appeared to me to have
a single and pure unified aspect, and I learned
therein *to rejoice with trembling* (Ps 2:11).

In my search I found that whatever I had read of
truth in those other books was here said also, but
with the commendation of Your grace, so that he
who sees *should not glory as if he had not received* not
only that which he sees, but also his ability to see.
For what has he that he has not received? (1 Cor 4:7).

It was also made clear to me that he who from
afar off cannot see may nevertheless walk in the way
by which he may come and see and possess, because
though a man *be delighted with the Law of God according to the inner man,* yet what shall he do with the
*other law in his members, warring against the law of his
mind, and leading him away captive in the law of sin
that is in his members* (Rom 7:22-23)?

*For You are just, O Lord, but we have sinned and
committed iniquity and behaved impiously* (Dn 3:27-
29), *and Your hand has fallen heavy upon us* (Ps
32:4). As a result we have been justly delivered over
to that ancient sinner, the governor of death, because he persuaded our will to become like his will,
which stood not in Your truth (Jn 8:44).

What shall wretched man do? *Who shall deliver
him from the body of this death but Your grace through
Jesus Christ our Lord?* (Rom 7:24-25). It is He

Whom You have begotten coeternal to Yourself and created *in the beginning of Your ways* (Prv 8:22), in Whom the *Prince of this world* (Jn 14:30) found nothing worthy of death, yet slew Him, thus *canceling the handwriting that was against us* (Col 2:14).

Those other books have nothing of this. They lack the feature of this piety, failing to mention the tears of confession, *Your sacrifice, a troubled spirit, a contrite and humbled heart* (Ps 51:19), the salvation of the people, *the bridal city* (Rv 21:2), the *pledge of the Holy Spirit* (2 Cor 1:22), or the cup of our ransom.

No one there sings: *Shall not my soul be subject to God, for from Him is my salvation? For He is my God and my Savior, my Protector, and no more shall I be moved* (Ps 62:2-3). No one there hears Him calling, *Come to Me, you who labor* (Mt 11:28). They scorn to learn from Him, *because He is meek and humble of heart* (Mt 11:29). For You have *hidden these things from the wise and prudent and have revealed them to little ones* (Mt 11:25).

It is one thing from a wooded mountaintop to see at a distance the "land of peace," but to find no path that leads to it, and to make vain efforts to reach it through impassable ways, besieged on every side and waylaid by fugitive deserters, with their leader "the lion and the dragon." It is another thing to keep to the way that leads there, safeguarded by the care of our heavenly Commander, where no deserters of the heavenly army lie hidden, awaiting an opportunity for thievery. For they shun that way as they would a torture. These things were wonderfully instilled into my soul when I read the *least of Your Apostles* (1 Cor 15:9) and meditated upon Your works and I was struck with fear.

BOOK 8—Conversion

Augustine reaches his thirty-second year. From Simplicianus he hears the history of the conversion of Victorinus. He is also influenced by Ponticianus who relates how two of his companions were converted by reading the life and miracles of St. Antony. During a severe mental struggle, Augustine hears a voice from heaven, opens the Scriptures, and is converted to God together with his friend Alypius.

CHAPTER 1 — Simplicianus

MY God, let me remember You with thanksgiving and confess Your mercies to me. Let my bones be pierced with Your love, and let them say, *O Lord, Who is like You?* (Ps 35:10). *You have broken my bonds. I will offer to You the sacrifice of praise* (Ps 116:16-17). I will relate in what manner You broke them, and all who worship You, upon hearing it, shall say, "Blessed be the Lord in Heaven and on earth. *Great and wonderful is His Name*" (Ps 76:2).

Your words had stuck fast in my heart, and You encompassed me on every side. Of Your life eternal I was certain, though I had only seen it *in a dark manner, and, as it were, through a glass* (1 Cor 13:12). However, I had no doubt at all of Your incorruptible substance, from which all substances have their being. Nor did I wish to be more certain of You, but merely to be more firmly fixed in You.

However, my temporal life was totally unsettled, and my heart had yet to be cleansed of *the old leaven* (1 Cor 5:7). The Way, which is our Savior Himself, pleased me, but I did not as yet have the courage to venture forth upon so narrow a path.

You did put into my mind, and it seemed good to me, to turn to Simplicianus, who appeared to me to be Your good servant, for Your grace shone in him. And I had heard that from his youth he had most devoutly served You. By now he had grown old, and I thought that in so long a time spent in Your service, he must have experienced many things and learned many things. And so it was in reality. I desired to lay open to him my troubles, hoping that he would show me what course of life was most suitable for one so affected, as I then was, to walk in Your way.

I saw that the Church had a great many members, and that in it some followed one way of life and some another. I myself was dissatisfied with the life I led in the world. It had become burdensome to me, for my former desires no longer inflamed me as they did before with hopes of honor and riches, yet I hesitated to bear Your heavy servitude.

My former hopes no longer gave me any delight in comparison to Your sweetness and *the beauty of Your house that I loved* (Ps 26:8). Yet, my passion for women still captivated me. Nor did the Apostle forbid me to marry, though he exhorted me to what was better, much wishing that all men were even as he himself was (cf. 1 Cor 7:7).

However, I, who was weaker, chose the easier state, and because of this I was tossed about in other respects, languishing and pining away with consuming cares, being forced to conform to things that I was otherwise unwilling to suffer, for the sake of a conjugal life, to which I was enthralled by so strong an inclination. I had heard from the mouth of Your Truth that *there are eunuchs who have made themselves such for the Kingdom of Heaven* (Mt 19:12) but, He added, *let him accept it who can.*

All men are certainly vain in whom there is not the knowledge of God and who, by these good things that are seen, cannot find Him (Wis 13:1). However I was not now encumbered by that vanity, but had moved beyond it and, by the testimony of Your whole creation, had found You, our Creator, and Your Word, God with You, and the Holy Spirit, one God, by Whom You have created all things.

There is another kind of wicked men *who, knowing God, have not glorified Him as God, nor given thanks* (Rom 1:21), and into this category also I had fallen. But *Your right hand, O God, raised me up* (Ps 18:36) and, rescuing me from its clutches, placed me where I might recover. For You have said to man, *Behold, the fear of the Lord is wisdom* (Jb 28:28), and again, *Do not desire to seem wise* (Prv 3:7), *for they who say that they are wise are fools* (Rom 1:22). And I had now discovered the precious pearl that I could possess by selling all that I had (cf. Mt 13:46). And yet I hesitated.

CHAPTER 2 — Victorinus

I WENT, therefore, to Simplicianus, the spiritual father of Ambrose (then a bishop) in receiving Your grace, and whom Ambrose truly loved as a father. To him I related all my wanderings along the paths of error. And when I told him that I had read certain books of the Platonists that had been translated into Latin by Victorinus, formerly professor of rhetoric in Rome, who, as I had heard, died a Christian, he congratulated me because I had not wasted time on the writings of other philosophers, "full of fallacies and lies, *according to the elements of this world* (Col 2:8)," but rather on these works of the Platonists in which God and His Word were by all means propounded.

Then, to exhort me to the humility of Christ, which is *hidden from the wise and revealed to little ones* (Mt 11:25), he took occasion to speak of this same Victorinus with whom, when he lived at Rome, he was intimately acquainted, and told me something of him, which I will not pass over in silence because it contains considerable insight into Your Grace, for which praise and glory ought to be offered to You.

He related, therefore, that this most learned old man, truly expert in all the liberal sciences, had read and examined and explained many of the works of the philosophers and had taught numerous noble senators. Hence, as a memorial, he had deserved and obtained an honor highly prized by the citizens of this world, namely, of having his statue set up in the Roman Forum.

Up to old age, Victorinus had been a worshiper of idols and a partaker of their sacrilegious rites, as almost all the nobility of Rome was at that time. The people also honored "a monstrous race of all kinds of gods and the barking Anubis, who had formerly stood in arms against Neptune and Venus and Minerva" (Virgil), so that Rome then worshiped the deities that she had formerly conquered. And the aged Victorinus had over the course of many years defended those things with his inspired eloquence.

Nonetheless, Simplicianus related, this old man was not ashamed to become a child of Your Christ and an infant at Your font, submitting his neck to the yoke of Your humility and his forehead to the reproach of the Cross.

O Lord, Lord, You Who *bowed down the heavens and descended, Who touched the mountains and they smoked* (Ps 144:5), by what ways did You insinuate Yourself into that breast? He read, as Simplicianus said, the Holy Scriptures, and he most diligently sought out and examined all the Christian writings. And he said to Simplicianus, not publicly, but secretly as to a friend, "Know that I am now a Christian." Simplicianus answered, "I will not believe it, nor reckon you among Christians, till I see you in the Church of Christ."

Victorinus jested with him, saying, "Do the walls then make people Christians?" He often repeated that now he was a Christian, and when Simplicianus just as often would make the same reply, he always repeated the jest about the walls. For he was afraid of offending his friends (the Roman senators), proud devil worshipers, and he imagined that great storms of malice would fall upon him from the height of their Babylonian dignity, as from the cedars of Lebanon that the Lord had not yet broken in pieces (cf. Ps 29:5).

But after that, by much reading and meditating, he gained strength, and began to fear that he would *be denied by* Christ *before His holy Angels* if he was ashamed *to confess Him before men* (Mt 10:33; Lk 12:9). He considered himself to be guilty of a great crime in being ashamed of the mysteries of the humility of Your Word, whereas he had not been ashamed of the sacrilegious rites of proud devils, of which he had been a partaker, imitating them in their pride.

Ceasing to be ashamed because of his vanity and becoming ashamed of his reluctance to admit the truth, he suddenly and unexpectedly said to Simplicianus, as Simplicianus himself told me, "Let us go to the church. I wish to become a Christian." And the latter, being transported with joy, accompanied him there.

Having been initiated in the first instructions, Victorinus not long after gave in his name, so that he might be regenerated by Baptism, to the astonishment of Rome and the joy of the Church. *The proud saw and were angry, they gnashed their teeth and pined away* (Ps 112:10). But as for Your servant, the Lord God *was his hope, and he regarded not vanities and lying follies* (Ps 40:5).

Finally the time came for making his profession of faith. At Rome those who are about to receive the grace of Your Baptism usually make their profession from an elevated place in a set memorized formula in the presence of all the faithful.

According to Simplicianus, the priests suggested to Victorinus that he make his profession in private, as was usually permitted to some who seemed likely to be afraid through bashfulness. But he rather chose to profess the Faith of his salvation in the presence of the saintly congregation. For what he taught in his profession of rhetoric was no matter of salvation, and yet this he had publicly professed. How much less then ought he to fear Your meek flock in proclaiming Your Word, when he had not been afraid to deliver his own words before large crowds of hostile listeners?

Therefore, as soon as he went up to make his profession, everyone who knew him—and who was there who did not?—repeated his name to his neighbor with joy and congratulations. And in the joyful mouths of all was heard with a low murmur, "Victorinus, Victorinus." They suddenly made this sound through the delight of seeing him, and just as quickly they fell silent again so that they might hear him. He made the profession of the true Faith with a wonderful confidence, and all desired to take him into their hearts. Indeed they placed him there by their love and joy, and these were the hands with which they embraced him.

CHAPTER 3 — Joy at the Conversion of Sinners

O GOD of goodness, what happens in man that he rejoices more for the safety of a soul that was despaired of and delivered out of a greater danger, than if he had always had hopes, or if the danger had been less? For You also, most merciful Father, *rejoice more over one sinner who repents than over ninety-nine just who have no need of penance* (Lk 15:7).

And it is with great delight that we hear in Your Word with how much joy the shepherd brought home on his shoulders the sheep that had gone astray, and with what congratulations of the neighbors Your coin was brought back into Your treasures by the woman who found it (cf. Lk 15).

Moreover, the joyousness of the solemn festivities in Your Church draws tears when in Your house is read the story of the younger son *who had been dead and was returned to life, who had been lost and was found* (Lk 15:24). You rejoice in us, and in Your Angels who are holy by holy charity. For in Yourself You are always the same, Who always know all things forever and in the same manner, though they neither always exist nor continue in the same manner.

What takes place in a soul that causes it to be more pleased with the things it loves when they are found or restored than if it had never ceased to possess them? Many things bear witness to this, and all places are full of testimonies that cry out, "It is so."

A conquering emperor returns in triumph, but he would never have gained the victory if he had not fought, and the greater danger there was in the fight, the greater is the joy of his triumph. A tempest at sea tosses a ship to and fro and threatens shipwreck; all aboard grow pale with the apprehensions of approaching death, but when the heavens and sea become serene and calm, their joy is now as excessive as their fear was before. A dear friend falls sick, his pulse indicates danger, and all who wish him well are sick with worry over him; when he recovers, though he is not yet able to walk with his former strength, there is more rejoicing for him than there was before when he was sound and strong.

Men acquire the very pleasures of human life by experiencing previous pains, even those that were not foreseen and involuntary but purposely procured. There is no pleasure in eating and drinking unless the discomfort of hunger and thirst has preceded. Drunkards eat salted foods deliberately so that they may afterward find pleasure in allaying their deliberately heightened thirst by drinking. And custom usually dictates that the promised bride should not be given immediately in marriage, lest the husband should hold cheap, when given to him, the woman whom he had not first longed for while the marriage was deferred.

This is always true even in regard to filthy and accursed delights. This also holds true in joys that are lawful and allowed, as well as in the most pure honesty of friendship, and in him *who had been dead and was returned to life, who had been lost and was found* (Lk 15:32). Everywhere greater uneasiness ushers in a greater joy.

Why is this, O Lord my God, since You are to Yourself Your own eternal joy and since there are always some about You who rejoice in Your presence? Why does this inferior part of Your creation thus alternately ebb and flow with pains and pleasures?

Is this the measure of their being? Is this what You have allotted them when, from the heights of Heaven to the lowest part of the earth, from the beginning to the end of time, from the angel to the worm, from the first motion to the last, all sorts of good things and all Your just works were set by You in their proper places and enacted in their proper times?

Ah! How high are You in the highest, and how deep are You in the depths! Never do You depart from us, and yet we seldom return to You,

CHAPTER 4 — More Joy at the Conversion of Famous Men

COME, Lord, and act within us. Arouse us and call us back. Inflame us with love for You. Breathe forth Your fragrance and become sweet to us. Let us love You and run to You.

Are there not many who return to You out of a deeper hell of blindness than Victorinus, who approach You and are illumined, receiving the light that, to all who receive it, gives *the power to become Your sons* (Jn 1:12)? Yet, if they are less known among the people, even those who know them rejoice less for them. For when we rejoice with many, the joy of each one is greater because we are enkindled and inflamed by one another.

Besides, those converts who are known to many have greater influence upon many in their salvation and give an example that many will follow. Therefore, even those who came in before them rejoice the more because they rejoice not for them alone, but for many.

Far be it from me to believe that in Your house the rich persons should be accepted before the poor, or the noble before the lowly, when *rather You have chosen the weak things of the world to confound the strong, and have chosen the base things of this world and the contemptible things and the things that are not, as if they are, that You might bring to naught the things that are* (1 Cor 1:27-28).

It was *that least of Your Apostles* (1 Cor 15:9) by whose tongue You did speak these words. Yet even he—when by his preaching he had overcome the pride of the proconsul Sergius Paulus and brought him under the gentle yoke of Your Christ and made him a subject of the great King (cf. Acts 13:6-12)—chose to be called Paul rather than by his former name, Saul, as a token of so great a victory.

For the devil is much more conquered in one on whom he has a stronger hold and through whom he holds many more. He has a stronger hold on the proud because of their nobility, and through them and on account of their authority he possesses many others.

Therefore, the more the heart of Victorinus was esteemed, which the devil had so long held as an impregnable fort, as well as Victorinus' tongue, with which, as with a great and sharp weapon, he had murdered many, the greater ought to be the joy of Your children because our King *has bound the strong man* (Mt 12:29). For they now saw his *vessels taken away and cleansed, and made fit for Your honor and serviceable to the Lord for every good work* (2 Tm 2:21).

CHAPTER 5 — Obstacles to Conversion

WHEN Your servant Simplicianus had related these things to me concerning Victorinus, I was inflamed with a desire to imitate him, for he had related them for this very purpose. Afterward, he also added that in the days of the emperor Julian a law was enacted by which the Christians were forbidden to teach the sciences or oratory, in consequence of which law Victorinus chose rather to quit his oratorical school than Your Word, which *makes eloquent the tongues of infants* (Wis 10:21). On hearing this I did not so much admire his fortitude as envy his happiness because by this means he found the opportunity to employ himself wholly in Your service.

Now this was the thing I longed for, bound fast as I was not with another's irons, but by my own iron will. The enemy held my will, and of it he had made a chain with which he had bound me fast. From a perverse will proceeded lust; serving this lust produced habit, and habit not resisted became necessity.

As with certain links fastened one to another—for which reason I have called it a chain—I was kept closely shackled by this cruel slavery. The new will which I began to have to serve You freely, and to enjoy You, O God, the only sure delight, was not yet strong enough to overcome the former, which had been strengthened by age. So these two wills of mine—the one old, the other new, the one carnal, the other spiritual—were in a conflict with one another, and by their discord wasted my soul.

Thus I understood by my own experience what I had read, *how the flesh lusts against the spirit, and the spirit against the flesh* (Gal 5:17). And it was I in them both, but more I in that which I approved in myself than in that which I disapproved; for in this it was not so much myself because in great part I rather suffered it against my will than acted willingly.

Yet, the custom that warred against me had gained power by my own doing, for it was willingly that I had come where I now did not wish to be. And who can deny that it is right that a just punishment should follow sin? Nor did I have any excuse, such as I formerly pretended, when I delayed to forsake the world and to serve You because I had not yet certainly discovered Your truth. For now I was certain of this truth, but I was still bound to the earth and refused to fight in Your service, being as much afraid of being disengaged from my burden as I would fear to remain encumbered by it.

The burdens of the world thus weighed me down sweetly, as in a restful sleep. The thoughts by which I meditated on You were like the efforts of those who want to get up but, overcome with drowsiness, fall back into their former slumber.

There is no man who would wish to sleep forever, and everyone's sound judgment holds it best to be awake. Yet, many times a man delays shaking off his sleep when a heavy laziness benumbs his limbs, and he more willingly resumes his slumber, even though his reason tells him it is wrong and it is now high time to get up. So it was with me, for I was satisfied that it was better for me to give myself up to Your love than to yield to my own lusts.

However, while the one course pleased me but gained not the mastery, the other both pleased and mastered me. I had nothing now to reply to You when You said to me, *Awake, sleeper, and arise from among the dead, and Christ will enlighten you* (Eph 5:14). And when on every side You did show me that You spoke the truth and I was thoroughly convinced of this, I had nothing at all to reply except some lazy and drowsy words: "Soon." "Presently." "In a little while." But this "Soon" never came, and this "In a little while" turned out to be a long time.

In vain did *I delight in Your law according to the inner man, when another law in my members warred against that law of my mind and led me captive to the law of sin, which was in my members* (Rom 7:22-23). For the law of sin is the violence of custom, with which the mind is dragged along and held against its will, but deservedly because it willingly fell into it. *Who then will deliver me, unhappy man as I was, from the body of this death, but Your grace only through Jesus Christ our Lord?* (Rom 7:24-25).

CHAPTER 6 — The Visit of Ponticianus

I WILL *now declare and confess to Your Name* (Ps 54:8), *O Lord, my Helper and Redeemer* (Ps 19:15), by what means You delivered me from the bond of lustful inclinations that bound me so tightly, and from the slavery of worldly affairs. I went about my accustomed tasks with an increasing anxiety, as I daily sighed for You, and I frequented Your church, as much as my affairs would permit, under the load of which I then groaned.

Alypius was with me, having a vacation from his law business after the third term, and he was awaiting clients to whom he might sell his legal skills, as I also sold the art of speech, as far as this can be taught. As for Nebridius, he had agreed because of our friendship to teach under Verecundus, a citizen and grammarian of Milan, a most intimate friend of all of us, who urgently needed a faithful assistant, and earnestly begged, as the law of friendship in our group required, that it might be one of our number.

It was not any desire for profit that drew Nebridius to that employment, for his learning would have entitled him to a higher post. However, being of a kind and compliant disposition, his good nature would not allow him to ignore the request of his friends. He acted most prudently in this position, shunning the opportunity to become known by the great ones *according to this world* (Eph 2:2), so that he might better avoid all distraction of mind, which he desired to have free as many hours as possible to seek or read or hear something concerning wisdom.

One day when Nebridius was absent—I do not recall for what reason—there came to our house to visit me and Alypius a man named Ponticianus, our countryman inasmuch as he was an African, who held an honorable post in the emperor's court. I do not know what he wanted of us, but when we sat down to talk together, he happened to notice a book lying upon a game table before us. He took it up and opened it and, contrary to his expectations, found it to be the writings of St. Paul. For he imagined that it would be one of the books dealing with my profession, which was now wearing me down.

Thereupon, smiling, and looking at me as if to offer congratulations, he expressed his wonder that he found those and only those writings before me. For he was a Christian and one of the faithful, and he often prostrated himself before You, our God, in church, in frequent and prolonged prayers.

When I told him that those Scriptures were now my chief study, he began a discourse concerning Antony, an Egyptian monk, whose name was highly illustrious among Your servants, but which up to that time was unknown to us. Perceiving this, he dwelt at greater length upon that subject, informing us of the life of so great a man and wondering why we had heard nothing of him.

We were astonished to *hear of Your wonderful works* (Ps 145:5) so well attested, done so lately and almost in our own days, in the true Faith and the Catholic Church. All of us marveled—we, that they were so great, and he, that they were unknown to us.

Then he turned his conversation to the flocks in the monasteries and their manner of life, yielding a sweet odor to You, and to the fruitful deserts of the wilderness, of which we had heard nothing. There was at Milan, outside the walls of the city, a monastery full of good brothers, under the care of Ambrose, and we had not known it. He proceeded with his discourse, as we listened in attentive silence.

Then he related to us how, at a time when the court was at Trier and the emperor one afternoon was attending the games of the circus, he and three of his companions went out walking among the gardens near the walls of the city. And there, as they chanced to go in pairs, one pair taking one way and the other another, these two companions, as they were wandering about, came upon a cottage where some of Your servants dwelt, *poor in spirit, of whom is the Kingdom of Heaven* (Mt 5:3). There they found a book in which was written the life of Antony.

One of them began to read this book, to admire it, and to be inflamed with it, and, as he was reading, to think of embracing the same kind of life and quitting his worldly office to become Your servant, for he was one of those whom they call agents in the emperor's affairs. Then, suddenly filled with a holy love and a sober shame and angry at himself, he cast his eyes upon his friend, and said to him.

"Tell me, I beg of you, what will we gain with all these labors of ours? What do we seek? What is the aim of our service? Can we have higher hopes in court than to become friends of the emperor? What is found there that is not brittle and full of dangers? Through how many dangers must we ascend to a greater danger? And when shall we reach our goal? On the contrary, if I wish it, I can now become immediately the friend of God."

Having said this, and troubled with the travail of a new life, he turned his eyes again to those pages. As he read, he was changed within, where You beheld it, and his mind was stripped of the world, as soon became apparent. As he read and rolled to and fro on the billows of his heart, he groaned for a while, and at last discerned and resolved upon better things.

Then, wholly Yours, he said to his friend: "I have now broken loose from these, our former hopes,

and am fully resolved to serve God, and I shall
begin from this hour, in this place. If you are unwilling to follow me, at least refrain from opposing my
resolution." The other replied that he would cling to
him as a companion for so high a reward and so glorious a service. Thus, both of them belonging to
You, they laid out the course proper for building
that "costly tower," by leaving all and following You.

By this time, Ponticianus and the one who had
walked with him through other parts of the garden
came to the same place in search of them, and, having found them, reminded them that they should return home because the day was far spent. But the
latter, relating their purpose and determination and
in what manner this resolution had been formed
and confirmed, requested of Ponticianus and his
companion, if they were not pleased to join them, at
least not to try to dissuade them.

Thereupon the others, being in no way changed
from their former selves, nevertheless wept at hearing their decision (as he stated), and piously congratulated them and recommended themselves to
their prayers. Accordingly, with hearts weighed
downward toward the earth, they went to the palace,
while the other two, with hearts fixed on heaven, remained in that cottage. Both of the latter had
prospective brides, who, as soon as they heard these
things, likewise consecrated their virginity to You.

CHAPTER 7 — The Effect of Ponticianus

THIS was the story Ponticianus related to us. But
You, O Lord, while he was speaking, forced me
to face myself, while I tried to avoid observing myself. You set me face to face with myself, so that I

might see how disgraceful I was, how deformed and filthy, spotted and ulcerous. I beheld and abhorred myself, but there was no way for me to flee from myself.

If I tried to turn away my sight from myself, as he continued his narration, You would bring me back again and set me before my eyes so that I might discover my iniquity and hate it. I knew it indeed, but I feigned ignorance, refused to acknowledge it, and put it out of my memory.

But now the more ardently I loved these persons, of whom I heard these wholesome resolutions, by which they had given themselves up without reserve to be healed by You, the more bitterly I hated myself when compared with them. Many years (I think about twelve) had passed since, in my nineteenth year, I had been stirred, upon reading Cicero's *Hortensius,* to the study of wisdom.

And yet I still continued to delay despising worldly happiness in order to apply myself wholly to a search for wisdom—the very search for which, and not simply the finding of it, was to be preferred to the finding of all the treasures and kingdoms of the world and all the pleasures of the body, however freely and abundantly they might be enjoyed.

In my youth, miserable wretch that I was, yes, most wretched from the first dawning of adolescence, I had begged You for chastity, and said: "Give me chastity and continence, but not for a while," for I was afraid that You might hear me too soon and heal me of the disease of concupiscence, which I wished rather to satiate than to extinguish. I had gone "through wicked ways" in a sacrilegious superstition [the Manichean heresy], not, indeed, as feeling certain of its validity, but as preferring it to other things that I did not seek religiously, but fought against as an enemy.

I believed that the reason I had deferred from day to day my intent to follow You alone, despising all worldly hopes, was because as yet there had appeared nothing certain by which I might steer my course. But now the day had come in which I was to be laid naked before my own eyes, and my conscience taunted me: "Where are you, my tongue? You used to say that you would not cast off the load of vanity for truth as yet uncertain. Lo, now it is certain, and yet this load oppresses you still, while others with lightened shoulders take wing and fly upward, who have neither been so worn out as you have been in the search of truth nor have spent ten years and more in thinking on it."

Thus was I inwardly corroded and extremely confounded with a horrible shame while Ponticianus was relating these things. Having ended his discourse and finished the business for which he had come, he went his way, and I turned inward. What did I not say against myself? With what lashes of condemnation did I not whip my soul, that it might follow me, who strove to go after You? And it still hung back; it refused, though offering no excuse. All its arguments were now spent and refuted, and there only remained a dumb fear, dreading no less than death to be restrained from that course of habit by which it was wasting to death.

CHAPTER 8 — In the Garden

THEN in this great conflict of my inner being in which I was hotly engaged with my soul in the private chamber of my heart, troubled equally in countenance and in mind, I set upon Alypius and cried out: "What is this we suffer? What is this you have been hearing? The unlearned arise and take Heaven by force, and we, heartless, with all our learning, behold how we still wallow in flesh and blood! Are we ashamed to follow them because they have gone before, and are we not ashamed if we do not so much as follow?"

I said some such words to this effect, and the tumult of my mind caused me to hurry away from him, while he stood silent, beholding me with astonishment. For I had not spoken as I usually did, and my forehead, cheeks, eyes, color, and the tone of my voice expressed more clearly the state of my mind than did the words I uttered.

There was a little garden belonging to our lodging. We had the use of it, as of the whole house, since our friend, the master of the house, did not live there. The tumult of my heart had caused me to go there, where no one might interrupt the hot conflict in which I was engaged with myself, until it might come to the resolution that You already knew, but I did not. For I was as yet only wholesomely raging at myself and dying in order to live, well knowing how wicked I was but not knowing how good, within a little while, I was to be.

I went away, therefore, into the garden. Alypius followed close after me, for I did not consider myself to have less privacy for his being there, and he had never seen me so greatly disturbed. We sat down as far removed from the house as possible. And I groaned in spirit, angry at myself with a most violent indignation, because I had not yet embraced Your Will and *entered into a covenant with You* (Ez 16:8), my God. *All my bones cried out* (Ps 35:10) that I should enter into that covenant, and they lifted me to the heavens with their praises.

I did not need ships, or coaches, or feet to go there, nor even did I need to move as far as I had come from the house to the place where we were sitting. For not only to go, but even to arrive there, nothing else was needed than to will to go. However, that had to be done resolutely and with a perfect will, not with a maimed and struggling will, turned and tossed this way and that, with one part rising and another collapsing.

In these very struggles with indecision, I made a number of movements in my body, which men are not always able to do when they will if either they have not those parts or they are bound in chains or are weak through sickness, or hindered in any other way. If I then tore my hair or struck my forehead or clasped my hands about my knee because I had a will to do it, I did it.

And yet, it was possible that I might have a will to do such things as those, but not be able to do them if my limbs were not pliant to obey my will. I did then so many things, the willing of which was not the same as to be able to do them, and yet I did not do that which pleased me incomparably more, and which I would be able to do as soon as I had the will to do it, because as soon as I had the will I should doubtless be truly willing.

In my case, the ability was the same as the will, and the very willing was doing, and yet it was not done. And the body more easily obeyed the slightest wish of my soul to make limbs move according to its beck and call than the soul obeyed itself in order to execute its important decrees that were to be fulfilled within the will alone.

CHAPTER 9 — The Two Wills

WHENCE comes this monstrous state, and why should it be? Let Your mercy shine forth, that I may inquire, if perhaps an answer can be given by the secret punishments of men and the darkest sufferings of the sons of Adam.

Whence and why this monstrous state? The mind commands the body, and is immediately obeyed; the mind commands itself, and is opposed. The mind commands that the hand should move, and it is so quickly executed that the command can hardly be distinguished from the obedience, and yet the mind is mind and the hand is body. The mind commands that the mind itself should will a thing, and yet, though it be the same mind, it does not do what is commanded.

Whence and why this monstrous state? It commands, I say, that it should will a thing, which if it did not will already, it would never command, and yet that is not done which it commands. But it does not entirely will it, and therefore it does not entirely command. For it commands only insofar as it wills, and that which it commands is not done insofar as it does not will. It is the will that commands that there should be a will, not any other will but itself. It is not then a full will that commands, and therefore that is not done which it commands, for if there were a full will, it would not command that *to be* because it would be *present* already.

It is then no monstrous thing that one should be partly willing and partly not willing. Rather, it is a sickness or weakness of the mind that, being weighed down by evil custom, it does not entirely arise when lifted up by truth.

There are, therefore, two wills, for one of them is not entire, and what is wanting to one is possessed by the other.

CHAPTER 10 — One Nature

*L*ET *them perish from before Your face* (Ps 10:4), O God, as *vain talkers and seducers* (Ti 1:10) of souls perish, who, because they observe two wills whenever we deliberate, affirm that there are in us two natures of two minds, the one good, the other bad.

They themselves are indeed evil when they entertain such evil sentiments; and yet the same persons will be good, provided that they entertain true sentiments and consent to things that are true, as the Apostle says to them: *You were once darkness but now you are light in the Lord* (Eph 5:8). In effect they want to be light not in the Lord, but in themselves, thinking that the nature of the soul is that which God is. Thus, they become deeper darkness because they go farther off from You by a horrid arrogance, from You, *the true Light that enlightens every man who comes into the world* (Jn 1:9).

Consider what you are saying, and be ashamed of yourselves. *Draw near to Him and be enlightened, and your face shall not be ashamed* (Ps 34:6). When I was thus deliberating to come now to the service of the Lord my God, as I had proposed for a long time, it was I who willed it, and I who willed it not. It was the same I, but as yet I neither fully willed it nor fully willed it not. Therefore, I was in conflict with myself, and was divided from myself.

This same division was indeed against my will, yet it did not manifest in me the nature of another mind, but the punishment of my own. And therefore it was not now I who did it, *but the sin that dwelt in me* (Rom 7:17), the punishment of a sin more freely committed because I was a son of Adam. For if there are as many contrary natures in us as there are opposite inclinations of the will, there will not be two only, but many.

If any man deliberates whether he shall go to the Manichees' meeting house or to the theater, the Manichees cry out: "See, there exist two natures. The one that is good leads this way; the other is bad that draws the other way. For what else could be the cause of this wavering of wills that results in their fighting against each other?" I say that both these wills are bad, both that which leads to their meeting-house and that which draws to the theater. But they do not believe that the will can be otherwise than good that leads to them.

Suppose then that one of us should deliberate and, by reason of the conflict of two wills, should waver and doubt whether he should go to the theater or to our church. Will not these men be at a loss what to answer? For either they must confess—a thing they are unwilling to do—that the will is good by which men go to our church, as they who are instructed in their mysteries go to theirs and are held by them, or else they must think that there are two evil natures and two evil minds that are at strife in the same man. And so, that will not be true which they are accustomed to say, that there is one that is good, another that is bad, or they would be converted to the truth, and confess that when any man deliberates, it is but one and the same soul that is tossed by different wills.

Let them then no longer say, when they find two wills in the same man contrary to each other, that two contrary minds, from two contrary substances, and from two contrary principles, are upon those occasions in conflict with each other, the one good, the other bad.

For You, the God of truth, disapprove and rebuke and convict them—as in cases where both wills are bad. For example, someone deliberates whether he should kill a man by poison or the sword, whether he should seize this or that possession of his neighbor when he cannot have both, whether he should indulge his luxury by spending his money upon his pleasures or keep it to serve avarice, whether he should go to the circus or to the theater if both are open on the same day, or—and now I add a third alternative—commit a theft if the opportunity presents itself, or, adding a fourth, commit adultery if there be at the same time an opportunity for this crime also.

Let us suppose that all these possibilities will occur at the same point in time, and all are much desired but cannot all be done at once. In such cases the soul is rent by four wills opposite to one another, or even by more in so great a variety of things as may be desired, and yet these men are not accustomed to admit such a multitude of different substances.

The same happens also in good wills, for I ask of them whether it is not good to be delighted with reading the Apostle, and whether it is not good to be pleased with a sober psalm, and whether again it is not good to discourse upon the Gospel? They must answer to each of these interrogations that it is good.

What then if all these together should at one and the same time offer their delight? Will not diverse wills divide the heart of man, while he deliberates as to what course he should choose? And all these wills are good, and they struggle among themselves, until one thing is chosen that may now be pursued by the whole unified will that before was divided into many parts.

So also when eternity delights us above, while the pleasure of temporal good holds us fast below, it is the same soul that with a will in conflict must choose one or the other. Therefore, it is rent and torn, suffering grievous embarrassment, while, for the sake of truth, it prefers the one, but out of habit does not relinquish the other.

CHAPTER 11 — The Conflict Between Flesh and Spirit

THUS I was sick and tormented, and I accused myself much more bitterly than I was wont to do. I twisted and turned in my chain until that should be entirely broken by which I now was scarcely held but was still held all the same. And You, O Lord, were still probing the hidden depths of my soul with a severe mercy, redoubling the lashes of fear and shame, lest I should delay once more, and the small connecting strand that still remained should not be broken off, and so might regain strength and bind me more tightly.

I said within myself, "Behold, let it be done now, let it be now." And as I said it, I came near to making the commitment. I almost did it, and yet did not do it. However, I did not fall back to where I was before, but stood very firm and regained my breath. And I tried again and came a little nearer, just a short distance away, and very close to touching and laying hold of it, but still I was not there, nor did I touch or lay hold of it, still hesitating to die unto death and to live unto life.

The evil that I had been long accustomed to had still more power over me than that which was better, but which I had not experienced. And the nearer the point of time approached in which I was to become another man, the greater the horror it struck into me, yet it did not make me recoil or turn away, but held me in suspense.

Those trifles of trifles and vanities of vanities, my former attachments, deterred me. Pulling me by the garment of my flesh, they whispered to me, "Will you then forsake us? And from this moment shall we no more be with you forever? And from this moment shall you no more be allowed to do this or that forever?"

And what did they suggest to me under what I call "this or that," what things did they suggest, O my God? Let Your mercy keep far from the soul of Your servant the filth, the shameful things they did suggest. And now I heard them much less than half as much, not as boldly confronting me and opposing me to my face, but as muttering behind me and stealthily pulling me as I was departing, that I might look back upon them. Yet they somewhat retarded me, while I hesitated to snatch myself away and shake them off and to leap forward where I was called, the violence of evil habit still saying to me, "Do you think you can live without these things?"

But now it said this very faintly. For there appeared to me on the side toward which I turned my face, though as yet I trembled to pass over, the chaste dignity of continence, serene and modestly cheerful, kindly enticing me to come forward and to doubt nothing, and stretching forth her pious hands to receive and embrace me, full of a multitude of good examples.

There were numerous boys and girls, there was a multitude of youths, and persons of all ages, grave widows, and aged virgins. And in all these continence herself was not *barren,* but by You, O Lord, her Bridegroom, a fruitful *mother of children* (Ps 112:9) of joy.

She turned to me with an encouraging smile by way of drawing me on, as if to say, "Are you not able to do what these youths and these maidens do? Or do they draw their power from themselves, and not from the Lord their God? The Lord their God gave me to them. Why attempt to stand relying upon yourself, and hence failing to stand up? Cast yourself upon Him! Fear not! He will not withdraw Himself to let you fall. Cast yourself upon Him without apprehension! He will receive and heal you."

I was very much ashamed that I should still hear the whispers of those vanities and hang in suspense. And she began again as if to say: "Stop your ears against your unclean members that are upon the earth, so that they may be mortified. They tell you of delights, but not as does the Law of the Lord your God" (see Ps 119:85). Such was the conflict within my heart but only between me and myself. And Alypius, who kept close by me, waited in silence for the outcome of this unusual conflict that I was enduring.

CHAPTER 12 — The Voice in the Garden

BUT when deep reflection had gathered from the secret recesses of my soul and heaped together all my misery in the sight of my heart, there arose in me a mighty squall, bringing with it a very great shower of tears.

That I might more freely pour it forth with its proper words, I arose and left Alypius, for I considered solitude to be more fitted for the business of weeping. And I moved away to such a distance that even his presence might not be burdensome to me.

This then is what was going on in me, and he realized it, for I think I must have said something, when I arose, in which the sound of my voice was heavy with tears. Therefore, he remained in the place where he had been sitting, greatly amazed.

I threw myself down, I know not how, under a certain fig tree, and there gave full vent to my tears. Floods gushed forth from my eyes, *an acceptable sacrifice to You* (Ps 51:19). And not indeed in these same words, but to this purpose I said many things to You: *And You, O Lord, how long?* (Ps 6:4). *How long, O Lord, will You be angry forever? Remember not our former iniquities* (Ps 79:5, 8). For I perceived myself to be held by them. And I uttered these words of complaint: "How long, how long, tomorrow and tomorrow! Why not now? Why not in this very hour put an end to my uncleanness?"

I spoke these things, and I wept with a most bitter contrition of my heart. And behold I heard a voice from a neighboring house, like that of a boy or a girl, I know not which, saying in a singsong voice, and often repeating, "Take up and read, take up and read." Immediately my countenance changed, and I began to consider most intently whether in any kind of play children were wont to sing such words, but I could not remember that I had anywhere heard any such thing.

And so, repressing the course of my tears, I got up, interpreting that childlike chant to be nothing less than a divine admonition that I should open the Bible and read the first chapter I should come upon. For I had heard about Antony that he had taken the text of the Gospel, which was being read when he came into the church, as particularly addressed to him: *Go, sell what you have, and give to the poor and you shall have treasure in heaven, and come, follow Me* (Mt 19:21). And by this divine oracle he was in that instant converted to You.

Therefore, I returned in haste to the place where Alypius was sitting, for when I arose, I had there laid down the book of the Apostle. I snatched it up, opened it, and read in silence the lines on which I first cast my eyes: *Not in reveling and drunkenness, not in debauchery and wantonness, not in strife and jealousy. But put on the Lord Jesus Christ, and as for the flesh, take no thought of it for its lusts* (Rom 13:13-14).

I would read no further, nor was there any need for me to do so. For with the conclusion of this sentence, it was as if a light of confidence and security had streamed into my heart, and all the darkness of my former hesitation was dispelled.

Then putting my finger or some other mark at that spot, I closed the book, and with a countenance that was now calm I related all to Alypius. And he in the following manner showed me what had been going on in himself, which I did not know. He asked to see what I had read, and I showed it to him. He also looked on further than I had read, but I knew not what followed.

These were the next words: *Receive him who is weak in faith* (Rom 14:1), which he applied to himself, and so told me. This admonition strengthened him, and without any disturbance of mind or hesitation, he joined with me in this holy purpose and resolution, which was very suitable to his moral state, in which he had long before far surpassed me.

We then went in to my mother. We told her what had occurred, and she rejoiced. When we told her how it came about, she was filled with a sense of exultation and triumph, and she blessed You, *Who are able to do above what we ask or understand* (Eph 3:20).

For she now saw that so much more had been granted to her by You in my regard than she had been wont to ask with tearful and lamentable sighs. For You had converted me to Yourself so that I now sought neither a wife nor any lofty position in this world, relying now upon that rule of Faith where, so many years before, You had shown me to her in a vision.

And You turned her mourning into a much more plentiful joy than she had wished for, a joy much more precious and chaste than what she expected from grandchildren of my flesh.

BOOK 9—The New Life

Augustine determines to abandon his profession of rhetoric in order to devote his life to God. He receives Baptism at thirty-three years of age, together with his friend Alypius and his son Adeodatus. On his way to Africa, Monica, his mother, dies at Ostia at fifty-six years of age. He describes her life and character.

CHAPTER 1 — Free from Worldly Cares

*L*ORD, I am Your servant. I am Your servant and the son of Your handmaid. You have broken my bonds. I will offer to You the sacrifice of praise (Ps 116:16-17). Let my heart and my tongue praise You, and let all my bones say, *Lord, who is like You?* (Ps 35:10). Let them say this, and I beg You to answer and *say to my soul, I am Your salvation* (Ps 35:3).

Who am I, and what am I? What was there in me that was not evil either in my deeds or, if not in my deeds, in my words, or, if not in my words, in my will? But You, O Lord, are good and merciful, and Your right hand has regarded the depth of my death, and from the bottom of my heart it has emptied out the abyss of corruption. This all consisted in not willing what I willed and willing what You willed.

But where for all these years was my free will, and out of what hidden and deep recess was it called forth in an instant, that I might submit my neck to Your sweet yoke and my shoulders to Your light burden, O Christ Jesus, *my Helper and my Redeemer* (Ps 19:15)?

How sweet did it suddenly become to me to be without the sweetness of vain pursuits! Those pleasures that previously I had so much feared to lose, I now cast from me with joy. You expelled them from me, You Who are the true and sovereign sweetness, You expelled them, and came in Yourself instead of them—sweeter than all delight, but not to flesh and blood; brighter than any light, but more interior than any secret; higher than any honor, but not to those who are high in their own estimate.

Now was my mind free from the gnawing cares of ambition, of the acquisition of riches, and of weltering in filth and scratching the itch of lusts. And my infant tongue spoke freely to You, my glory, my wealth, and my salvation, my Lord and God.

CHAPTER 2 — Leaving the Profession of Rhetoric

IT SEEMED good to me in Your presence not noisily to break off, but gently to withdraw the service of my tongue from that business of loquacity, so that youths—not students of Your Law, nor of Your peace, but of lying follies and the conflicts of the Law—might no longer purchase from my mouth the weapons for their madness.

By a happy coincidence there now remained just a few days before the vintage holidays, and these I resolved patiently to endure, so that I might leave my school at the usual time and, having now been ransomed by You, might never again put myself up for sale.

This design of ours was manifest to Your sight, but was not known by others, except by our own friends. And we had agreed among ourselves that the news should not be divulged everywhere, although to us ascending from *the vale of tears* (Ps 84:7), and singing to You *a song of ascents* (Ps 120:1), You had given *sharp arrows and consuming coals against the deceitful tongue* (Ps 120:3-4) that opposes us under the guise of counsel, and, as men do with food, loves us so as to devour us.

You had pierced our heart with Your love. Your words, like arrows, were fixed in our innermost parts. The examples set by Your servants, whom You had brought from darkness to light and from death to life, being laid up together in the bosom of our thought, inflamed and consumed our heavy torpor, so that we would no longer tend downward to the things below. They enkindled in us so strong a flame that any wind of opposition that could blow from a deceitful tongue would only have increased it, instead of extinguishing it.

Nevertheless, since You have sanctified Your Name throughout the earth, our vow and resolution would be regarded by some as acts deserving of high praise. Therefore, it would appear ostentatious if we were not to remain until the vacation that was now so near at hand but to resign before then with a public profession of my intentions, allowing all those who knew of it to conclude that I had done so deliberately to take advantage of the approaching vintage holidays and spread their opinion that I had done so to make myself seem important. And what would it profit me if men should be spreading their opinions and disputing about my intentions, and if *our good-will should be reviled* (Rom 14:16)?

Moreover, that same summer my lungs began to fail under the heavy strain of teaching, and I had great difficulty breathing. The pains in my breast signified that my lungs were damaged, and since they could not allow me to deliver any clear or lengthy discourse, I was faced with the troubling decision either to lay down that burden of my profession, or, if I could be cured and recover, at least to give it up for a time. But after I had now taken a full resolution to *devote my leisure time to the acknowledgement that You are God* (Ps 46:11), and I was steadfast in my resolve, You know, O my God, how I began even to be glad that I had this excuse that was in no way fabricated, to assuage the unhappiness of those men who, for the sake of their children, were unwilling that I should be free from teaching.

Therefore, being full of such joy, I patiently endured that interval of time till it should run out. I do not know whether it lasted as long as twenty days, but I endured that period with fortitude, for the desire for money, which had formerly helped me to bear so heavy a burden, was now completely absent. I would have been quite overwhelmed by that lack, had not patience succeeded in its place.

Some of Your servants, my brethren, may say that it was sinful for me, with my heart now completely devoted to Your service, to allow myself to sit in the *chair of lies* (Ps 1:1) even for a single hour. And I will not attempt to dispute it. But, most merciful Lord, have You in Your sacred waters not pardoned and remitted this sin along with so many others much more horrible and deadly?

CHAPTER 3 — Verecundus' Offer of a House

VERECUNDUS was quite upset about this path we had determined to follow, for he saw that now he would be deprived of our company because of the bonds by which he was so strictly tied to the world. He was not yet a Christian, though his wife was one of the faithful, and yet she was the chief fetter that retarded him from following the course of life that we proposed to enter upon. And he said that he would not become such a Christian because the terms for his admission would not be acceptable to him. However, he very kindly offered us the use of his country house for the time we would remain in that area.

You will reward him, O Lord, in the resurrection of the just, since You have already rewarded him with the lot of the just. For when we were absent on a journey to Rome, he was seized with some bodily illness, in the course of which he became a Christian, one of the faithful, and so departed this life. Thus, You were pleased to show mercy not just to him, but also to us, lest, in remembering the great kindness of this friend toward us and not numbering him among Your flock, we would have been tormented with an unbearable grief.

Thanks be to You, O God! We are Yours, as You have shown through Your encouragement and consolations. And You are faithful in Your promises. In return for his country house at Cassiciacum where, retired from the tumult of the world we reposed in You, You granted to Verecundus the joys of Your ever verdant paradise. For You have forgiven him for his sins here upon earth, *in the mountain of abundance, Your mountain, that fertile mountain* (Ps 68:16).

At that time, therefore, Verecundus was very much concerned, but Nebridius rejoiced with us. Although before he became a Christian he had fallen into the pit of that most pernicious error, to believe the flesh of Your Son to have been no more than a phantasm, he had now rejected that concept, and though he was not as yet initiated in any of the Sacraments of Your Church, he was a most earnest inquirer after truth. Not long after our conversion and regeneration by Your Baptism, he himself became a faithful Catholic and served You in perfect chastity and continence in Africa among his kindred. Once he had converted his entire family to the Christian Faith, he was freed by You from the chains of the flesh, and now he lives *in Abraham's bosom* (Lk 16:22).

Whatever it is that is signified by that bosom, there my Nebridius lives—that dear friend of mine, Your adopted son, and no longer a freed man only. What other place could receive such a soul? There he lives, concerning which place he asked so many questions of me, a poor inexperienced mortal. He now no more lays his ears to my mouth, but places his spiritual mouth at Your fountain, and there he drinks to his fill true wisdom with a thirst ever fresh, happy without end. And yet I cannot think that he is so inebriated from the fountain of Your wisdom as to forget me, since You, O Lord, the fountain at which he drinks, are pleased to be mindful of us.

So were we then, comforting Verecundus who was grieved because of our conversion, though without any lessening of friendship. We exhorted him to accept the Faith proper to his station, namely, in married life. And we waited anxiously for Nebridius to follow us, which he was so well-disposed to do and was just upon the point of doing, when, behold, those days finally came to an end. They had seemed endless and many to me, by reason of the longing desire that I had to be at liberty, so that I might sing to You from the depths of my heart: *My heart has said to You, I have sought Your face; Your face, O Lord, I will still seek* (Ps 27:8).

CHAPTER 4 — At Cassiciacum

FINALLY the day arrived when I was indeed to be released from my professorship of rhetoric, from which I had already been released in mind. Now it was over. You previously had freed my heart from that profession; now You delivered my tongue.

Rejoicing, I blessed You and retired to the country with my closest friends. The kind of writing I did there—now indeed dedicated to Your service, but still panting with something of the school of pride during this sort of breathing spell—may be seen in all the books composed there, whether discussed with those who were with me or with myself alone in Your presence. But what passed between me and Nebridius, who was absent, appears in my letters.

When shall I find enough time to commemorate all Your great benefits bestowed upon us at that time, especially when hastening now to other still greater things? My remembrance calls me back to those times, and it becomes sweet to me to confess to You, O Lord, with what inward scourges You did then break and tame me, and in what manner You did make me plain and level, *making low the mountains and hills* of my thoughts, *making straight what was crooked* in me, *and smooth what was rough* (Lk 3:5).

In like manner You also subdued Alypius, the brother of my heart, to the Name of Your only-begotten Son, *our Lord and Savior Jesus Christ* (2 Pt 3:18), which Name at first he was unwilling to have inserted in our writings. For he had preferred that they rather should savor of the *cedars* of the schools, *which the Lord has now broken in pieces* (Ps 29:5), than of the wholesome herbs of the Church, the antidote against serpents.

What cries did I send up to You, my God, when I read the Psalms of David, those canticles of faith and songs of devotion that cast out a proud spirit when I was as yet but a novice in Your sincere love, a catechumen on vacation in a country house with Alypius, who was also a catechumen. However, my mother was also with us, in a woman's garb, yet with a virile faith and having the security of old age, the charity of a mother, and the piety of a Christian.

What affectionate words did I utter to You in those Psalms, and how much was I inflamed by them with the love of You, and burned with a desire to recite them, if I could, all the world over, to abate the swelling pride of mankind! And indeed they are sung all the world over, *nor is there anyone who can hide himself from Your heat* (Ps 19:7).

With what a vehement and sharp indignation was I incensed against the Manichees, and how again did I pity them, that they were ignorant of our Sacraments, these sovereign medicines, and were violently opposed to the antidote that might have cured them of their madness!

I could have wished that they had then been somewhere near me, without my knowing of their being there, and could have seen my countenance and heard my words when I read Psalm 4 in that time of rest, and been able to observe the effects it wrought upon me: *When I called upon You, You heard me, O God of my justice, in tribulation You have enlarged me. Have mercy on me, O Lord, and hear my prayer* (Ps 4:2).

Would that they could have heard, without my knowing that they heard me, that they might not think I spoke for their sakes when I recited those words. Indeed, I would not say the same things, nor in the same manner, if I perceived that I was heard and seen by them. Even if I were to say the same things, they would not understand that I was speaking with myself and to myself in Your presence, out of the natural feelings of my soul.

I trembled with fear, and again I was inflamed with hope and with rejoicing in Your mercy, O Father! And all these things issued forth from my eyes and from my voice, when Your good Spirit turned to us and said: *You sons of men, how long will you be dull of heart? Why do you love vanity and seek after lying?* (Ps 4:3). For I had loved vanity, and sought after lying.

And You, O Lord, had now magnified Your Holy One, raising Him from the dead, and placing Him at Your right hand (Eph 1:20), whence He should send from on high His promise, *the Paraclete, the Spirit of Truth* (Lk 24:49). Actually He had already sent Him, but I knew it not.

He had sent Him because He was already glorified, rising from the dead and ascending into Heaven. For till then *the Spirit was not given, because Jesus was not yet glorified* (Jn 7:39). And the Prophet cries out: *"How long will you be dull in heart? Why do you love vanity and seek after lying? Know that the Lord has glorified His Holy One"* (Ps 4:3). He cries out, *"How long";* he cries out, "Know"; and I, so long not knowing, loved vanity and sought after lying.

Therefore, I heard and trembled, because this is said to such as I remembered I had been. For in those phantoms that I had held for truth, there was vanity and lying. And I broke forth into many strong

and vehement expressions in the bitterness of my remembrance, which I wish they might have heard
who still love vanity and seek after lying. Perhaps
they would have been troubled and would have cast
it away, and so You would hear them when they
would cry to You, because He *has died* for us a true
death of the flesh, *Who intercedes to You for us* (Rom
8:34).

I read also: *Be angry and sin not* (Ps 4:5). And
how greatly I was moved, O my God, for by this
time I had learned to be angry with myself for my
past sins so that in the future I would sin no more.
And I had good reason to be angry with myself, because it was not another nature emanating from a
race of darkness that sinned in me, as is the attitude
of those who refuse to get angry with themselves,
and so *treasure up anger against the day of anger and of
the revelation of Your just judgment* (Rom 2:5).

Neither were my "good things" in the outer
world, nor were they sought under this sun by the
eyes of the flesh. Those who seek their joy in outward things easily become vain and expend their en-
ergies upon things that are seen and that are temporal, and they savor these images with hungry
thoughts. Would to God that they were weary of this
hunger, and would say: *Who shall send us good
things?* (Ps 4:6). And we might answer them, and
they would hear: *The light of Your countenance, O
Lord, is sealed upon us* (Ps 4:7). For we ourselves are
not *the light that enlightens every man* (Jn 1:9), but we
are enlightened by You so that *we who were sometimes
darkness may now be light in You* (Eph 5:8).

Oh, if only they could see that internal eternal
light! Having tasted it, I was troubled because I

could not show it to them, as long as they brought me their heart with their eyes averted from You and said: *Who shall show us good things?* (Ps 4:7). For there it was, within my bedchamber, where I was angry with myself, where I had compunction, and where I had sacrificed to You, slaying my old life, and had begun to meditate upon a new one, hoping in You. There it was that You had now begun to grow sweet to me and *had given a gladness in my heart* (Ps 4:8).

And I cried out, reading these things outwardly, and experiencing them within me. Nor did I now desire a multiplication of time consuming earthly goods, and to find myself consumed by the things of time, for I had in Your eternal simplicity another sort of *corn, wine and oil* (Ps 4:8).

With a loud cry of my heart, I cried out in the next verse: *Oh in peace, Oh in the Selfsame!* Oh for what reason does he say: *I will sleep and I will take my rest* (Ps 4:9)? For who shall withstand us when that *word will come to pass that is written: Death is swallowed up in victory* (1 Cor 15:54)? And You are that Selfsame indeed Who are never changed, and in You is rest that forgets all labors, for there is none with You. Nor should we seek many other things that are not what You are, *for You, O Lord, singularly have established me in hope* (Ps 4:9).

I read this and I was afire with zeal, but I did not discover what to do for those who were deaf and dead. One of them I had been, as pestilent as any of them, a bitter and blind ranter against those writings that were sweetened with the honey of Heaven and luminous with Your light. And I was distraught as I thought about the enemies of these Scriptures.

When shall I be able to call to mind all that took place during those blessed days? But I have not forgotten, nor will I pass over in silence, the sharp scourge with which You afflicted me and the wonderful swiftness of Your mercy. At that time You greatly tormented me with a toothache, and when it had intensified to such a degree that I could not speak, my heart conceived the desire to request of all my friends who were there to pray for me to You, the God Who is the source of all health.

I wrote this petition on wax and gave it to them to read, and as soon as we knelt down in humble prayer, the pain left me. But what kind of pain was this and how did it go away? I admit, *my Lord and my God* (Jn 20:28), that it terrified me, for I had never experienced any such pain from my earliest days. The power of Your slightest nod in the depths of our misery was thus shown unto me, and rejoicing in faith I praised Your Name. But the same faith did not allow me to have peace of mind as regards my former sins, which had not yet been remitted to me by Your Baptism.

CHAPTER 5 — Resignation Tendered

WHEN the vintage holidays were over, I gave notice to the people of Milan to provide for their scholars another teacher of rhetoric because I had resolved to dedicate myself to Your service. Moreover, by reason of my difficulty in breathing and the pain in my chest, I was no longer able to continue in that profession.

By letters I revealed to Your prelate, that holy man Ambrose, my former errors and my present desire, and I asked for his advice as to what part of

Your Scriptures it would be most proper for me to read so that I would be better prepared and suited for so great a grace. He told me to read the Prophet Isaiah, undoubtedly because his writings foreshadow the Gospel and the calling of the Gentiles more than any others. However, I did not understand much of what he said in his early chapters, and, supposing that all the rest would be the same, I laid Isaiah aside, to be taken up again when I was more expert in our Lord's way of speech.

CHAPTER 6 — Baptism

AND so, when the time had come for me to submit my name for Baptism, we left the country and returned to Milan. Alypius also decided to be reborn in You with me, having now put on the humility that is suitable to Your Sacraments. He had subjected his body, even to the extent that, with exceptional daring, he would walk barefoot on the frozen ground of Italy. We joined with us also the boy Adeodatus, carnally born of my sin. You had fashioned him well; he was then about fifteen years of age and surpassed in intelligence many grave and learned men.

I confess Your own gifts to You, O Lord my God, the Creator of all and possessing great power to reform our deformities. There was nothing in that boy that was mine, save for the sin. If he was brought up in Your discipline, it was what You alone had inspired in us. I confess Your gifts.

There is a book of mine, entitled *On the Teacher,* where he is introduced discoursing with me. You know that all the things there spoken by him in dialogue with me were his thoughts when he was only sixteen years old. I experienced many other more admirable things in him and was perfectly astonished at his great intelligence. Who but You could be the Source of such wonders?

You soon took away his life from the earth [at seventeen], and now with greater peace of mind I remember him, having no concern about any character deficiency in his childhood or his youth, or even in any way as a young man. We joined him to us, to be of equal age with us in Your grace and to be educated by us in Your discipline. Once we were baptized, any anxiety about our past life fled from us.

Nor was I satiated in those days with the wonderful sweetness I enjoyed as I considered the depth of Your counsel concerning the salvation of mankind. Oh how many tears I shed in hearing Your hymns and canticles, being exceedingly moved by the voices of Your harmonious Church. Those voices flowed into my ears, and Your truth was distilled into my heart. Then the affection of devotion overflowed and tears ran down, and I found much comfort in them.

CHAPTER 7 — Sts. Gervasius and Protasius

THE Church of Milan had recently begun to practice mutual consolation and exhortation in their worship, with the brethren singing with great devotion, united in voice and heart. For it was then about a year, or not much more, since Justina, the mother of Valentinian, the boy emperor, persecuted Your servant Ambrose in favor of her heresy, into which she had been seduced by the Arians. The pious people watched night and day in the church, ready to die with their bishop, Your servant. There also my mother, Your handmaid, bearing a chief part in the solicitude and watchings, lived in prayer.

We ourselves, though cold as yet with regard to the heat of Your Spirit, were stirred by the concern and trouble of the city. It was then instituted that hymns and psalms should be sung after the manner of the Eastern Churches, lest the people should languish with the weariness of sorrow. The practice is retained to this day, followed by many or almost all Your congregations throughout the world.

Then it occurred that through a vision You revealed to Your aforementioned bishop where the bodies of Your martyrs Gervasius and Protasius lay hidden, which for so many years You had kept uncorrupted in Your secret treasury. Now You opportunely decided to bring them forth to restrain the rage of a woman, who was also an empress. When they had been discovered and dug up and were with suitable honor transferred to Ambrose's church, those troubled with unclean spirits were delivered from their power, the same devils confessing their true nature.

At the same time, a certain citizen who had been blind for many years and was well known in the city, having inquired and learned the cause of the joyful gathering of the people, sprang to his feet and commanded his guide to conduct him there. When he arrived there he asked to be allowed entrance so that he could touch with his handkerchief the bier of the Saints *whose death is precious in Your sight* (Ps 116:15). When he had done this and applied the handkerchief to his eyes, they were immediately opened.

News of this miracle was immediately spread abroad, and Your praises were fervently celebrated. As a result, the mind of that enraged woman [Justina], though it was not brought to the health of faith, was repressed from the fury of persecution.

Thanks be to You, my God! From where and whither have You guided my remembrance that I should also confess these things to You? For though they were of considerable importance I had allowed them to escape my thoughts and had forgotten them. And yet, even then, when the *odor of Your ointments* was so fragrant, we did not *run after You* (Song 1:3). For this reason I wept all the more at the singing of these hymns in Your honor. I had formerly sighed after You, and now at I last was breathing in You, as far as there is room for this breath in this house of grass.

CHAPTER 8 — Monica's Religious Habits

*Y*OU *Who make men to live together of one mind in one house* (Ps 68:7) also added to our company Evodius, a young man of our city. While he was one of the court officers assigned to handle the emperor's affairs, he had been converted to You and had been baptized before we were. Now, having forsaken his worldly duties, he betook himself to Your service. We were unified in spirit and determined to live together as we pursued our holy purpose. We were in the process of seeking a place that would be most suitable for us who desired to devote ourselves to You, and were returning together to Africa. When we came to Ostia on the Tiber, my mother died.

I have passed over many things in my desire to be concise. Accept, O my God, my confessions and thanksgivings for innumerable things, even in my silence. But I will not pass over what my soul brings forth concerning that handmaid of Yours, who labored for me, both in the flesh that I might be born into this temporal light, and in her heart, that I might be born again into light eternal. Not her gifts but Yours in her are the gifts I shall here relate, for she had neither created nor educated herself.

It was You Who created her. Neither her father nor her mother knew what she would be when she was born of them. Though she was raised in a faithful family as a good member of Your Church, it was the rod of Your Christ, the discipline of Your only Son, that educated her in Your fear.

In regard to her good education, she was wont to extol not so much the diligence of her mother as the care of a certain very old maidservant, who had carried her father on her back when he was an infant, as older girls are assigned to carry little children. For this reason, and as a mark of respect for her old age and her excellent conduct, she was highly regarded in that Christian family by her masters.

Hence, the care of her master's daughters had also been committed to her, and this function she diligently discharged, using a holy severity when necessary in restraining them, and teaching them with a sober prudence. Except at the set hours when they were most moderately fed at their parents' table, she would not allow them, however thirsty they might be, to drink so much as a little water, thus preventing a bad custom, and adding this wholesome saying, "You are now drinking water because you cannot get wine, but when you are married, and thus mistress of the storerooms and the cellars, you will despise water, but the habit of drinking will remain."

By this prudent method of teaching and the authority of her commands, she reined in the greediness so common in children at that tender age, and she formed the very thirst of the girls to the measure of virtuous moderation, so that they no longer wanted what it was improper for them to have.

Yet, she had gradually fallen prey to—as Your handmaid related to me, her son—a love of wine. When, according to custom, she used to be sent by her parents, as a sober girl, to draw wine from the flask, in taking it out with a cup, before she poured it into the pitcher, she used to put her lips to it and sip a little, because she could not take more, her palate having a repugnance to it.

She did not do this out of any intemperate lust for drink, but out of a certain exuberance not uncommon to children of that age, which results in foolish actions that cause them to be admonished by their parents. Therefore, by slightly increasing her consumption each day, *for he who despises little things falls by little and little* (Sir 19:1), she had gradually fallen into such a habit, that now she would eagerly drink little cups that were almost filled to the brim with wine.

Why then were the advice of that sagacious old woman and her strong prohibition ignored? Would anything be efficacious against this secret disease if Your healing power, O Lord, were not watchful over us? In the absence of the fathers and mothers and guardians, You are present. You have created us, and even by those who are wicked, You bring about some good for the salvation of our souls. What did

You then do, O my God? How did You cure her? How did You heal her? Did You not subject her to a rude and sharp reproach from another soul, drawn out with a scalpel from Your hidden store, and with one stroke cut away that rottenness?

It so came to pass that a maidservant, with whom she was accustomed to go to the cellar, had a falling out with her young mistress when they are alone, and she taunted her for this fault with a most bitter insult, calling her a winebibber. Stung by this reproach, my mother realized the foulness of her fault, and she immediately condemned it and forsook it.

Just as flattering friends pervert us, so quarreling enemies many times cause us to amend our lives. However, You will repay such people not according to the good that You do through them, but according to their intentions. Being angry, this servant did not intend to cure her young mistress, but only to reproach and vex her. Hence, she did this secretly, either because such was the time and place when they happened to have their falling out, or perhaps because she also might have been condemned for reporting the matter so late.

It was You, O Lord, the Ruler of everything in Heaven and on earth—Who turn to Your uses even the depths of the torrent and dispose the turbulent madness of the times so as to make it subservient to Your designs—Who by the hostility of one soul reclaimed another. The lesson to be learned here is that no one should attribute to his own power the desired reformation of some individual should his words result in the amendment of life of that person.

CHAPTER 9 — Monica's Womanly Advice

M Y MOTHER was, therefore, raised chastely and soberly, and by You she was made subject to her parents, rather than by her parents to You. When she reached marriageable age, she was given to a husband, whom *she served as her lord* (Eph 5:22). She labored to gain him for You, continually preaching You to him by her conduct, in which You had made her very beautiful, an object of reverent love, and a source of admiration to her husband. And as for the violations he committed against her marriage bed, she tolerated them in such a manner as never to have any quarrel with her husband upon that subject. She waited for Your mercy upon him, that by coming to believe in You he might also become chaste.

He was, moreover, both as good-hearted and loving as he was hot-tempered. However, she learned not to oppose her husband when he was angry, not merely in deeds but even in words. Then after his anger had abated and he was calm, and she had found a suitable propitious moment, she would offer him her point of view in an attempt to soften his hostility.

When many women, though married to milder husbands, bore the marks of their beatings even on their disfigured faces, and in their familiar talks with her blamed the evil ways of their husbands, she, on her part, would blame their tongues. Thus, in this jesting way, she would soberly admonish them. She said that, from the time they had heard the so-called marriage contracts read to them, they ought to have regarded them as agreements whereby they were made servants. Being mindful, therefore, of their condition, she said that they should never act in a disrespectful way against their lords.

Such women, knowing what a hot-tempered husband she endured, expressed their amazement that it had never been heard or in any other way appeared that Patricius had struck his wife, or that they had ever, for so much as one day, entered into any domestic dispute. When in confidence they inquired of her the reason, she taught them her method mentioned above. Those who followed her advice found it good and thanked her. Those who did not follow it continued to suffer abuse.

Initially her mother-in-law, who had also been influenced against her by the malicious whispers of wicked maidservants, was at first incensed with her, but was finally won over by her respect and perseverance in patience and meekness. As a result she disclosed to her son how these meddling tongues had disrupted the peace of the family by causing a rift between her and her daughter-in-law, and she asked him to punish those servants.

Then, when he, in obedience to his mother and for the good order of the family and the harmony of its members, had acceded to her desire and punished with beatings those she had complained of, she pledged that anyone in the future who attempted to please her by spreading evil stories about her daughter-in-law could expect to be punished in a similar manner. And since no one now dared to do so, they thereafter lived together with remarkable harmony and benevolence.

You had also bestowed another marvelous gift on Your good servant, in whose womb You created me, *O my God, my Mercy* (Ps 59:18): namely that, whenever she could, she performed superbly her role as a peacemaker between any souls who held opposing views and were in disagreement. After listening to many most bitter things on both sides, such as a swelling and undigested discord is wont to produce when the crudities of hatred are belched forth by vicious comments to a friend who is present concerning an absent enemy, she never disclosed anything to one about what the other had said unless it was something that might lead to their reconciliation.

This might have seemed to me a small matter if sad experience had not shown me a great many people who, through some horrible and widespread contagion of sin, not only reveal to mutual enemies the angry comments of each other but also add things that were not said. On the contrary, a person who is kindly should not find it sufficient to avoid storing up or increasing, by evil speaking, the animosities and understandings of others, but also should endeavor to allay them, and extinguish them by kind words. She was such a person, taught by You, her interior Master, in the school of her heart.

She also effected the conversion to You of her husband, toward the end of his temporal life, and then she no longer had any occasion, now that he was a faithful Christian, to lament those difficult times that she had endured before his conversion.

In addition, she was a servant of Your servants. Those who knew her praised and honored and loved You very much in her, because they sensed Your presence in her, as evidenced by the testimony of the fruits of her holy life. For she had been *the wife of just one husband, she had rendered the duty of respect to her parents, she had piously managed her own house, and she had earned a reputation for good works* (1 Tm 5:4, 9-10). She had brought up her children and had been *in travail of giving birth again* (Gal 4:19) whenever she perceived them to go astray from You.

Lastly, of all of us Your servants, O Lord (for so You graciously permitted us to call ourselves), who, before her death, lived already together associated in You, after having received the grace of Your Baptism, she took as much care as if she had been the mother of us all, and she served us as if she had been the offspring of us all.

CHAPTER 10 — The Vision at Ostia

WHEN the day was near that she was to depart from this life, a day known to You but not to us, it came to pass—and You, I believe, brought it about by Your secret ways—that she and I were standing alone, leaning out from a window that overlooked the garden of the house where we were staying, at Ostia on the Tiber. There, removed from the crowds after the fatigue of a long journey, we were refurbishing our strength for our voyage.

We two were alone, discoursing together very sweetly, and *forgetting what is behind, and straining forward to what lies ahead* (Phil 3:13), we were meditating between ourselves *in the presence of Truth* (2 Pt 1:12), which You are, about what the eternal life of the Saints was to be, *which eye has not seen or ear heard nor has it entered into the heart of man* (1 Cor 2:9). Even so, we panted with the mouth of our heart for the heavenly streams of Your fountain, *the fountain of life that is with You* (Ps 36:10), so that, being sprinkled from thence, according to our present capacity, we might, in some small measure, conceive so great a thing.

When our conversation had come thus far as to conclude that the greatest delights of the bodily senses, in however great a corporeal light, were not to be compared, or even mentioned, in respect to the pleasures of that life to come, rising yet higher, with a more ardent affection in pursuit of the *Selfsame* (Ps 4:9), we ascended by several steps through all corporeal things, and through that heaven itself, from which the sun, moon, and stars shine upon earth. We ascended still higher and higher in our interior thought, thinking and speaking of You and admiring Your works.

At last we came to our own minds, and passed beyond, so that we might reach that region of never-failing plenty where You feed Israel forever with the food of truth, and where the life is that Wisdom by which all these things are made, both those that have been and and those that shall be. That Wisdom itself is not made, but is such as it always was and always will be. For to "have been" and "to be in the future" do not pertain to that Wisdom, but only "to be," because it is eternal, and anything that "has been" or "is to be hereafter" is not eternal.

And while we were speaking and gasping after it, behold we just touched it a little with one whole beat of the heart, and we sighed, and there we left fastened the *firstfruits of the Spirit* (Rom 8:23); and we returned to the sound of our mouth, where the word has its beginning and its ending. For what is there in this word of ours like Your Word, our Lord, which ever remains in itself without becoming old and renews all things?

Therefore, we said to one another: Suppose that any soul encountered only silence in the presence of all tumult of the flesh and all impressions or images of the earth, water, or air; suppose that the heavens also were silent, and the soul were silent to itself and should pass beyond itself, by not thinking of itself; suppose that dreams and all imaginary revelations were silent, and every tongue, and every sign, and whatever has its being by passing away, were also absolutely silent (because if anyone could hear them, all these things would say: *"We did not make ourselves, but He made us Who abides forever"*) (Ps 100:3-5).

Suppose, we said, that after saying this, they should all be silent, having directed our ears to Him Who made them, and so He should speak alone, not by them, but by Himself, so that we would hear His word, not by the tongue of the flesh, nor by the voice of an angel, nor *by the sound of thunder* (Ps 77:18), nor by the obscurity of a similitude, but that we should hear His own self without any of these things, His own self, Whom we love in all these things (as just now we two had strained ourselves, and, with a swift thought, had touched upon the eternal wisdom that abides above all things).

Suppose such a thing were to be continued and all other sights, of a far inferior kind, were to be withdrawn, and this one were totally to ravish, and swallow up, and engulf the beholder into its interior joys, so that our life forever should be such as that one moment of understanding, for which we had sighed—would not this be what is written, *Enter into the joy of Your Master* (Mt 25:21)? And when shall that be? Shall it be when *we shall all rise again, but we shall not all be changed* (1 Cor 15:51)?

Such things we spoke, although not altogether in this manner or in these very words. Yet You know, O Lord, that on that day, while we were speaking of such things, this world with all its delights appeared contemptible to us as we spoke. And my mother said to me, "Son, for my part, there is nothing now in this life that gives me any delight. What I have to do here any longer or why I am here I do not know; all my hopes of this world are now at an end.

"One thing there was for which I did desire to stay a little longer in this life, which was that I might see you a Catholic before I died. And my God has granted me this more abundantly, in that I see you now despising all worldly happiness, devoted to His service. What have I now to do here?"

CHAPTER 11 — Monica's Ecstasy and Death

WHAT answer I made to her about these things I do not clearly remember. But scarcely five days or not many more had passed after this before she fell ill with a fever. One day, being very sick, she fainted away, and for a little while lost consciousness. We ran in, but she soon came to herself again, and looking upon my brother and me who were standing by her, she said to us inquiringly: "Where was I?" Then beholding us struck with grief, she said, "Here you shall bury your mother."

I held my peace and refrained from weeping, but my brother said something that manifested his wish for a more felicitous end—namely, that she would not die abroad, but in her own country. Hearing this, with an anxious look she reproached him with her eyes because he entertained such notions. Looking at me, she said: "Do you hear what he says?"

Then to us both she gave these instructions: "Lay this body anywhere. Do not be concerned about that. Only this I beg of you, that wherever you may be, you will continue to remember me at the altar of the Lord." And having expressed to us this sentiment with such words as she could, she said no more, being afflicted with her disease that was steadily growing worse.

I thought of Your gifts, O invisible God, which You sow in the hearts of Your faithful and which bring forth admirable fruits. I rejoiced and gave thanks to You, remembering what I had formerly known, how much concern she had always had about the tomb that she had provided and prepared for herself near the body of her husband. Because they had lived together in great harmony, she desired also (so little can the human mind embrace things divine) to have this added to their former happiness, and to have it commemorated by men, that it would be granted to her after her pilgrimage beyond the seas that what was earthly of this united pair would be permitted to be united beneath earth.

At what point that vain wish, by the fullness of Your goodness, had ceased to be in her heart, I did not know. However I rejoiced, admiring this change that was now revealed to me, although by the conversation that we had at the window, when she said, "What have I to do here any longer?" she did not seem to desire to die in her own country. And I heard afterward that when we were already at Ostia, she one day talked, in my absence, to some of my friends with the confidence of a mother concerning the contempt of this life and the good there was in death. Admiring the virtue and courage of the woman, which You had given her, they asked her if she was not afraid to leave her body so far from her own city. To this she answered, "Nothing is far from God; neither do I need to fear that He will not know at the end of the world whence He should raise me again."

Therefore, in the ninth day of her illness, the fifty-sixth year of her life and the thirty-third of mine, that religious and devout soul was released from the body.

CHAPTER 12 — Augustine's Grief

I CLOSED her eyes, and a mighty grief came flowing into my heart and overflowed into tears. Immediately thereafter, in obedience to an insistent command of my mind, my eyes drank up their source again until it was dry, and in this inward conflict my suffering was intense. As soon as she had breathed her last, the boy Adeodatus broke out into a loud lamentation, but after being hushed by all of us, he lapsed into silence. In the same manner also some immaturity in me that was leading me to the verge of tears was checked and silenced by the youthful voice of my heart.

We did not consider it fitting to memorialize her death with lamentations and groans, because these for the most part express grief over the wretchedness of those that die, or even their apparently total extinction. However, she neither died in misery nor ceased in reality to exist. Of this we were assured without any doubt by the purity of her life and the sincerity of her *faith unfeigned* (1 Tm 1:5).

What grieved me so deeply was that I had received a fresh wound from the sudden breaking off of that most sweet and beloved custom of living together. I indeed had cause to rejoice because in the same last sickness of hers, appreciatively noting the services that I was performing for her, she called me a dutiful son, and related with much tenderness and affection that she had never once heard from my mouth any harsh or reproachful words toward her.

But yet, O my God Who made us, what comparison could there be between the honor I showed her and her life of service on my behalf? Being then left destitute of that great comfort I had in her, my soul was wounded, and my life was, as it were, torn in two, for it had, in a certain sense, become one life with hers.

The boy Evodius, therefore, being restrained from crying, took up the Psalter and began to sing the Psalm, *Of mercy and judgment, I will sing to You, O Lord* (Ps 101:1), and all of us who were in the house answered him. Many brethren and devout women, on learning of our loss, came to us, and, fulfilling the duties of their office, arranged for the funeral in the usual manner. Meanwhile, in another part of the house where it could properly be done, I discussed subjects that were suitable for that occasion with those who thought it not proper to leave me alone at such a time. And with this balm of truth I soothed my pain about which You were fully aware, although those who were there knew nothing of it and listened to me attentively, thinking me to be without any feeling of sorrow.

However in Your ears, O Lord, where none of them could hear me, I was chiding myself for the weakness of my affection and restraining the flood of my grief. Sometimes it yielded to me a little, and then again with violence it rushed upon me, yet not to such an extent as to cause me to burst into tears or to make apparent any change in my countenance. And because it caused me great distress that these human occurrences should have such a powerful effect upon me, which in due order and by the lot of our condition must necessarily come to pass, I grieved for this my grief with another grief, and so was afflicted with a double sorrow.

When the body was carried out to the burial, I went and returned without tears. Nor in those prayers that we poured forth to You, when the sacrifice of our redemption was offered to You for her, the body being set down by the grave before its interment, as is the custom in that place—nor in those prayers, I say, did I shed more tears.

However, throughout that entire day I was secretly overwhelmed with deep grief, and with a troubled spirit I begged You, to the best of my ability, to heal my sorrow, and You did not do it. I believe You did not answer my prayer because You wanted me to always remember by this one experience how strong is the bond of any habit, even upon a mind that is no longer fed with any deceitful word.

It also seemed good to me to go and bathe myself, for I had heard that the bath (*balneum*) received its name because the Greek word *balaneion* signifies something that drives away anxiety from the soul. Behold, I confess this also to Your mercy, *O Father of orphans* (Ps 68:6), because after I bathed myself, I was the same as before. I could not thereby sweat out of my heart the bitterness of my grief.

After this I slept and awoke, and found my sorrow somewhat eased. And when I was alone in bed,

I called to mind those most true verses of Your servant Ambrose:

> Maker of all things! God most high!
> Great Ruler of the starry sky!
> Who, robing day with beauteous light,
> Have clothed in soft repose the night,
> That sleep may wearied limbs restore,
> Make fit for toil and use once more;
> May gently soothe the careworn breast,
> And lull our anxious griefs to rest.

Then, little by little, my thoughts turned back to Your handmaid, recalling her conduct, so pious and holy toward You, so kind and devoted toward us, of which I was now so suddenly deprived. And I had a desire to weep in Your presence for her and for myself, on her behalf and on my own.

I gave vent to my tears, which I had kept in before, allowing them to flow as much as they pleased, and I reposed my heart upon them and found rest therein, for I addressed Your ears only, and not those of a mortal man who might have scornfully misinterpreted my weeping.

And now, O Lord, I confess all this to You in writing. Let him read it who wishes to do so and interpret it in his own way. And if he should find it to have been a sin that I wept for my mother for a small fraction of an hour—for my mother so lately dead from my eyes, who for so many years had wept for me, that I might live in Your eyes—let him not deride me for it, but rather, if his charity be great, let him weep also for my sins to You, the Father of all the brethren of Your Christ.

CHAPTER 13 — Prayers for Monica

NOW that my heart is healed of that wound for which it might be reproached for succumbing to a carnal affection, I pour out to You, our God, on behalf of that servant of Yours, a far different sort of tears, flowing from a spirit troubled by the consideration of the perils afflicting every soul that dies in Adam. She had found the joy of life in Christ even before being set loose from the flesh, and she had lived in such a manner that her faith and character gave glory to Your Name. But even so I would never dare to assert that from the time You regenerated her by Baptism, no word fell from her lips that was in violation of Your Commandments.

And Your Son, Who is the Truth, has said: *"If anyone shall say to his brother, 'You fool,' he shall be liable to the fire of Gehenna"* (Mt 5:22). And woe even to men who have led commendable lives if You were to judge them, setting aside Your mercy! But because You do not so meticulously scrutinize our sins, we confidently hope to find some place with You. Should someone attempt to compute his true merits before You, what else would he count except for Your gifts? Oh that men would recognize their true worth, and that *those who glory would glory in the Lord* (2 Cor 10:17).

Therefore, O my Praise and my Life, the God of my heart, I will put aside for a while any consideration of her good deeds, for which I joyfully give thanks to You, and I now entreat You in regard to any sins committed by my mother. Hear me, I beseech You, through that Medicine of our wounds Who hung upon the tree, and *Who at the right hand of God also intercedes for us* (Rom 8:34). I know that she acted mercifully to others, and that from her heart she forgave her debtors their debts.

Please likewise forgive her her debts, if she also contracted some in those many years she lived after receiving the saving waters of Baptism. Forgive them, O Lord, forgive them, I beseech You. *Enter not into judgment with her* (Ps 143:2), but let *Your mercy triumph over Your justice* (Jas 2:13), for Your words are true, and You have promised mercy to the merciful. It was by Your gift that they were such, for *You will have mercy on whom You will have mercy, and You will show pity to whom You will show pity* (Rom 9:15).

I believe that You have already done what I ask, but *give Your approval to these free offerings of my mouth, O Lord* (Ps 119:108). For when the day of her dissolution was at hand, she gave no thought to have her body sumptuously clothed or embalmed, nor did she desire a fine monument, nor was she solicitous about being buried in her own country. None of these things did she require of us. She only desired that we should remember her at Your altar, where she was present every day without fail.

For she knew that on the altar was offered the Holy Victim, a sacrifice that *canceled the decree that was against us* (Col 2:14). Through that sacrifice our enemy was triumphed over, who reckons up our sins and seeks what he may lay to our charge, but finds nothing in Him in Whom we conquer. Who shall repay Him for that innocent blood He shed for us? Who shall repay Him the price with which He bought us so that he could rescue us from the clutches of the enemy? To this sacrament of our redemption Your handmaid bound fast her soul by the bond of faith.

Let no one separate her from Your protection. Let not the *lion or the dragon* (Ps 91:13) either by force or by fraud establish itself as a barrier between her and You. She will not plead that she owes nothing, lest she should be convicted and fall under the power of that crafty Accuser. Rather, she will plead that her debts have been discharged by Him to Whom no one can repay what He, Who Himself had incurred no debt, paid for us.

Let her, therefore, rest in peace with her husband, before whom and after whom she was given in marriage to no man. Him she dutifully served, *bringing forth fruit* to You *in her great patience* (Lk 8:15) through which she was also able to win him to You. Inspire, O Lord my God, inspire Your servants who are my brethren, Your children who are my masters, whom I serve with my voice, my heart, and my writings, that as many as shall read this may remember at Your altar Your handmaid Monica, along with Patricius, formerly her husband, by whose flesh You brought me into this life, how I know not.

Let them remember with a pious affection these who were my parents in this transitory light, my brethren under You our Father in our Catholic Mother, and my fellow citizens in the eternal Jerusalem, for which Your pilgrim people here below continually sigh from their setting out until their return. In that way, more abundantly than by my personal prayers, my mother's final request to me may be granted through the prayers of many, influenced by these my confessions.

Book 10 — The Power of Memory

Augustine describes what he is since his conversion, professing his love for God, and searches the depths of his soul to discover by what means we know God. He then discusses the nature of memory. He examines himself with regard to the lust of the flesh, the lust of the eyes, and the pride of life, and confesses that his whole trust lies in Jesus Christ, the Mediator between God and man.

CHAPTER 1 — The Truth of the Confessions

LET me know You, O Lord, Who know me. *Let me know You, as also I am known by You* (1 Cor 13:17). O power of my soul, enter into it, and make it fit for You, that You may have it and possess it *without spot or wrinkle* (Eph 5:27). This is my hope; therefore do I speak, and in this hope I find joy when I rejoice in a wholesome manner.

As for the other things of this life, they are so much the less to be sorrowed for, the more they are sorrowed for, and they are the more to be sorrowed for, the less men sorrow for them. *For behold, You have loved truth* (Ps 51:8), because *he who does the truth comes to the light* (Jn 3:21). This I desire to do in my heart, in my confession to You, and in my writing before many witnesses

CHAPTER 2 — Universal Knowledge

AS for You, O Lord, before Whose eyes the abyss of man's conscience lies naked, what could there be in me that could be concealed from You, even if I did not will to confess it to You? For I would only be hiding You from myself and not myself from You. But now, when my groans bear witness that I am displeased with myself, You shine forth, and I look upon You as pleasing to me, and as loved and longed for, causing me to become ashamed of myself and to renounce myself and choose You, and to be able to please neither You nor myself, otherwise than in You.

To You, therefore, O Lord, I am an open book, whatever I am, and I have already stated what advantage there is in confessing to You. Nor do I accomplish this by words of the flesh and outward sounds, but by the words of the soul and the loud cry of the thought that is known to Your ear. When I am evil, to confess to You is nothing else than to be displeased with myself, and when I am good, to confess to You is nothing else than not to attribute this worthy condition to myself. For You, O Lord, bless the just man, but first You impose Your *justice on the impious* (Ps 5:13).

Let my confession to You, therefore, O my God, *in Your sight* (Rom 4:5), be made silently, and yet not be silent. It is silent in the sound of the voice, but cries aloud in the affection of the heart. Neither do I speak any good thing to men which You have not first heard from me, nor do You hear any such thing from me which You have not first said to me.

CHAPTER 3 — The Confession of Sins

BUT then what have I to do with men, that they should hear my confessions, as if they were to *heal all my infirmities* (Ps 103:3)? They are curious to know about the lives of others, but careless to amend their own. Why do they seek to hear from me what I am and yet will not listen to You about what they are themselves?

And when they hear me talk about myself, how do they know whether I tell the truth, since no man *knows what goes on within a man, but the spirit of man that is in him* (1 Cor 2:11)? But when they hear from You about themselves they cannot say: "The Lord is lying." For what does it mean to hear from You about themselves except to know themselves? And who can know the truth about himself, and say: "It is false," unless he is a liar?

But because *charity believes all things* (1 Cor 13:7) among those whom it unites together by a mutual bond, I also confess to You in such a manner that men may hear me, although I cannot demonstrate to them that I confess the truth. Yet those whose ears charity opens to me believe me.

But You Who are my inmost Physician, deign to reveal to me what fruit there is in this confession. For when they are read or heard, those confessions of my past sins—which You have remitted and obliterated so that You might make me happy in You, changing my soul by faith and Your Sacrament—excite the heart, so that it may not sleep in despair, and say, "I cannot," but that it may awake in the love of Your mercy and the sweetness of Your grace.

By this grace a weak man becomes conscious of his own weakness and grows strong. And good men are delighted when they hear of the past evils committed by those who are now delivered from them—not that they take delight in the evils, but only because these evils have been and now are not.

But what fruit is derived, O Lord my God, to Whom my conscience confesses daily, much more secure in the hope of Your mercy than in its own innocence—what fruit is derived, I ask You, from the fact that now in these my writings I confess also to men in Your presence, not what I once was, but what I now am? For I have seen and related the fruit derived from confessing my past evils. But what am I now, at this very time of writing my confessions, many desire to know, both those who have known me and those who have not. Perhaps they have heard something from me or about me, but their ear is not near my heart, where I am whatever I am.

Therefore, they desire to hear me confess what I am within, where neither their eyes nor their ears nor their minds can penetrate. They wish this, and they are ready to believe, but there is no other way for them to be certain. For charity, whereby they are good themselves, persuades them that I do not lie in what I confess of myself, and it is this charity in them that causes them to believe me.

CHAPTER 4 — The Fruits of Confession

BUT what fruit do they desire from gaining this knowledge? Do they wish to rejoice with me when they hear how much I have advanced toward communion with You by Your gifts, and will they pray for me when they hear how far I have still fallen short of my goal because of my own shortcomings?

To such men I will freely lay myself open. For this is no small fruit, O Lord my God, that *many should return You thanks on our behalf* (2 Cor 1:11) and that many should pray to You for us.

Let a brotherly mind love in me whatever You teach ought to be loved, and lament in me whatever You teach ought to be worthy of lament. Let the mind of a brother do this, not that of a stranger, not that *of strange children, whose mouth has spoken vanity, and whose right hand is the right hand of iniquity* (Ps

144:7-8). Let it be that brotherly mind which, when it approves me, rejoices for me, and, when it has reason to approve my actions, is sorry for me, because in both cases it loves me.

To such men I will freely reveal the innermost secrets of my soul. Let them rejoice with pleasure in my good deeds, let them lament my wickedness. My good deeds have been ordained by You and are Your gifts. My wicked deeds are my faults, subject to Your judgment. Let men take pleasure in my good deeds and lament those that are evil, and let both their rejoicing and their sighs rise to You from the censers of their brotherly hearts.

O Lord, in Your delight with this sweet odor rising from Your holy temple, *have mercy on me according to Your great mercy* (Ps 51:3), for Your Name's sake. Forsake in no way what You have begun in me, but rather perfect what is as yet imperfect in me.

This then is the fruit of my confessions of what I am rather than of what I have been: I can make my confession not only before You *with a secret joy and trembling* (Phil 2:12) and with secret grief lightened by hope, but also in the ears of the believing sons of men, the companions of my joy and co-partners of my mortality, my fellow citizens, and my fellow pilgrims traveling before me, or behind me, or with me in this life.

These are Your servants, my brethren, whom You have chosen to be Your children, my masters, whom You have commanded me to serve, if I am to live in You and with You. Your Word would mean little to me if He had simply given us commands and had not also gone before me by setting the example. And this is what I now do, by both words and actions.

This I do *under Your wings* (Ps 17:8) with exceedingly great danger to myself, were not my soul subject to You under Your sheltering wings and my weakness known to You.

I am a little one, but my Father lives now and always, and as my Protector He is sufficient for me. For He is the very One Who begot me and watches over me, and this is none other than Yourself Who are all good things to me, You the Almighty, Who are with me even before I am with You. I will declare then to such as these, whom You command me to serve, not what I have been, but what I now am, and what I still am. *I do not even judge my own self* (1 Cor 4:3). Therefore, in this manner, let me be heard.

CHAPTER 5 — Imperfect Knowledge of Self

YOU, O Lord, are my Judge. For although no man *knows the things of a man save the spirit of man that is in him* (1 Cor 2:11), yet there is something in man that even the spirit of man that is in him does not know. But You, O Lord, Who have made him, know all things that are in him. Although I despise myself in Your presence and regard myself as nothing but *dust and ashes* (Jb 42:6), yet I know something concerning You that I know not concerning myself.

Indeed, *we see now through a mirror in an obscure manner, and not yet face to face* (1 Cor 13:12). Therefore, as long as I wander far from You, I am more present to myself than to You. Yet I know concerning You that You can in no manner be violated. But as for myself, what temptations I am able and not able to withstand I do not know.

Nevertheless, my hope is strong, for *You are faithful, and You will not allow us to be tempted beyond our strength, but in time of temptation You will also give us a way out to enable us to bear it* (1 Cor 10:13). Let me confess then what I know of myself, and let me also confess what it is that as yet I do not know of myself. What I know of myself, I know by the light of Your wisdom, and what I do not know, I shall remain ignorant of until *my darkness be made like the noonday* (Is 58:10) in Your countenance.

CHAPTER 6 — Love for God

NOT with a doubting but with a certain knowledge, O Lord, do I love You. You have pierced my heart with Your Word, and from that moment I have loved You. Moreover, behold, both heaven and earth and all things that are in them cry out to me on every side that I should love You. Nor do they cease to say this to all men, so that they cannot claim ignorance. Yet, in a higher way, *You will have mercy on whom You will, and will show pity to whom You will* (Rom 9:15). Otherwise heaven and earth would speak Your praises to deaf ears.

What then is it that I love when I love You? Neither the beauty of the body nor temporal glory, nor the brightness of light that is so pleasant to our eyes, nor the sweet melodies of all kinds of songs, nor the fragrant scents of flowers, ointments, or spices, nor manna and honey, nor limbs created for carnal embraces—none of these things do I love when I love my God.

Yet I do love a certain light and a certain voice and a certain fragrance and a certain food and a certain embrace when I love my God, the light, the voice, the fragrance, the food, and the embrace of my inner man, where His light that no place can contain shines into my soul, and where sounds reverberate which no period of time can carry away, and where aromas rise that no wind can disperse, and where food abounds that no eating can diminish, and where that is embraced which no satiety can separate. This is what I love when I love my God.

And what is this? I asked the earth and it said, "I am not he." And all things therein confessed the same. I asked the sea and the deeps and the creeping forms of living things, and they answered, "We are not your God! Seek higher above us." I asked the passing winds above, and the whole air with its inhabitants cried out, "Anaximenes [the philosopher] is mistaken. I am not God." I asked the heavens, the sun, the moon, and the stars. They replied: "Neither are we the God Whom you seek."

And I said to all the earthly creations that surround my corporal body: "You have told me concerning my God that you are not He; tell me something of Him." And they all cried out with a loud voice, "*He made us.*" My question was the gaze I turned on them, and their answer was their beauty.

I then turned my eyes upon myself, and I said to myself, "Who are you?" And I answered, "A man." And behold, in my existence are presented to my consideration the body and the soul, the one exterior and the other interior. Now by which of these ought I to seek my God, Whom I had already sought by the body from the earth even to the heavens, as far as I could send my messengers, the beams of my eyes?

But the interior being is certainly more suitable for this purpose. For it was to this being that interiorly presides in me and judges all those answers of heaven and earth and all things in them that those bodily messengers reported back their replies when they said: "We are not God, but He made us." It was the interior man who knew these things through the ministry of the exterior man. It was I, the person within, who understood these things—I, the soul, through the senses of my body.

I asked the whole structure of the world concerning my God, and it answered me, "I am not He, but He made me." Does not the world appear the same to all those whose senses are sound? Why then does it not speak the same to all? Living creatures great and small see it, but they cannot ask questions, for there has not been granted to them the power of reason by which they can judge the discoveries of the senses. But men can ask questions, enabling them to behold the *invisible things of God, understood by the things that have been made* (Rom 1:20).

However, by loving these things they are made subject to them, and being subject to creatures they cannot judge them. Nor do creatures offer an answer to those who ask unless those who ask can judge them. Neither do they change their voice, that is, their appearance, when one man simply sees them while another both sees and questions them, so as to appear one way to one man and another way to the other. While appearing to both in the same manner, they are dumb to one and speak to the other.

In truth, they speak to all, but only those understand who compare the voice that is received from without with the truth within. For truth tells me: "Neither heaven nor earth is your God, nor any corporal thing." And the nature of these things says to us that the world is a great mass, smaller in any part than in its whole. However, I can speak to you, my soul, and assert that as a part you are superior, for you animate the mass of a body, giving it life, and this no body can impart to another. But your God is still to you the life of your life.

CHAPTER 7 — The Soul's Longing for God

WHAT is it then that I love when I love my God? Who is He Who is above the summit of my soul? By this very soul of mine I will ascend to Him. I will pass beyond that power by which I adhere to this body, and give life and motion to its whole frame. Not by this power can I find my God, for then in the same way *a horse and a mule that have no understanding* (Ps 32:9) would also find Him, for in them there is the same energy by which their bodies also live.

However, there is another power in me that gives not merely life alone, but sense to my flesh. This the Lord has fashioned for me. He has ordered that the eye should not hear and that the ear should not see, but that I should see by the eye, and hear with the ear. In like manner He has assigned to the rest of the senses what is proper to each of them in their various organs and purposes. But no matter how diverse they are, I, as an individual soul, act by means of them. However, I will pass by this power also, for the horse and mule have the same, since they have sense perception as well as I.

CHAPTER 8 — The Realm of Memory

THEREFORE I will also pass beyond this faculty of my nature, ascending higher, as it were, by steps, until I find Him Who made me. And behold, I come into the spacious fields and vast palaces of my memory, where are stored up countless images of various treasures conveyed into it from such things as have been perceived by the senses. There also are stored up whatever else we have thought, either by enlarging or diminishing or in any other way modifying the things that our senses have discovered, as well as whatever else has been committed to it for safekeeping and has not yet been swallowed up and buried by oblivion.

When I am in that realm, I request that whatsoever I wish should be brought out. Some things appear immediately. Others are sought for a longer time before they are found, and are ferreted out, as it were, from some more secret repositories. Still others rush forward in crowds, and while I am calling for and requiring another thing, they will make their presence known, as if to say: "Aren't we the ones you want?" And I put them aside with the hand of my heart from before the face of my memory until the thing that I desire is unveiled and comes forth in my sight from its hidden cell. Other things come up, as they are called for, easily and in regular order, so that what goes before gives place to what follows, and having given way they are laid up, ready to come again when I want them. All this takes place when I recount anything by memory.

In my memory all things are kept distinct and by their various kinds, which have been brought in through their several avenues such as light and all

colors and bodily shapes through the eyes, and all
kinds of sounds through the ears, and all smells
through the avenue of the nostrils, and all tastes by
the door of the mouth. And the sense of feeling is
spread through the whole body—what is hard, what
is soft, what is hot or cold, smooth or rough, heavy
or light, either within or without the body.

All these things are taken into the vast storehouse,
the hidden and unsearchable caverns of the memory, to be called to mind when the need arises. All of
them come in by their respective gates, and are
stored up in the memory. The things themselves do
not enter there, but their images are there ready at
hand to our thought when it remembers them.

Though it is plain enough by which of the senses
they have been received and brought in, who can tell
how these images are formed? For even when I am
both in darkness and in silence, I represent colors in
my memory when I please, and distinguish between
white and black, and between what others I please.
Nor do sounds come in and disturb what I am considering that has been taken in by the eyes—although those sounds are also there all this while,
and lie hidden and stored apart, as it were. For I
summon them also, if I please, and they come forth
immediately.

Although my tongue is quiet and my throat is
silent, I sing there as much as I will. Those images
of color, which are nevertheless there, do not in-
trude themselves nor interrupt me when I am sur-
veying another grouping that came in through the
ears. Thus, also, the other things that have been
brought in and stored up together by the other
senses I recall to mind as I please. I distinguish the

scent of lilies from that of violets, although I am smelling neither one. I prefer honey to new wine, and smooth to rough, not by tasting or handling either at that time, but simply by remembering.

All this I transact within the great hall of my memory. There, heaven, earth, and sea are presented to me, with all things in them that my senses have ever perceived, as well as those I have forgotten. There I also encounter myself and review my life—what I have done, when, and where, and how I was affected when I did it. There are all the things I have myself experienced or believed on the word of others, so far as I remember them.

From that same abundant storehouse I also form other likenesses, and to those that are past I add more and more things either experienced by me or believed from what I had experienced. From these again I mentally picture future actions, or events, or hopes, and meditate on them all, as if they were present.

"I shall do this or that," I say to myself, within this vast bosom of my mind, full of the images of so many and so great things, "and this or that will follow. Oh, if such or such a thing might occur! And God forbid that this or that should happen!" Such things I say to myself, and when I do so, the images of all these are before me, out of the same treasury of my memory. Nor would I say any of these things at all if such images were lacking.

Great is this power of the memory—exceedingly great, O my God, a spacious and boundless room. Who can sound its depths? This is a power of my soul and belongs to my nature, and I myself am not able to comprehend all that I myself am. Is the soul then too limited to contain itself, so that it cannot comprehend where it is and what it is? Is it then outside itself and not in itself? How then does it not contain or comprehend itself? This is to me a subject of great wonder, and I am astonished at it.

Men travel a great distance to see and admire the heights of mountains and the vast billows of the sea and the courses of great rivers and the vastness of the ocean and the motions of the heavenly bodies, and yet do not bother to examine themselves. And they do not wonder that when I named all these things, I did not see them at that very moment with my eyes.

Yet I could not have named them if I had not then represented inwardly in my memory mountains and waves and rivers and stars that I have seen, and the ocean that I have heard of, and with their proper bulk and extension, as if I saw them abroad. Yet when I saw them with my eyes, I did not draw them into myself, nor are they present to me, except through their images. And I know by which of the senses of the body I received my various impressions.

CHAPTER 9 — The Memory of Knowledge

BUT these are not the only things that are lodged in this immense capacity of my memory. Here also are all those precepts learned from my studies in the liberal arts, which are not as yet forgotten, but simply removed as it were into a more inward place. Yet there is no such place, nor do I carry about with me their images, but the things themselves.

For what literature is, what skill in disputation is, how many kinds of questions there are—whatever I know of these things is in my memory in such a way that I have not kept only the image and left the thing outside. It is not like a voice that should have sounded and then passed away, leaving behind it an impression made by the ears, by which it may be represented again as if it were sounding when it no longer sounded. Nor is it like a scent, which, while it passes and is dispersed in the air, affects the smell so as to convey into the memory its image that by re-membering we may again call before us.

It is not like meat that has now no taste in the stomach, and yet still is, as it were, tasted in the memory. Nor is it like something perceived by the touch or feeling of the body, which, when it is at a distance, is still imagined by the memory.

These things themselves are not part of the mem-ory; only their images are taken in with marvelous speed, and are there stored up, as it were, in won-derful cells, and no less wonderfully are brought forth again in remembering.

CHAPTER 10 — The Senses and the Memory

WHEN I hear that there are three kinds of ques-tions—whether a thing exists, what it is, what properties it possesses—I have indeed within me the images of those sounds by which these words were formed, and I know that the sounds themselves passed through the air with a noise, and are now no more.

But as for the things themselves that are signified by those sounds, I did not meet with them by any of the senses of my body, nor did I ever see them ex-cept in my own mind, and I stored up in my mem-ory not their images but the things themselves. How they came in to me, let them tell if they can. For I examine all the portals of my flesh but cannot find any gate by which they entered.

For my eyes say, "If they were clad with any color, we discovered them." The ears say, "If they made any noise or sound, we reported them." The nostrils say, "If they had any smell, they passed through us." The sense of taste says, "Unless they had a savor, ask me no questions about them." The touch says, "If they had no body, I could not feel them, and therefore could give no notice of them."

From where, then, and how, did these things enter into my memory? I cannot tell how it was, for when I learned them it was not by giving credit to another's judgment, but by acknowledging them in my own, and there finding them to be true. Thus, I recommended them to my memory, laying them up there, as it were, from where I might call for them when I pleased. They were therefore within me, even before I learned them, but they were not in my memory.

Where, then, were they? Or how, when they were first mentioned to me, did I readily acknowledge them and say, "So it is; it is true," unless they were already in my memory, but so pushed back and removed out of the way, as it were, into certain hidden recesses that, had they not been drawn out by some other reminder, I would perhaps not have thought of them at all.

CHAPTER 11 — Thought and Memory

WE FIND then that to learn these things, of which we do not take in the images through the senses but without any images see them within us as they are in themselves, is nothing else but this:

by thinking of and noting various things that have been stored in the memory without any unity or sense of order, we observe such things and ensure that they are now stored in an orderly fashion where before they lay scattered and neglected and thus may more easily occur to our mind that is already familiar with them.

And how many things of this nature does my memory contain that have already been discovered and, as I said, stored up, as it were, at hand, which we are said to have learned and come to know? If I should cease for a short space of time to call them to mind, they would again sink down and slip away into the more remote recesses, so that I must, in order to know them, think them out again as if new, and gather them together within the same place—for they have no other region.

And they must be collected *(cogenda)* again so that they may be known, that is, they must, as it were, be brought together *(colligenda)* from their dispersion, whence we speak of *cogitare* (to think, to put together in the mind). For, in Latin, we say *cogo* (I bring together) and *cogito* (I cogitate), as we say *ago* (I do) and *agito* (I do constantly), or *facio* (I make) and *factito* (I make often).

Yet the mind has appropriated this word *cogito* (I think) to itself in such a way that not what is gathered elsewhere, but what is collected *(colligitur)*, that is, gathered *(cogitur)*, is properly said to be cogitated *(cogitari)*, thought by the mind.

CHAPTER 12 — Mathematics and Memory

THE memory also contains the innumerable forms and laws of numbers and dimensions, none of which have been imprinted by any sense of the body. For they have neither color, nor sound, nor smell, nor have they been either tasted or touched at any time. I have heard indeed the sounds of the words by which they are signified when they have been discussed, but these sounds are one thing, and the things themselves are quite another. For the sounds are different in Greek from what they are in Latin, but the things themselves are neither Greek nor Latin, nor any other kind of language.

I have also seen the lines drawn by architects, some of them as fine as a spider's web, but those lines are different: they are not the images of these lines which my bodily eye has revealed to me. A person knows them who recognizes them interiorly without any concept of any kind of body. I have also perceived by all the senses of my body the numbers that we enumerate, but those by which we number are different. They are not the images of these others, but even so they really exist. He who does not see them may laugh at me while I am saying these things, and I shall pity him for laughing at me.

CHAPTER 13 — The Memory in Relation to Itself

ALL these things I retain in my memory, and how I learned them I also retain in my memory. Many things I have heard, which in dispute have been very falsely urged against them, and these also I retain in my memory. Even should these things be false, yet my remembrance of them is no falsehood. Furthermore I also remember that I distinguished between those truths and the false things that were said against them. And I see that I now discern these things in another way than I remember myself formerly to have discerned them when I oftentimes thought upon them.

Therefore, I remember that I have often thought upon these things, and what I now discern and understand I lay up in my memory, so that I may afterward remember that now I understand them. Therefore, I also remember my having remembered. And if afterward I should remember that I could not remember them, this also would be by the same power of the memory.

CHAPTER 14 — Memory and the Passions

THE same memory contains likewise the passions and affections of my soul, not in the same manner as the soul has them when it experiences them, but in another far different manner proper to the power of the memory. For when I am not joyful I can remember my former joy, and at a time when I am not sorrowful I can remember my past sorrows. I can reflect without fear upon my former fears, and I can remember my former desires without desiring. Sometimes, on the contrary, it is with joy that I remember my past sorrows and with sorrow that I remember my former joys.

This should not be considered a source of wonder with regard to the body, for the mind is one thing, the body another. Therefore, it is not so unusual that I should remember with joy some past pain of the body. But here the wonder is because the memory itself is the mind. Hence, when we recommend anything to be remembered, we say, "See that you keep it in mind," and when we forget something, we say, "It was in my mind," or "It has slipped out of my mind," still referring to the memory as the mind.

Since this is so, what does it signify, that when with joy I remember my past sorrow, there should be joy in my mind and sorrow in my memory, and that my mind should be joyful from the joy that is there, and yet my memory should not be sorrowful from the sorrow that is there? Does not the memory belong to the mind? Who will assert this?

The memory, then, is, as it were, the stomach of the mind, and joy and sorrow are like sweet and bitter food. When they are committed to the memory, they are, as it were, passed down into the stomach, where they may be deposited but cannot be tasted. It would be ridiculous to think that these things are alike, and yet they are not totally dissimilar.

But behold, when I say there are four movements of the mind—desire, joy, fear, and sorrow—I bring this forth from my memory. And whatsoever I can say concerning them by defining and dividing each of them into their different kinds, it is in the memory that I find it, and it is from my memory that I bring it forth. Yet, I am not disturbed by any of these passions while I am remembering and speaking of them. And they were there even before I was considering and recalling them—otherwise I could not have brought them out by remembering them.

Perhaps, then, just as food is brought out of the stomach by chewing the cud, so these things are brought up out of the memory by recollection. But why then is not the sweetness of joy or the bitterness of sorrow felt in the mouth of the thought of him who discourses on them and remembers them? Or is it in this particular aspect that these things are unlike, since they are not alike in all things? Who would ever willingly mention or speak of such things if, as often as we name sorrow or fear, we should be compelled to be sad or fearful?

Yet we would not speak of them if we did not find in our memory not only the sounds of their names according to the images imprinted through the senses of the body, but also the concepts of the things themselves, which we did not receive through any of the doors of the flesh. However, the mind itself, perceiving them by the experience it has of its own passion, committed them to the memory, or the memory itself retained them without their being committed to it.

CHAPTER 15 — Remembrance of Things Past

BUT whether this occurs by means of images or not, who can easily tell? For if I name a stone or name the sun, when those things themselves are not present to my senses, their images nevertheless are present to my memory. If I name a pain of the body, it is not present when I am not suffering any pain, and yet if the image were not in my memory, I would not know what I was speaking of, nor could I distinguish it from pleasure in my conversation.

I speak of health of body, and when I am in health, the reality itself is indeed with me, but if the image of it was not also in my memory, I could by no means remember what the sound of these words signified. Nor when the word health is used would the sick know what was meant by it, unless that same image were retained by the power of the memory even when the thing itself is absent from the body.

I name the numbers by which we calculate, and they are present in my memory—not their images but the numbers themselves. I name the image of the sun, and this same image is present in my memory, for it is not the image of this image that I recall, but the image itself is present to me as I call it to mind. I name memory, and I know what I name, and where do I know it except in the same memory? Is the memory present to itself by its image, and is not present by its own self?

CHAPTER 16 — Memory and Forgetfulness

WHEN I name forgetfulness, I know very well what it is that I name, but would I know it if I did not remember it? I am not speaking of recalling the same sound of the word, but the thing that it signifies, for if I had forgotten that, I would not be able to know what that sound meant. Therefore, when I remember memory, this same memory is by itself present to itself, and when I remember at once both forgetfulness and memory, both are also at the same time present—memory, by which I remember, and forgetfulness, by which I do not remember.

Yet what is forgetfulness but the privation of memory? How then must it be present that I may remember it, when, if it is present, I cannot remember? But if we retain in our memory whatever we remember, and we certainly remember forgetfulness, or if we could not upon hearing that name know the thing signified by it, then forgetfulness also is retained in the memory.

Therefore, it is present with us in order that we may not forget, yet when it is present, we tend to forget. Or are we to gather from this that forgetfulness, when we remember it, is not in the memory by itself, but by its image, because if it were there present by itself, it would not make us remember but cause us to forget?

Who can find this out? Who can comprehend how it is? Here, O Lord, I truly labor, and I labor in myself. I have become to myself a land of hardship that requires much sweat. For I am not now searching into the regions of the heavens, nor measuring the distances of the stars, nor inquiring into the balancing of the earth. It is I myself who remember, I the soul.

I do not regard it as so wonderful that what is not myself should be far from me. But what can be nearer to me than myself? And behold, the power of my memory is what I cannot comprehend, without which I cannot so much as name myself. For what shall I say, being certain as I am that I do remember forgetfulness? Shall I say that the thing that I remember is not in my memory? Or shall I say that this forgetting is in my memory so that I should not forget? Both answers are highly absurd.

What shall I say of the third possibility? How can I say that it is not forgetfulness itself but the image of it that is in my memory when I remember it? But how can I maintain this, since when the image of anything is imprinted on the memory, the thing itself must first be present, from whence the image may be imprinted?

For it is in this manner that I remember Carthage and all the places where I have been. In this manner I remember the faces of the men whom I have seen and the things reported by the other senses. In this manner I remember the health or pain of the body itself. When these things were present, my memory borrowed from them images, which being present to me I might consider and reconsider as often as I should afterward remember the things that were themselves absent.

If, therefore, forgetfulness is retained in the memory, not by itself, but by its image, it certainly must first have been present itself, that its image might be taken. Now when it was present, how could it imprint its image in the memory when the nature of forgetfulness is to efface by its presence what it finds already noted there? And yet, however it is, though the manner of it be incomprehensible and inexplicable, I am certain that I remember forgetfulness itself, by which what we remember is destroyed.

CHAPTER 17 — Three Powers of Man's Nature

GREAT is this power of the memory, and something that is awe-inspiring, O my God, profound and infinite in its multiplicity. And this is my soul, and this is myself.

What then am I, O my God? What nature defines me? My life is various and multiform, and unfathomable in its immensity. Behold, the myriad fields and dens and caverns of my memory are innumerably full of countless kinds of things, either through images, as of all bodies, or by their presence, as of the arts, or by certain notions or impressions, as with the passions of the mind that the memory retains even when the mind does not experience them (for whatever is in the memory is also in the mind).

Through them all I fly this way and that, I dive as far as I can, and nowhere can I find an end. So great is the power of the memory! So great is the power of life even in the mortal life of man.

What then shall I do, O You Who are my true life, my God? I will pass even beyond this power of mine, which is called the memory; I will pass beyond that so that I may come to You, the sweet light. What do you say to me? Behold, I am ascending by my mind to You, Who remain above me. I desire only to reach You where You may be reached, and to cling to you there where You may be clung to.

Even the beasts and birds have memory; otherwise they could not return to their dens or nests, nor to many other things that they are accustomed to. And they could not be accustomed to anything except through the memory. Therefore, I will pass beyond the memory, so that I may arrive at Him Who has separated me from the four-footed beasts and made me wiser than the fowls of the air. I will pass beyond the memory.

But where then shall I find You, O true Good and secure Sweetness? Where then shall I find You? If I find You without my memory, then I have no remembrance of You. And how shall I find You if I have no remembrance of You?

CHAPTER 18 — Reminiscence

WHEN the woman had lost her drachma and sought it with a lamp (cf. Lk 15:8), how could she have found it if she had not remembered it? And when she had found it, how could she know that it was the same if she had no remembrance of it? I remember that I have sought and found many things that I have lost. How do I know this? Because when I was seeking any of them, if anyone should have said to me, "Is it not this or that?" I should have answered, "No," until that was brought forth which I sought after. If I had not remembered, whatever it was, even if it had been offered to me, I would not have found it because I could not recognize it. Thus is always the case when we seek for something that is lost, and find it.

But when a thing such as any visible body is only lost from sight and not from the memory, the image of it is kept within us, and by our memory the thing is sought until it is restored to our sight. And when it is found, it is recognized by that image which is within. Neither do we say that we have found what was lost if we do not recognize the thing to be the same, nor can we recognize it if we do not remember it. It was only lost to the eyes, but preserved in the memory.

CHAPTER 19 — Forgetfulness

BUT what shall I say about when the memory itself loses something, as it happens when we forget and seek to remember it again? Where is it we seek but in the memory itself? And there, if one thing perchance be offered to replace another, we reject it until the thing comes to mind that we are seeking, and when that occurs we say, "This is it!" We would not say this if we did not recognize it, nor could we recognize it unless we remembered it.

It is certain, therefore, that we had forgotten it. For the whole had not escaped us, but by the part that was still retained, the other part was sought, because the memory—perceiving that it did not represent accurately all the parts of what was sought in memory, and maimed, as it were, by the cutting off of some part of its accustomed object—called for the restoration of what was wanting.

Thus, when we see or think of a man whom we know, and, having forgotten his name, endeavor to recall it, any other name that comes to mind is rejected because it has not usually been joined in our thought with him. Therefore, it is turned aside until that comes up which our thought was wont to represent together with him, and our knowledge accepts it without any objection.

But where does this name come to mind except from the memory itself? For even when we recognize it after being reminded of it by another, it is from there that it comes. We do not receive it as something new, but, remembering it, we approve what was said as being right. However, if it has been totally erased from our mind, we do not remember it, even when we are reminded of it. For we have not altogether forgotten a thing of which we can only remember that we have forgotten it. Therefore, what we have utterly forgotten we cannot even seek for as for a thing lost.

CHAPTER 20 — Desire for Happiness

HOW then do I seek You, O Lord? For when I seek You, my God, I seek a happy life. I will seek You *so that my soul may live* (Is 55:3). For my body lives by my soul, and my soul lives by You. How then do I seek a happy life? For I do not possess it until I can say: "Enough! It is there!"

How then do I seek it? Is it by way of remembrance, as if it were a thing that I had forgotten but still retain in mind that I had forgotten it? Or is it by way of desiring to learn a thing unknown, which I either never knew or have so absolutely forgotten as not even to remember that I have forgotten it?

But is not a happy life the thing that all desire, and is it not true that there is no man who does not desire it? Where then have they known it, that they should so desire it? Or where have they seen it, that they should so love it? We have it then, but I do not know how.

There are others who are happy because of their accomplishments, and there are those who are happy because of their hope. These have it in a lower manner than they who already are happy in deed, but yet are they better than those who are happy neither in deed nor in hope? Yet even the latter would not be so desirous of being happy if they did not possess it in some manner, and it is clear that they most certainly desire it.

I do not know how they came to know it, and therefore I am not aware what sort of notion they have. I do not know whether the source of their knowledge is in the memory. If it be there, then we all must at some time have been happy, whether everyone individually or all in the person of him who first sinned, *in whom we all died* (Rom 5:12) and from whom we are all born with misery.

I do not examine at present this question. I only seek whether a happy life is in our memory, for we would not love it if we had no knowledge of it. We hear this name, and we all confess that we desire the thing itself, for it is not the mere sound of the word that delights us. When a Greek hears this in Latin, he is not delighted because he does not know what has been said. But we are delighted with it, as he also is when he hears the same word in Greek. The thing itself is neither Greek nor Latin, and both Greeks and Latins and men of all other languages long for it with eagerness. It is known, therefore, to all, because if they could all be asked in one language whether they desired to be happy, they would all answer without the least hesitation that they desired this. This could not be, unless the thing signified by that word were retained in their memory.

CHAPTER 21 — The Happy Life

IS this similar to the situation when, having seen Carthage, one remembers that city? No. For a happy life is not seen by the eyes, because it is not a body. Or is it similar to the way we remember numbers? No. For one who has these in his knowledge seeks no longer to acquire them. However, we have a happy life in our knowledge, and therefore we love it, but nevertheless we want to acquire it, that we may be happy.

Is it then similar to when we remember eloquence? No. For although they who as yet are not eloquent, upon hearing that name, remember the thing itself, and many of them desire eloquence, and thus it appears that they have knowledge of it, yet these men by the bodily senses have observed others who were eloquent and have been delighted by them, and hence desire to be such. However, were it not for that interior knowledge, they would not have been delighted, nor would they wish such eloquence unless they were delighted. But the happy life we do not experience in others by any bodily sense.

Is it then similar to the way we remember joy? Perhaps it may be so. For I remember joyful times even when I am sorrowful, as I recall a happy life when I am miserable. Neither did I ever, by any bodily sense, either see or hear or smell or taste or touch my joy. But I have experienced it in my mind, when I was joyful, and the notion of it stuck in my memory, so that I am able to remember it some-times with contempt, sometimes with desire, ac-cording to the diversity of the things in which I re-member to have rejoiced.

For even in foul things I have been filled with a kind of joy, and when I now remember feeling such joy, I hate and detest myself. I also have experienced joy in good and virtuous things, which I remember with desire, although perhaps these are not with me now. Therefore, with sorrow I remember my former joy.

Where, then, and when have I experienced a happy life, that I should remember it and love it and desire it? And not only I, or just a few with me, but all of us, without exception, desire to be happy. Now if we did not know this with a certain knowl-edge, we would not desire it with so resolute a will.

But how does it happen that if you ask two men whether they will serve in the army, it may be that one will answer that he will, the other that he will not. But if you ask them whether they desire to be happy, both without the least hesitation shall answer that this is what they desire. Moreover, for no other reason but to be happy is one willing to serve and the other is unwilling. Is it perhaps because one man finds joy in one thing, another in another thing?

All agree then in affirming that they desire to be happy, as they would all agree, if they were asked, in affirming that they desire to have joy, and that this same joy is what they call a happy life. Though one man seeks joy in this, another in that, yet this one thing all aim to attain, namely, joy. Now since this is a thing that no man can say he has not experienced, it is, therefore, found in the memory and recognized whenever the words "happy life" are used.

CHAPTER 22 — True Happiness

FAR be it, O Lord, far be it from the heart of Your servant who confesses to You, far be it from me to think that the experience of any sort of joy can make me think I am happy. For there is a *joy that is not given to the wicked* (Is 48:22), but to those who worship You for Your own sake, whose joy You Yourself are.

And this is the happy life, to rejoice to You, in You, and for You: this is it, for there is no other. But they who think there is some other beatitude seek after some other joy. It is not a true joy, and yet their will is not turned away from some semblance of joy.

CHAPTER 23 — Truth and Happiness

IT IS not certain then that all desire to be happy, in the sense that those who do not wish to rejoice in You, wherein alone can be achieved a happy life, do not truly wish a happy life. Or do all desire this? But because the *flesh lusts against the spirit and the spirit against the flesh* (Gal 5:17), so that they do not do what they will, they simply restrict themselves to that which they are able to do, and are satisfied with their lot. Perhaps this is the result of their insufficient desire to acquire the skill to accomplish what they presently are unable to do.

When I ask people whether they would rather rejoice in truth or in falsehood, they do not hesitate in answering that they would rather rejoice in the truth any more than they do in saying that they desire to be happy. And there is no doubt that joy in the truth is the basis of a happy life. For this is joy in You, *Who are the Truth, O God, my Light, the Health of my countenance, my God* (Ps 27:1). This happy life all desire, this life, which alone is happy, all desire, and to rejoice in the truth, all desire.

I have known many who are willing to deceive, but I have not known anyone who was willing to be deceived. Where then have they known this happy life, except where they have known the truth also? For this also they love, since they do not wish to be led into error. And when they love a happy life, which is nothing else but joy in the truth, they also love the truth. Nor would they love it if they had not some knowledge of it in their memory.

Why then do they not rejoice in it? Why then are they not happy? Because their greatest efforts are devoted to other things, which have far greater power to make them miserable than does that which they so faintly remember to make them happy. For as yet there is *but little light in men.* Oh let them walk, and walk on, *lest the darkness overtake them* (Jn 12:35).

But why does truth often bring forth hatred? Why did Your servant who preached the truth to men become their enemy, and yet they love a happy life, which is nothing else but rejoicing in the truth? Simply because truth is so loved that those who love anything else would regard that to be the truth which they love. And because they are not willing to be deceived, they are not willing to be convinced that they were in error.

Therefore, they hate the truth for the sake of that thing which they love instead of truth. They love the truth when it shines upon them, they hate it when it shows them the error of their ways. Because they are unwilling to be deceived and willing to deceive, they love the truth when it reveals itself, and they hate it when it reveals them. Therefore, truth will justly repay them, so that they who are unwilling to be made manifest by the truth will be manifested by it against their will, while the truth itself will not be manifested to them.

The end result is that while the mind of man does not wish it to be revealed that it is blind and sick and filthy and impure, desiring to keep itself concealed, it is not willing that anything should be hidden from its knowledge. The contrary justly happens to it—the mind cannot lie hidden from the truth, but the truth lies hidden from the mind. And yet, however miserable it is, it rather chooses to rejoice in true things than in false. Only then will it be truly happy when, without any impediment or distraction, it will rejoice in that sole Truth Who is the Source of all truth.

CHAPTER 24 — God, the Truth Itself

BEHOLD how far I have traveled in my memory, seeking You, O Lord, and I have not found You outside of it. Nor have I found anything concerning You that I did not store in my memory since I first learned of You. From the time I first learned of You, I have not forgotten You. Wherever I found truth, there I found my God, Who is the Truth itself, and since I first learned that truth I have not forgotten it.

Hence, from the time when I first learned You, You have dwelt in my memory, and there I find You when I remember You and take my delight in You. These are my holy delights, which You have bestowed upon me by Your mercy, having regard for my poverty.

CHAPTER 25 — God Found in the Memory

BUT where do You, O Lord, abide in my memory? Where do You abide there? What kind of lodging have You made there for Yourself? What kind of sanctuary have You built for Yourself? You have bestowed such great honor to my memory by deigning to abide therein. But in what parts thereof You are lodged is what I now wish to consider.

When I remembered You, I passed beyond those parts that beasts also possess, for I did not find You there among the images of bodily things. And I came to its parts where are stored up the affections of my mind, but neither could I find You there. And I entered into the seat of my mind itself (which is also there in my memory, because the mind remembers also itself). Neither were You there—for as You are not a corporeal image, nor an affection of the mind, such as we experience when we rejoice or are sorrowful, when we desire or fear, when we remember or forget or the like, so neither are You the mind itself, because You are the Lord God of the mind.

All of these things have been subjected to change, but You remain forever unchangeable, high above all things, and yet You have vouchsafed to dwell in my memory from the time that I first learned of You. Why then do I inquire in what place You dwell there, as if there were places there? Yet I am certain that You dwell there, because I remember You from the first time that I learned of You, and I find You there whenever I recall You to mind.

CHAPTER 26 — Finding God

WHERE then did I find You so that I might learn to know You? For You were not in my memory before I learned about You. Where then did I find You so that I might learn about You but in Yourself above me? And here there is no such thing as place. We depart from You and we approach You, and yet here there is no such thing as place.

You, the Truth, reside everywhere, listening to all who consult You, and at the same time You answer them all, despite the fact that they consult You on different subjects. You answer them all clearly, but all do not hear You clearly. All consult You upon what they please, but they do not always hear from You what pleases them. He is Your best servant who desires not so much to hear from You what may be conformable to his own will, but rather to conform his will to whatever he shall hear from You.

CHAPTER 27 — Saved by God's Love

TOO late have I loved You, O Beauty so ancient, O Beauty so new, too late have I loved You! Behold, You were within me and I was outside, and it was there that I sought You. Deformed as I was, I ran after those beauteous things that You have made. You were with me, but I was not with You, for those things kept me far from You, which, unless they existed in You, would have no being.

You have called. You have cried out and pierced my deafness. You have poured forth Your light. You have shone forth and dispelled my blindness. You have sent forth Your fragrance, and I have inhaled and panted after You. I have tasted You, and I hunger and thirst for You. You have touched me, and I am inflamed with the desire for Your peace.

CHAPTER 28 — Life, a Continual Warfare

WHEN I shall finally be united to You with my entire being, then never again will I be burdened with sorrow and toil. My life shall be truly alive, wholly filled with You. But inasmuch as everyone whom You fill You also bear up, I am a burden to myself because I am not yet filled with You.

My joys that ought to be lamented contend with my sorrows, in which I ought to rejoice, and to which side the victory inclines, I know not. Alas! Have pity on me, O Lord! Again, my evil sorrows contend with my honorable joys, and on which side the victory stands, I know not. Alas! O Lord, have pity on me! Behold, I hide not my wounds. You are the physician, I am sick. You are merciful, I am miserable. Is not *man's life upon earth a warfare* (Jb 7:1)?

Who would choose troubles and difficulties? You command that they should be endured, but not that they should be loved. No one loves what he endures, though he loves to endure it. For though he is glad that he patiently endures it, yet he would much prefer that there were nothing for him to endure. In time of adversity I long for prosperity; in time of prosperity I fear adversity. What middle ground exists between these where man's life can be without trial?

Woe to the prosperities of the world, once and again, because of the fear of adversity and the corruption of joy! And woe to the adversities of the world once and again and a third time, from the longing after prosperity, and because adversity itself is hard and the power of endurance may erode away! Is not man's life upon earth a trial without any period of respite?

CHAPTER 29 — Hoping in God

ALL my hope is only in Your exceeding great mercy. Give me what You command, and command what You will. You command continence. As someone has said, *I knew that I could not otherwise be continent except God gave me the strength; and this also was a point of wisdom: to know whose gift it was* (Wis 8:21). For by continence we are gathered up and brought back to the One from Whom we had been separated and attracted by many other things.

Too little does he love You who loves anything else together with You, but which he does not love because of You. O Love, Who are ever burning and are never extinguished, O Charity, my God, set me totally afire. You command continence; give what You command, and command what You will.

CHAPTER 30 — Illusive Dreams

ASSUREDLY You command continence as regards *the lust of the flesh, the lust of the eyes, and the pride of life* (1 Jn 2:16). First You have commanded continence from concubinage, and as for marriage itself, You have counseled me to follow a more worthy course than what You have permitted.

And because You granted me this privilege it was preordained even before I became a dispenser of Your Sacrament.

However there still live in my memory, of which I have spoken so much, the images of such things that were implanted there by my former habits. They haunt me when I am awake, but they are lacking in power to seduce me. But when I am asleep they not only afford pleasure but even consent, so closely do they seem to correspond with reality. And the illusion of the image in my soul and in my flesh has such great power that such false representations persuade me, when asleep, to do what the realities, when I am awake, are not able to do.

Am I not then myself, O Lord, my God? Yet there is a tremendous difference between my sleeping and my waking self during the moment in which I pass from waking to sleep or return from sleeping to waking.

Where is then that reason which, when awake, resists such suggestions and remains unmoved when such actions present themselves before me? Is it shut up together with the eyes? Is it lulled asleep together with the senses of the body? How is it then that even in our sleep we oftentimes resist, and being mindful of our resolution, and chastely persevering in it, give no manner of assent to such allurements? Yet there is so much difference that when it happens otherwise, we recover peace of conscience as soon as we awake, and by this very difference we discover that we have not done what we are grieved to recall was in some way done within us.

Is not Your hand, O omnipotent God, able to heal all the infirmities of my soul and, with a more abundant grace, to extinguish also the lascivious actions of my sleep? Increase, O Lord, more and more in me Your gifts, that my soul may follow me toward You, freed from the birdlime of concupiscence, that it may not rebel against itself, and that even in sleep it may not only not commit such filthiness of corruption by those sensual images that lead to the pollution of the flesh, but not even consent to them.

That nothing of this nature should give me the least pleasure, not even something that may be subdued by sheer willpower or be in any way harbored in my chaste affection when asleep, not only in this life but also at my present age, is no great matter for the Almighty to grant, Who *is able to accomplish all things in a measure far beyond what we ask or conceive* (Eph 3:20).

But now I have confessed to my good Lord at what stage I am now in this path of my evil, *rejoicing with fear* (Ps 2:11) in what You have already given me and mourning for that in which I am yet imperfect. And I trust that You will perfect Your mercies in me till I arrive at the full peace that both my interior and exterior being shall then enjoy, *when death is swallowed up in victory* (1 Cor 15:54).

CHAPTER 31 — Excess in Eating and Drinking

THERE is another *evil of the day,* and would to God it were *sufficient for the day* (Mt 6:34). By eating and drinking we repair the daily decays of the body until *You destroy both the food and the stomach* (1 Cor 6:13), when You shall bring an end to our hunger by an admirable satiety and *shall clothe this corruptible body with eternal incorruption* (1 Cor 15:54).

But now this necessity is sweet to me, and against this sweetness I fight, that I may not be taken captive by it. I wage a daily war against it by fasting, often *bringing my body into subjection* (1 Cor 9:27), and my pains are removed by pleasure. For hunger and thirst are pains, and like a fever they burn and kill, unless they be aided by the medicine of our nourishment. Now because food is always at hand, through the comfort of Your gifts, with which the land and the water and the air supply our infirmities, our calamity is called delight.

You have taught me this so that I should come to take nourishment as a medicine. But while I am in the process of passing from the discomfort of hunger to the satisfaction of being filled, the snare of concupiscence lies in wait for me. For the very passing is a pleasure, and there is no other way to pass but this, a path to which I am forced by necessity.

Thus, whereas health is the cause of eating and drinking, yet a dangerous delight accompanies those activities and for the most part endeavors to take precedence so that I may do for its sake what I pretend and desire to do for health's sake. Nor do both of these operate under the same standard, for what is sufficient for health is insufficient for delight. And often it becomes uncertain whether it is the necessary care of the body that is asking for sustenance or the voluptuous deceit of greediness that proffers its services.

The unhappy soul rejoices in this uncertainty and prepares herein the protection of an excuse. It is glad that it is not evident what is sufficient for the maintaining of health, so that under the cloak of health it may disguise the pursuit of gratification.

These temptations I daily strive to resist, and I summon Your right hand to my assistance. To You do I refer my anxieties, for I have not as yet resolved these problems in my own mind.

I hear the voice of my God commanding me, *Let not your hearts be overburdened with self-indulgence and drunkenness* (Lk 21:34). Drunkenness is far, far from me, and Your mercy will keep it from ever coming near me. But the tendency to overeat sometimes steals upon Your servant. May Your mercy remove that temptation far from me. For *no one can be continent unless You give us the strength* (Wis 8:21).

You grant many things in answer to our prayers, and whatever good we received before we prayed had You as its source. And that we afterward know and acknowledge our receiving these things from You is also Your gift. I never was a drunkard, but I have known drunkards who have been made sober by You. Hence, it was Your design that they should not be drunkards who never were such, and also Your design that they should not always remain drunkards who for some time had been such. Furthermore, it was also Your Will that both groups should know that this was all according to Your design.

I have also heard another command of Yours, *Go not after your lusts, but turn away from your own will* (Sir 18:30). By Your gift I have heard also the sentence that I have loved much: *Neither shall we suffer any loss if we do not eat, nor if we do eat shall we gain any advantage* (1 Cor 8:8). That is to say, neither shall the one course make me happy nor the other course cause me to be miserable. Again, I have heard: *For I have learned to be self-suffering in what-*

ever circumstance I am. I know how to live humbly and I know how to live in abundance. . . . I can do all things in Him Who strengthens me (Phil 4:11-13). Such words are fitting for a soldier of the heavenly camp, and not of the dust that we are.

But remember, O Lord, *that we are dust* (Ps 103:14), and out of dust You made man, and *he was lost and is found* (Lk 15:32). Nor could he do it of himself, because he himself was dust, whom I so loved to hear saying through the breath of Your inspiration: *"I can do all things in Him Who strengthens me"* (Phil 4:13) Strengthen me that I also may be able to do all things. Grant what You command, and command what You will.

Such a man confesses that he has received this from You, and when *he glories, he glories in the Lord* (1 Cor 1:31). I have heard another praying that he might also receive help: *"Take from me the greediness of the belly"* (Sir 23:6). From this it is clear, my holy God, that You give when that is done which You command to be done.

You have taught me, O good Father, that to the clean *all things are clean, but a thing is evil for the man who by eating gives scandal* (Rom 14:20), that *every creature of God is good, and nothing is to be rejected that is received with thanksgiving* (1 Tm 4:4), and that *food does not commend us to God* (1 Cor 8:8). We have also been commanded: *Let no one call you to account for what you eat or drink* (Col 2:16), and *let not him who eats despise him who does not eat, and let not him who does not eat judge him who eats* (Rom 14:3). These things I have learned, thanks be to You and praises to You, my God, and praised be You, my Master, Who knock at my ears and enlighten my heart!

Deliver me from all temptations, for it is not then the uncleanness of the food I fear but the uncleanness of wrongful desire. I know that every kind of flesh that was good to be eaten was permitted to Noah, that Elijah was fed with flesh meat, and that John, though a man whose abstinence was praiseworthy, was not defiled by using animals, i.e., locusts, for his food.

And again, I know that Esau was deceived by a lust for lentils, that David reprehended himself for the desire of a drink of water, and that our King was tempted, not by flesh meat but by bread. Therefore, also, the people of the wilderness were justly condemned, not for their desiring flesh meat but because through the desire for such meat they murmured against the Lord.

Therefore, being placed as I am in the midst of these temptations, I engage in a struggle every day against concupiscence in eating and drinking. This is not something that I can resolve to cut off once and for all and touch no more, as I could do with regard to concubinage. The reins that restrain the throat must be held neither too loosely nor too tightly.

Is there anyone, O Lord, who is not carried sometimes a little beyond the bounds of necessity? Whoever he is, he is truly great; let him magnify Your Name. But I am not such a person, *for I am a sinful man* (Lk 5:8). And yet I also magnify Your Name. He Who has *overcome the world* (Jn 16:33) intercedes to You for my sins, numbering me among the weaker members of His body, because *Your eyes have seen that which is imperfect in me, and in Your book all shall be written* (Ps 139:16).

CHAPTER 32 — Delight in the Sense of Smell

A S FOR the allurement of sweet odors, I am not much concerned. When they are absent, I want them not; when they are present, I refuse them not; yet I am ready to live completely without them. So it seems to me, but perhaps I am mistaken. Also to be lamented is that darkness which does not permit me to discern what abilities I have. Therefore my mind, in questioning itself concerning its own powers, does not readily discern what to believe, because even that which is in it lies mostly concealed unless revealed by experience.

Therefore. in this life, which is aptly called a trial, no man can assert with certitude that someone who is capable of becoming better instead of worse will not become actually worse instead of better. Our only hope, our only confidence, our only solid promise is Your mercy.

CHAPTER 33 — Delight in the Sense of Hearing

T HE pleasures of the ears had more strongly entangled and captivated me, but You have loosed these snares and set me at liberty. Now, I confess, I take some satisfaction in the melodies that are enlivened by Your words, when these are sung with a sweet and skillful voice, yet not to the extent that I am held entranced by them, for I can disengage myself at will. However, coming as they do, together with those words that animate them and procure my acceptance, they are apt to seek a place of some dignity in my heart, and I find it difficult to offer them one that is suitable.

Occasionally I seem to allow them more honor than is becoming, when I find my mind more religiously and ardently raised to a heightened devotion by those holy words when they are sung in that manner than when they are not, and all the affections of our spirit, according to their variety, seem to have their proper modes in the voice and in the singing, stirred up by some hidden sympathy. But this sensual pleasure, which should not be allowed to enervate the mind, often deceives me.

For sense is not content to wait upon reason in such manner as to follow it patiently, but since it is only admitted for the mind's sake, it strives to run before it and lead it. Thus, in these things I sin without perceiving it, but afterward I am aware of it.

Sometimes again, being too immoderately fearful of this very deception, I err on the side of too much severity—sometimes to such an extent that I begin to wish that all the melodies and sweet tunes, in which David's Psalter is usually sung, were banished from my ears and from the Church. Then I wonder if the safer course would be that which I remember to have often heard told of Athanasius, the Bishop of Alexandria, who instructed the lector to intone the Psalms with such a slight inflection of the voice that it was more like reading than singing.

But then, when I remember those tears that I shed at the singing of the chants of the Church in the early period of my recovered faith, and also how much I am now also moved, not with the singing, but with the things that are expressed in song when they are delivered with a clear voice and a most suitable modulation, I acknowledge once more the great benefit of this institution.

Thus, I fluctuate in my feelings of trying to choose between pleasure with its attendant danger and the profit to be derived from wholesome experience. While not ready as yet to pronounce an irrevocable judgment, I am rather inclined to approve the custom of singing in church, so that, by the delight of the ears, weaker souls may be raised to the affection of devotion. Yet, when it happens that I am more moved with the singing than with the things that are sung, I confess my sin and am sorry for it, and then I would rather not hear the singing.

Behold in what a state I am! Weep with me and weep for me, you who do something good within yourselves, from which proceed our good actions. For you, who are not doing so, are little moved with these things. But You, O Lord, my God, *hearken, look down upon me, and see; and pity and heal me* (Ps 13:4); for in Your sight I have thus become an enigma to myself, and this is my infirmity.

CHAPTER 34 — Dangerous Enticements from the Sense of Sight

THERE remains the pleasure I derive from these eyes of my flesh, of which I will now voice confessions to be heard by the brotherly and loving ears of Your temple. Thus, we may conclude the enumeration of the temptations derived from concupiscence that still molest me, while *I groan, yearning to be clothed over with that dwelling of ours which is from Heaven* (2 Cor 5:2).

The eyes love fair and varied forms, bright and pleasant colors. Let not these things have any hold upon my soul. Let God alone possess it, He Who made these things that are exceedingly good indeed, but He is my good, not they. And these things affect me, when awake, all the day long. Nor do I find any respite from them, as I do from melodious voices, and sometimes from all other sounds, as when I am in silence.

For this very light, the queen of colors, bathing all things that we see, wherever I am during the day, flowing in varied forms about me, soothes me while I am engaged in other things and am not observing it. And so strongly does it insinuate itself into my existence that, if it should be suddenly withdrawn, it is sought for with longing, and if it is long absent, it saddens the mind.

But the true Light is the Light that Tobit beheld when, with his blind eyes closed, he taught his son the way of life, and walked before him with the feet of charity, without making one false step. It is the Light that Isaac saw when, his carnal eyes being heavy and closed by old age, it was granted to him to bless his sons while not knowing them, yet in blessing them to know them.

It is the Light that Jacob saw when he, also blind through great age, with an enlightened heart foresaw in his sons the various races of the future people that should descend from them, and imposed his hands mystically crossed upon his grandchildren by Joseph, not as their father outwardly regarded them but as he himself inwardly discerned them (cf. Gn 48:11-12). This is the true Light, and it is one, and all are one who behold it and love it.

However, that other corporeal light, of which I have spoken, seasons the life of this world for its blind lovers with an enticing and dangerous sweetness. But those who know how to use it to give glory to You, O God, the Creator of all things, take hold of it when they sing Your praise, and they are taken

up by it in their sleep. And such I desire to be. I resist the seductions of the eyes, lest my feet, with
which I enter upon Your way, should be entangled,
and to You I lift up my inward eyes so that You *may
pull my feet out of the snare* (Ps 25:15). From time to
time You disengage them, for they are ensnared.
You cease not to free them, but I am often entangled
with these nets that are prepared on all sides, because *You will neither sleep nor slumber Who are the
keeper of Israel* (Ps 121:4).

How innumerable are the things made by every
kind of skill and workmanship. With clothes, shoes,
vessels, and similar handicrafts, with pictures also
and every kind of statues, and these far exceeding all
necessary and moderate use and pious signification,
men have added to the allurements of the eyes. In
doing so, they have outwardly followed what they
have made, but they have inwardly forsaken Him by
Whom they themselves were made and destroyed
what they were made to be.

O my God, and my Glory, even from these things
do I now sing a hymn to You and offer a sacrifice of
praise to Him Who offers his sacrifice for me. For
all these beautiful patterns, which pass from souls to
the skillful hands of artists, are derived from that
beauty which is above the soul and for which my
soul sighs day and night.

However, those who fashion and admire these exterior beauties, while they take from that first beauty
the rule of judging them, do not take from it the rule
of using them. It is there, but they do not see it, so
as to stop there and go no farther, and *keep their
strength for you* (Ps 59:10), and not scatter it abroad
upon wearisome pleasures.

As for me, while I speak and discern these things, I am also apt to have my steps entangled in these beauties. But You pluck me out, O Lord, You pluck me out, because *Your mercy is before my eyes* (Ps 26:3). For I fall miserably into these snares, and You draw me out again mercifully—sometimes without my perceiving it because I had only lightly fallen upon them, and sometimes with pain to me because I had become stuck fast in them.

CHAPTER 35 — Curiosity in Knowledge

TO this may be added another sort of temptation that poses numerous dangers. For besides the concupiscence of the flesh, which is found in the delight of all the senses and their several pleasures, the slaves of which are lost when they stray far from Your path, there is in the soul a certain foolish and curious inclination. It is a desire not to take delight in the flesh, but to experiment with various sensual pleasures cloaked under the name of knowledge and scientific investigation.

Because this is rooted in the appetite for knowledge and since of all the senses the eyes are the principal instruments of knowledge, this is called in Scripture *the concupiscence of the eyes* (1 Jn 2:16).

Seeing belongs properly to the eyes. However, we also use this word with relation to the other senses whenever we employ them in search of knowledge. Thus, we do not say, "Hear how it flashes," or "Smell how it shines," or "Feel how bright it is." All these things are said to be seen. And we do not only say, "See how it shines," which the eye alone can perceive, but we also say, "See how it sounds," "See how it smells," "See how it tastes," "See how hard it is." Therefore, the general experience of all the senses is called, as I have said, the concupiscence of the eyes, because the office of seeing, which principally belongs to the eyes, is by a certain analogy exercised also by the other senses when they are in the pursuit of knowledge.

Now what is done by the senses for pleasure and what is done for curiosity may be more clearly discerned by this, that pleasure seeks objects that are beautiful, melodious, fragrant, savory, or soft, but curiosity often seeks their opposites, not for the sake of undergoing some troubling experience but merely through a desire for experimentation and knowledge. For what pleasure is there in beholding a mangled corpse that will make you shudder? And yet if something like this lies anywhere, people flock to see it, only to grow sad and to turn pale. And they are also afraid of seeing it in their sleep—as if anyone had obliged them to see it when they were awake, or any report of its beauty had urged them to behold it.

The same thing happens with respect to the other senses, which it would take far too long to cover the subject adequately. This disease of curiosity also is the reason why monstrous perversities are shown in theaters. As a result men proceed to search into the secrets of nature, the knowledge of which is beyond our scope and of no advantage, and yet such knowledge is the object of their study. Such curiosity also lies at the basis of why magical arts are employed in the search for perverted objects of knowledge. Therefore, even in religion itself we put God to the test when the signs and miracles that are asked for are not desired for the attaining of any good, but only for the chance to experience them.

In this vast forest, full of snares and dangers, behold how many of them I have cut off and cast away from my heart, as You have enabled me to do, You, the God of my salvation. Yet, when shall I dare to say—since so many things of this kind buzz on all sides around our daily life—when shall I dare to say that no such thing at all makes me desire to behold it or arouses a vain curiosity? It is true that the theaters do not capture my interest. I do not care to know the courses of the stars, nor did my soul ever seek for answers from dead spirits—all sacrilegious mysteries I detest.

But with how many suggestions and artful stratagems does the enemy seek to tempt me to ask for some sign from You, O Lord, my God, to Whom I owe humble and sincere homage? I beseech You, by our king and our honorable and chaste country Jerusalem, that just as the consent to any such temptation is far from me, so it may be removed still farther and farther away. But when I ask You for the welfare or salvation of anyone, I have quite another end and intention, and You give me, and will ever give me, the grace to acquiesce to Your holy Will, whatever You are pleased to do.

Nevertheless, in how many petty and contemptible things is our curiosity daily tempted? And who can count how often we fall? How often, when people are relating vain and empty things, do we at first, as it were, tolerate them, so as not to give offense to the weak, and afterward little by little willingly give our attention to them?

I do not now go to the circus to see a dog chasing a hare, but should such a sight present itself to my eyes when I chance to be passing by a field, it may well divert me from some important thought to concentrate on that chase and cause me to turn aside not with the body of my mount but rather with the inclinations of my heart. And unless You be pleased on these occasions, after having shown me my weakness, quickly to remind me by this sight either to aspire by some pious consideration toward You or totally to despise it and pass on, I stand fixed in this vain stupidity.

When I am sitting at home and a lizard is catching flies or a spider is entangling them in its web, how often does this capture my attention? Is it a different sight to observe because the creatures are small? I go on from them to praise You, the wonderful Creator and Ordainer of all things, but it was not with this thought that I first began to observe them. It is one thing quickly to rise again, but another not to fall.

Of such things my life is full, and my one great hope is in Your exceedingly great mercy. For when our heart becomes the receptacle of such things and is overcharged with the distractions of this abundant vanity, then our prayers also are often interrupted and disturbed, and while in Your presence we direct the voice of our hearts to Your ears, this important process is broken off by the inrush of idle thoughts, the source of which I am unaware.

CHAPTER 36 — The Desire To Be Loved and Feared

SHALL we account this also a contemptible matter, or is there any room here for hope except in Your mercy because You have begun to change us? And You know how greatly You have already reformed me, You Who have healed me first from the desire for revenge, so that You might also forgive all the rest of my iniquities, and might heal all my maladies and redeem my life from corruption and crown me in Your compassion and mercy and satisfy my desire with good things, You Who crushed my pride with Your fear and tamed my neck to Your yoke. Now I bear that yoke, and to me it is light, for so You have promised, and so You have made it. And indeed it was so, but I knew it not when I was afraid to submit to it.

But yet, O Lord, You Who alone rule without pride because You alone are the true Lord and have no lord over You, can I say that this third kind of temptation has wholly passed from me or can ever cease during this whole life—to desire to be feared and to be loved by men, for no other end but to have the resultant joy, which is no true joy?

Such is a wretched life and a shameful boastfulness, and, because of this, men neither love You nor chastely fear You. Therefore, *You resist the proud and give Your grace to the humble* (1 Pt 5:5). And You thunder down upon the ambitions of this world, and the *foundations of the mountains tremble* (Ps 18:7).

Now, because certain roles in human society require us to be loved and feared by men, the enemy of our true happiness presses close upon us, spreading his snares with the words "Well done, well done." He does this so that while we greedily pick up the bait, we may be drawn into displacing our joy from Your truth and placing it in the falsehood of man, and so that we will be pleased to be loved and feared, not for Your sake, but in Your stead.

Thus, we having been made like that enemy, he will have us with him, not in the concord of charity but in the fellowship of punishment. *For he has sought to establish his throne in the North* (Is 14:13), so that as many as in a perverse and crooked way imitate You might serve him there in cold and darkness.

But we, O Lord, are Your little flock. Deign to keep us as Your own possession. Spread Your wings and let us flee for shelter under them. Be our glory. Let us be loved for Your sake, and may Your Word be feared by us. Whoever wishes to be praised by men while he is blamed by You shall not be defended by men when he shall be judged by You, nor rescued by men when he shall be condemned by You.

Now when it is not *a sinner who is praised in the desires of his soul, nor the unjust man who is blessed* (Ps 10:3), but when a man is praised for some real good, which You have given him, and he rejoices more within himself for his being praised than for his having that gift for which he is praised, such a man also is praised by men while You blame him. And, in this case, better is the man who praises than he who is praised, for the former is pleased with the gift of God in man, but the latter is more pleased with the gift of man than with the gift of God.

CHAPTER 37 — Praise and Despair

WE ARE daily assaulted, O Lord, with these temptations; we are tempted without ceasing. The tongues of men are our furnace in which we are daily tried. You command continence for us in this way also. Grant what You command, and command what You will.

You know the groans of my heart to You concerning this matter and the flood of tears from my eyes. For I cannot easily discover what progress I have made in becoming more cleansed from this plague, and I very much dread my secret sins, which are known to Your eyes, but not to mine.

For other kinds of temptations I have some way by which I may more or less accurately gauge my progress, but none at all in this. As regards sensual pleasures and the vain curiosity of knowledge, I perceive to what extent I have weaned my mind from them when I forego them, either by my will when they are absent, or by necessity when they are not present. For at such times I ask myself how much more or less burdensome it is to be without them.

As for riches, which men covet so that they may pursue one of the three kinds of concupiscence, or two of them or all of them, if the mind cannot discover whether or not it despises them when it possesses them, it can test itself by parting with them.

But what must we do to rid ourselves of all forms of praise, so that we may test ourselves to see how able we are to forego it? Must we live badly and follow so profligate a course of life that all who know us may abhor us? Could a greater madness be named or imagined? However, praise both usually is and ought to be the companion of a good life and of good works. Therefore, just as we must not renounce a good life, so we cannot avoid its being attended with praise. Yet I do not know what I can forego contentedly or what I cannot part with without pain unless it be absent.

What do I then confess to You, O Lord, in this kind of temptation? What else except that I am delighted with praises, but more with the truth itself than with praises? For if I were asked which I would rather be—mad or erring in all things and praised by men or constant or confirmed in the truth and blamed by all—I know what I should choose. Yet I would not wish the approbation of another's mouth to increase my joy for any good that I may possess. Yet, I confess not only that it increases it, but also that disparagement diminishes it.

When I am troubled at my misery, an excuse occurs to me. How just it is, You know, O God, but I confess that it leaves me perplexed. You have not only commanded continence, that is, from what things we are to restrain our love, but also justice, that is, on what we are to bestow our love. And since it is Your will that we should not only love You, but also our neighbors, I often am delighted with what I regard as the proficiency or promise of my neighbor when I am pleased to receive the commendations of one who understands things rightly, and again am grieved for the evil in him when I hear him disparage what he is ignorant of or what is good.

I am also grieved sometimes at praises I receive, either when those things are praised in me that I dislike in myself, or when things good indeed, but slight and inconsiderable, are valued more than they deserve. But then again, how do I know whether I am not thus affected, because I would not want the person who praises me to entertain a different opinion of me from that which I have of myself? And this is so not because I am concerned by what is good for him, but because the same good things that please me in myself become more pleasant to me when others also are pleased with them. For in some fashion I do not regard that I am praised when it is not my own judgment of myself that is praised, as when those things are praised in me that displease me, or those things are praised more that please me less. Am I not, therefore, still in the dark about myself in this matter?

Behold, I see in You, O Truth, that I ought not to be pleased for being praised for my own sake, but only for my neighbor's good. But whether it be so with me I know not, for in this regard I know less about myself than You do. I beg You, O my God, show me a true picture of myself, so that I may confess my wounds to my brethren, who will pray for me. Let me yet more diligently examine myself.

If it be only in respect of my neighbor's benefit that I am touched with my own praises, why then am I less moved if any other be unjustly reviled than if it were myself? Or why am I more concerned at an affront offered to me than if, with equal injustice, it were offered to another in my presence? Can I pretend not to know that this is so? Or shall I delude myself so far as not to say the truth in Your presence, both in my heart and by my tongue? Such a folly as this keep far from me, O Lord, so that my own mouth may not be to me the *flattering oil of the sinner to anoint my head* (Ps 141:5).

CHAPTER 38 — Virtue and Vainglory

I AM needy and poor (Ps 70:6), but I am a better man when by inward groaning I displease myself and seek Your mercy, until what is defective in me is repaired and made whole again and I achieve the peace that the eye of the haughty cannot perceive.

Now the words that proceed from our mouths and actions that men perform arouse a most dangerous temptation—namely, the love of praise, which is ever striving to procure the approval of others in order to advance our own personal excellence. This tempts me even when I censure it in myself, taking occasion to attack me from my very censuring of it. And often a man is guilty of a greater vainglory as he glories in his avowed despising of vainglory. And thus it is no longer in true contempt of glory that he glories, for he does not really contemn it, since he meanwhile glories within.

CHAPTER 39 — Self-Love

THERE is yet within us another evil in this same type of temptation, by which persons are vainly conceited, self-satisfied in themselves, although they neither please nor displease others, and do not make the slightest attempt to please others. However, while they please themselves, they very much displease You, by taking pride not only in things that are not good, as though they were good, but also in good things that are Yours as though they were their own; or else they acknowledge them as Yours but conferred on them for their own merits; or, again, they know that they have received them from Your grace but begrudge others that grace and will not rejoice in it with them.

In all these and the other similar dangers and labors, You see the tremblings of my heart. And I realize that I would rather be healed by You again and again than to have no wounds at all.

CHAPTER 40 — Comforts and Desolations

WHERE have You not walked along with me, O Truth, teaching me what to avoid and what to desire, while I referred to You what my sight could discover here below, and sought counsel from You? I surveyed the outward world as far as my senses could reach and considered the life of my own body and those same senses of mine. Then I entered into the inner chambers of my memory, those manifold and spacious rooms, wonderfully filled with innumerable recesses. I considered them and was amazed, for none of them could I discern without You, and I found none of them to be You.

Neither was I the discoverer who examined all these and strove to distinguish and estimate each of them according to their dignity. I received some of them from my senses and subjected them to questioning. Others I encountered through my feelings and found that they were closely concerned with my own self. Enumerating the various messengers of the senses that brought these to me, I distinguished between them. Lastly, the great treasury of my memory yielded still other things that I examined; some of them I returned to the memory and others I drew out for study.

Yet neither I myself, I say, who was doing all this, nor my faculty itself, by which I did all this, was You; for You are that ever-abiding Light that I consulted concerning all these, whether they were, what they were, and of what value they were. I listened to You instructing me and commanding me, as I often do; this gives me great pleasure, and as often as I can have leisure from necessary duties I take refuge in this pleasure.

In all these things that I review in consulting You, I cannot find any safe place of repose for my soul except in You, where all my dissipations may be recollected. Therefore, nothing of me may go astray from You. And sometimes You do admit me into a most unusual affection of devotion within my innermost being, of such a sweetness that, if it were to be perfected in me, I do not know not what there could be in the next life which the present did not possess.

But then I fall back again into the things below, burdened by the weight of my misery, and I am again engulfed in the things I am accustomed to, and am held fast by them, and I weep much, but am still held fast. So much does the burden of custom weigh down the soul. Here I am able to be, but not willing; there I am willing to be, but not able. And in both ways I am miserable.

CHAPTER 41 — God Alone

THEREFORE I considered the maladies of my sins in the three kinds of concupiscence, and I invoked Your right hand to cure me. For I beheld Your brightness with my wounded heart, and, being struck back by it, I said, "Who can attain to that?" *I am cast forth from before Your eyes* (Ps 31:23). You are the Truth Who preside over all things.

Because of my covetousness, I was not willing to lose You, but wished to possess a lie together with You, just as no man desires in such manner to tell lies so as to be ignorant himself of the truth. Therefore I lost You, because You deigned not to be possessed together with a lie.

CHAPTER 42 — A False Mediator

AND now whom could I find who might reconcile me to You? Was that office to be undertaken for me by some Angel? By what prayers? By what Sacraments? Many who endeavor to return to You and are not able to accomplish this by themselves, I have heard, have attempted such ways, and fallen into the desire for curious visions, and so have deserved to suffer delusions.

For they sought You, being puffed up with self-importance as the result of their learning, and swelling out their chests with pride rather than beating their breasts. And they drew to themselves those of similar dispositions, *the powers of this air* (Eph 2:2), conspiring with them, and associated with them in their pride, only to be deceived by them through magical influence.

They were pretending to seek a mediator by whom they might be purged, and there was none, except for the Devil, who was *transforming himself into an Angel of light* (2 Cor 11:14). And it was a great allurement to proud flesh that they had lighted upon a spirit who had no body of flesh.

For they were both mortals and sinners, but You, O Lord, to Whom they proudly sought to be reconciled, are immortal and without sin. Now *the mediator between God and men* (1 Tm 2:5) should have something like to God and something like to men, lest if in both aspects he were like men, he should be at too great a distance from God, or if in both he were like God, he should be at too great a distance from men, and so not be a mediator.

Hence, that false mediator, by whom through Your secret judgment pride deserves to be deluded, has one thing in common with men, i.e., sin. And he pretends to have another thing in common with God, in that, not being clothed with mortal flesh, he proclaims himself as immortal. But *since the wages of sin is death* (Rom 6:23), he has this in common with men: to be condemned with them to death.

CHAPTER 43 —The Powerful Mediation of Christ

BUT the true Mediator, Whom by Your secret mercy You have manifested to the humble, and Whom You have sent so that by His example men might learn humility, *that Mediator between God and men, the Man Christ Jesus* (1 Tm 2:5), has appeared between mortal sinners and the immortal Just One, being mortal with men, just with God. Since the wages of righteousness are life and peace, He, allied to God by His righteousness, voided the death of justified sinners, which death He was pleased to have in common with them.

This Mediator was shown to the Saints of old, so that they might attain salvation by faith in His coming Passion, just as we can be saved by faith in His Passion now past. For He was Mediator, inasmuch as He was Man, but inasmuch as He was the Word He was not in a role that marked him as of lesser importance, because He was equal to God, and, God with God, and, together with the Holy Spirit, one God.

How greatly have You loved us, O good Father, You *Who have not spared even Your own Son but have delivered Him up for us sinners* (Rom 8:32). How greatly have You loved us, for whom He, Who *did not consider equality with God a thing to cling to, became obedient to death, even to death on a Cross* (Phil 2:6-8). He Who alone was *free among the dead* (Ps 88:6), *having the power to lay down His life and the power to take it up again* (Jn 10:18), became to You, on our behalf, both a Victor and a Victim, and therefore a Victor because He was a Victim.

For us, before You, He became both the Priest and the Sacrifice, and therefore the Priest because

He was the Sacrifice, making us Your sons instead of servants by being born of You and becoming our Servant.

Therefore I justly place a strong hope in Him that You will heal all my maladies through Him *Who sits at Your right hand and intercedes for us* (Rom 8:34); otherwise I would despair. For many and great are these my infirmities. But while they are many and great, greater still is Your medicine. We might have thought that Your Word was too remote from any union with man and have despaired of ourselves, had not this *Word become flesh, and dwelt among us* (Jn 1:14).

Terrified at my sins and at the burden of my misery, I had considered in my heart and actually planned to run away into the wilderness. However You prohibited this and gave me encouragement, saying that *therefore Christ died for all, in order that they who are alive may live no longer for themselves, but for Him Who died for them* (2 Cor 5:15).

Behold, O Lord, I cast all my care upon You, so *that I may live and consider the wonderful things of Your Law* (Ps 119:17-18). You know my ignorance and my weakness; teach me and heal me. He, Your only Son, in whom *are hidden all the treasures of wisdom and knowledge* (Col 2:3), has redeemed me by His Blood. *Let not the proud calumniate me* (Ps 119:122), for I meditate on the price of my ransom, and I eat and drink and communicate it to others, and being poor I desire to be filled therewith, among those who *eat and are filled, and they shall praise the Lord who seek Him* (Ps 22:27).

Book 11—Time and Eternity

St. Augustine is concerned with the interpretation of Holy Scripture, especially with the first chapter of Genesis. Eternity and time are thoroughly examined, especially the definitions of past, present, and future times.

CHAPTER 1 —The Reason for Writing This Book

LORD, since eternity is Yours, are You unaware of what I am saying to You? Or do You see in time what takes place in time? Therefore, why do I give You an account of so many things? It is surely not that You may learn them from me.

Rather, I say them to You that You may arouse my own love and that of my readers for You, so that we may all say: *The Lord is great and exceedingly to be praised* (Ps 96:4). I have already said, and I will say again, that it is for the love of Your love that I am writing this book.

We pray, although Truth has said: *Your Father knows what you need before you ask Him* (Mt 6:8). Therefore, we make known our love for You, while we confess our miseries to You and Your mercies toward us, so that You may free us wholly as You have begun to do.

Then we will cease to be wretched in ourselves and be happy in You. For You have called us to be poor in spirit, to be meek, and to mourn, to hunger and thirst after justice, and to be merciful, clean of heart, and peacemakers.

Thus, I have told You many things, such as I could relate and as I wished to do so, for first it was Your Will that I should confess to You, my Lord and my God, *because You are good and Your mercy remains forever* (Ps 118:1).

CHAPTER 2 — Seeking Truth in Scripture

BUT when will the voice of my pen be able to declare all Your exhortations, Your consoling words, and Your guidance, whereby You have drawn me to preach Your Word and to dispense Your Sacraments to Your people? And even though I might be able to set down these things in order, drops of my time are precious to me.

For a long time I have been aflame with a desire to meditate upon Your Law, and to confess to You both my knowledge and my ignorance of it—the first beginnings of Your enlightenment and the remains of my own darkness—until my weakness be swallowed up by Your strength. On no other task would I wish to waste such time as I find free from the necessity of reinvigorating my physical and mental powers and fulfilling the service that we owe to men or that, though we owe it not, we nevertheless render.

O Lord my God, *be attentive to my prayer* (Ps 61:2), and in Your mercy grant my desire, for it burns not for myself alone, but strives also to benefit fraternal charity. You see in my heart that this is so. To You I wish to offer the sacrifice of my mind and tongue; give me what I may offer You. *For I am needy and poor* (Ps 86:1), *but You enrich all who call upon You* (Rom 10:12), You Who, although being Yourself free from care, overflow with Your care for us.

Circumcise my lips from all rashness and lying, both within and without. Let Your Scriptures be my chaste delights. Let me neither be deceived in my interpretation of them nor deceive others in teaching them.

O Lord, be attentive to my prayer and have mercy on me. O Lord my God, Light of the blind and Strength of the weak, You Who are simultaneously the Light of those who see and the Strength of the strong, listen to my soul and hear it *crying from the depths* (Ps 130:1). If Your ears are not also with us in the depths, where shall we go, or to whom shall we cry? *Yours is the day, and Yours is the night* (Ps 74:16). At Your nod the moments fly away.

Grant us sufficient time to meditate on the hidden aspects of Your Law, and do not conceal them from those who knock. It was not without reason that You willed to have so many pages filled with the writing of such dark secrets, nor are those forests without their harts that might retire in them to strengthen themselves, wander about, feed, rest, and ruminate.

O Lord, perfect me and reveal these things to me. Behold, Your voice is my joy; Your voice exceeds the abundance of all pleasures. Grant me what I love, for I truly do love it, and even this love is Your gift. Forsake not Your own gifts, nor despise this plant that thirsts after You.

Let me confess to You whatsoever I shall find in Your books; let me *lift my voice in Your praise* (Ps 26:7), and drink of You, and *consider the wondrous things of Your Law* (Ps 119:18), from the very beginning, wherein You made Heaven and earth, until the everlasting reign with You in Your holy city.

O Lord, have mercy on me and grant my desire, for I think that I do not aspire to earthly things, to gold or silver or precious stones, or to temporal honors and power, or to the pleasure of flesh, or even to bodily necessities for the life of this our pilgrimage. *All these things shall be added unto us who seek the Kingdom of God and Your justice* (Mt 6:33). Behold, O my God, the motive of my desire! *The wicked have told me fables, but they have not spoken to me of Your Law* (Ps 119:85), O Lord. Behold the motive of my desire!

See, O Father, look down, consider, and approve, and let it be pleasing in the sight of Your mercy that I should find grace before You, so that the inner secrets of Your Word may be opened at my knock.

I beseech You by Your Son, our Lord Jesus Christ, *the Man of Your right hand, the Son of Man Whom You have established for Yourself* (Ps 80:18) as Your Mediator and ours. Through Him You sought us when we sought You not, and, moreover, sought us in order that we might seek You. He is Your Word, through Whom You had made all things, and among them also myself. He is Your only-begotten Son by Whom You did call to adoption the multitude of believers, and me among them.

I beseech You through Him *Who sits at Your right hand and intercedes for us* (Rom 8:34), *in Whom are hidden all the treasures of wisdom and knowledge* (Col 2:3). These same treasures do I seek in Your books. It is of Him that *Moses wrote* (Jn 5:46): This He says, and He is the Truth.

CHAPTER 3 — Language and Truth

LET me hear and understand how *in the Beginning You made Heaven and earth* (Gn 1:1). Of this Moses wrote. He wrote and passed away; he passed from this world to You. Neither is he now before me, for if he were, then would I hold him fast, and I would ask him and beg him in Your

Name to explain clearly these things to me. And I would lend these bodily ears to the sounds coming out of his mouth. If he should speak in Hebrew, in vain would it fall upon my ears, nor would I understand anything; but if he spoke in Latin, I would know what he said.

But how would I know whether or not he spoke the truth? And if I knew this also, would I know it from him? Yes, certainly, for within me, in that inner house of my thought, neither Hebrew, nor Greek, nor Latin, nor any barbarous tongue, but Truth Itself, without any instrument of mouth or tongue, and without the sound of any syllables, would say unto me, "He speaks the truth." Then I, being assured thereof, would confidently say to Your servant, "You speak truly."

But now, since I cannot ask him questions, I beg of You, O Truth, filled with Whom he spoke true things, I beseech You, my God, to *forgive my sins* (Jb 14:16), and as You enabled Your servant to speak these things, grant that I may also understand them.

CHAPTER 4 — The Cry of Creation

BEHOLD, Heaven and earth exist, and they cry out that they were created, for they change and vary, whereas whatsoever has not been made, and yet exists, has nothing in it now that it did not have before. Such is the very nature of change and variation.

They also cry out that they did not make themselves, saying, "Therefore, we exist because we have been made. We did not exist before we were made so that we might be able to give being to ourselves."

The voice of those who speak is clear evidence of this fact. Therefore, O Lord, You Who are beautiful made them, for they are beautiful; You Who are good made them, for they are good; You Who exist made them, for they exist.

They are not as beautiful or as good, nor do they exist in the same way as You, their Creator. In comparison with You they are neither beautiful, nor good, nor do they really exist! These things we know, thanks be to You, but our knowledge compared with Your knowledge is ignorance.

CHAPTER 5 — The Instrument of Creation

BUT how did You make Heaven and earth, and what was the instrument used for so great a work? For You are not like a human artisan, fashioning one body from another according to his fancy, which he sees in his mind by an inward kind of eye. And how would he be able to do this if You had not made that mind? He impresses a form upon what already exists and has the capacity to exist, such as earth, or stone, or wood, or gold, or the like. And how could these things have a being, unless You had made them?

It was You Who gave to the artisan his body, and a mind that might direct his limbs, the matter from which he might make anything, the intelligence whereby he might understand his art and might see inwardly what he produces outwardly, the senses of his body with which, as an interpreter, he conveys what he does from his mind to the material upon which he labors, and carries back word to the same mind of what has been accomplished, so that it may judge by the truth that presides there whether it is well done or not.

All these things praise You, the Creator of all things. But how do You make them? How, O God, did You create Heaven and earth? Certainly, neither in Heaven nor on earth did You make Heaven and earth. Nor did You do so in the air or in the waters, because these also are part of Heaven and earth. Nor in the whole world together did You make the whole world, for there was no place wherein it might be made before it was made so that it might have its being. Nor did You have anything in Your hand to make Heaven and earth, for how could You have anything to use as material that You had not made? Whatever has any existence at all does so only because You exist.

Therefore, *You spoke, and they were made* (Ps 33:9), and in Your Word You made these things.

CHAPTER 6 — The Manner of Creation

BUT how did You speak? Was it in that manner in which the voice came out of the cloud, saying, *This is My beloved Son* (Mt 3:17)? That voice sounded and passed away; it began and ended. The syllables did sound and so passed onward, the second after the first, the third after the second, and so on in order, until the last came after the rest, and after that there was silence.

Thus, it is clearly evident that the temporal movement of a creature expressed Your eternal Will. And these words of Yours were spoken in time, conveyed by the outward ear to the intelligent mind, whose internal ear was listening to Your eternal Word. But the mind compared these temporally sounding words with Your eternal Words in silence, and said, "It is far, far different. These words are far inferior to mine. Nay, they do not even exist at all, for they pass away and are no more, but the *Word of God* is far superior to me, and *endures forever*" (Is 40:8).

If, therefore, by audible and passing words You decreed that Heaven and earth should be made, and so created Heaven and earth, there would have to be a corporeal creature already existing before Heaven and earth, through whose temporal motions that voice might have its course in time. But before Heaven and earth there was no corporeal creature existing, or, if there were, You certainly created it without any transitory voice, that by it You might utter the transitory voice that bade Heaven and earth to be made. Finally, whatever it was that produced such a voice, it would not have existed at all unless it were made by You.

I ask then: By what Word of Yours did You command that a body be made, capable of uttering these words?

CHAPTER 7 — The Eternal Word

YOU call us, therefore, to understand the Word, God with You, God, which Word is spoken from all eternity, and in which all things are spoken eternally. That which was spoken does not come to an end, nor is the one thing said that the next may be spoken, but all things are spoken at once and eternally. Otherwise there would be time and change and neither true eternity nor true immortality. This I know, O my God, and *I thank You for it* (1 Cor 1:4). I know it, and I confess it to You, O Lord, and whosoever is not ungrateful to Your certain Truth knows it and joins me in blessing You for it.

We know, O Lord, we know that in proportion as anything is not what it once was, and is now what it once was not, in that same proportion does it die and begin anew. Therefore, nothing of Your Word gives place or is succeeded, because it is truly immortal and eternal. Therefore, by Your Word, which is coeternal with You, You speak those things that You say, once and for all, and all things are made that You will to be made. Nor did You create anything otherwise than by speaking, nor are all things made together, and everlasting, that You make by Your speaking.

CHAPTER 8 —The Word and the Beginning

WHY is this so, I implore You, O Lord my God? I see it after a fashion, but I know not how to express it, save that whatever begins to be, and then ceases to be, begins and ends at the moment when it is resolved in Your eternal reason, where nothing either begins or ends, that it ought to begin or end. This is Your Word, which is the beginning since it also speaks to us.

Thus, in the Gospel He speaks through the flesh, and this did sound forth outwardly in the ears of men, so that it may be believed and be sought for inwardly and be found in the eternal Truth, where the Master Who alone is good teaches all His disciples. There, O Lord, do I hear Your voice speaking to me, because only he who teaches us speaks to us. Anyone who does not teach us may be speaking, but not to us.

Moreover, who is it that teaches us unless it be this unchanging Truth? For when we are admonished by any changing creature, we are led to that unchangeable Truth, where we truly learn, as we *stand and hear Him and rejoice with joy because of the Bridegroom's voice* (Jn 3:29) restoring us to the source of our being.

Therefore, He is the Beginning, and if He did not remain, there would be nowhere for us to return to when we strayed from His path. Now when we return from error, it is by first acknowledging our failure that we return. And in order that we may know, He teaches us, because He is the Beginning, Who also speaks to us.

CHAPTER 9 — Wisdom and the Beginning

IN THIS Beginning, O God, You made Heaven and earth, in the Word, in Your Son, in Your Power, in Your Wisdom, in Your Truth, speaking and working in a wonderful manner. Who can understand it? Who can declare it? What is it that shines through me and strikes my heart without wounding it, causing me to shudder and burn with passion? I shudder inasmuch as I am unlike it; I burn with passion inasmuch as I am like it.

It is Wisdom, Wisdom itself, that shines into me, breaking through the dark clouds that overwhelm me as I faint under the gross darkness and the huge weight of my sins. *My strength is weakened through poverty* (Ps 31:11) so that I cannot endure my blessings until You, O Lord, *Who forgive me all my iniquities, shall also heal all my diseases. For You also shall redeem my life from destruction and shall crown me with mercy and compassion, and You shall satisfy my desire with good things, when my youth shall be renewed like that of an eagle* (Ps 103:3-5). *For by hope are we saved, and we await with patience* (Rom 8:24-25) the fulfillment of Your promises.

Let him who can do so hear Your voice speaking within him; I will cry out boldly in the words of Your oracle: *How great are Your works, O Lord! You have made all things in Wisdom* (Ps 104:24). This Wisdom is the Beginning, and in that Beginning You made Heaven and earth.

CHAPTER 10 — An Idle Question Concerning God

A RE they not guilty of the ancient error who say to us, "What was God doing before He made Heaven and earth?" And they continue: "For if He was at rest and did nothing, why does He not henceforth and forever cease working, as He did forever in times past?

"If any new motion or any new will came to exist in God to form a creature that until then He had never formed, how can this be a true eternity, where there arises a new will which did not exist before? For the Will of God is not a creature, but existed prior to the creature, since nothing would have been created unless the Will of the Creator first so willed it.

"The Will of God belongs to His very substance. Now if anything should appear in the substance of God that was not there before, that substance could not be truly called eternal. But if it were eternally the Will of God that there should be a creature, why was not the creature also eternal?"

CHAPTER 11 — The Wisdom of God and the Light of the Mind

T HOSE who speak in such a manner do not yet understand You, O Wisdom of God and Light of our minds. They do not yet understand how those things are made that are made by You and in You. They strive to comprehend eternity but their mind still flickers to and fro in the past and future movements of things, and it is still vain.

Who shall hold and steady it so that for a while it may be still, so as to catch a glimpse of the splendor of Your immutable eternity and compare it with the times that never stand fast? In that way he may see that there is no comparison, and he may come to realize how a long time is made long as the result of many transitory motions, which cannot be extended at the same instant, and comprehend that in eternity nothing passes away, but the whole is present, and no time can be present all at once. Let him see that all past time is driven away by the future, and that all future time follows upon the past, and that all past and future times are created and flow out from that which is always present.

Who shall hold fast to the mind of man so that it may focus its concentration and see how that ever-fixed eternity determines both past and future time, itself being neither past nor future? Can any mind reach so far, or can the hand of my mouth, by persuasion, accomplish so great a result?

CHAPTER 12 — Before the Creation of the World

BEHOLD, I answer him who asks, "What was God doing before He made Heaven and earth?" I do not answer jestingly as a certain person is said to have done, thereby avoiding the force of the question, when he said, "God was preparing hell for those who are over-curious." It is one thing to look into a matter, another to make sport of it. I make no such answer. I would much rather answer, "I do not know," when such is actually the case, rather than make a fool of someone who asks deep questions and then be commended for giving false answers.

Therefore it is my firm belief that You, our God, are the Creator of every creature. And if, under the name of Heaven and earth, all creation is meant, I say boldly: "Before God made Heaven and earth, He made nothing. For if He made anything, what could it have been but a creature?"

I wish that I knew everything that would be advantageous for me to know with the same certitude that I know that no creature was made before any creature was made.

CHAPTER 13 — The Eternity of God

BUT if the inquisitive mind of any man wanders through the images of the past and wonders why You, Who are the Omnipotent, All-creating and All-sustaining God, the Maker of Heaven and earth, did for innumerable ages abstain from producing so great a work before actually doing so, let him awake to reality and realize that he wonders at false things.

How could innumerable ages flow by which You, the Author and Creator of all ages, did not make? Or what times could there be which were not created by You? Or how could they flow by if they never existed in the first place?

Since, therefore, You are the Maker of all times, if there was a time before You made Heaven and earth, why is it said that You rested from Your labors? For You did make that very time, nor could times pass before they were made by You. But if there was no time before Heaven and earth, why is it asked, "What did You do then?" For there was no "then" when as yet there was no time.

Neither are You in time before all time; otherwise You could not have preceded all time. But You precede all the past by the sublimity of Your ever-present eternity, and You dominate the future because it is still to be, and when it shall have come it will be the past. *You are always the same and Your years shall never end* (Ps 102:28). Your years neither come nor go, but ours both come and go, so that they may all come in order. Your years stand all at the same time, because they are steadfast. Departing years are not obliterated by those that follow, because they never pass away, whereas these years of Yours shall all be ours when time shall be no more.

Your years are as a single day, and Your day is not every day, but today, because Your today neither gives place to tomorrow nor comes in place of yesterday. Your today is eternity. Therefore, You did beget Him coeternal with Yourself to Whom You did say, *"This day have I begotten You"* (Ps 2:7). You made all times, and before all times You are, nor at any time was there no time.

CHAPTER 14 — The Nature of Time

THEREFORE, there was no time when You had not made anything, because You had made time itself. And no time is coeternal with You, because You are changeless, but if time was changeless, it would not be time.

But what is time? Who can easily and briefly explain this? Who even in his thought can comprehend it and so express it in words? And yet, what more familiar and more common word do we use than time? And when we use it we understand its meaning, and likewise when others use it.

What then is time? If no man asks me, I know, but if I attempt to explain it to someone who does not ask me, I do not know. Yet, this I say confidently: I know that if nothing were passing, there would be no past time, and if nothing were coming, there would be no future time, and if nothing existed now, there would be no present time.

Those two times, therefore, the past and future, how can they exist, since the past is now no more, and the future is not yet? Moreover, if the present could be forever present and not pass on to become the past, truly it would not be time, but eternity.

If, then, the present, to be considered as time, only comes into existence because it passes on to the past, how can we say that it is, since the very cause of its being is that it will cease to be. Therefore, we can truly affirm it to exist only because it tends to nonbeing.

CHAPTER 15 — The Length of Time

AND yet, we speak of a long time and a short time, nor can we say this unless we mean the past or the future. For example, we call a hundred years ago a long time ago in the past, and we speak of a hundred years hence as a long time in the future. In contrast, we term ten days ago a short time ago in the past, and ten days hence a short time to come.

But in what sense is time either long or short if it does not exist? The time past is no more, and the future is not yet. Therefore, let us not say, "It is long," but of the past, "It has been long," and of the future, "It will be long." O *Lord* my God, *my Light* (Ps 27:1), will not Your Truth deride man here? For the past time that was long, was it long when it was already past, or while it was still present? For it might be long then, when it had a being that was long, but the past no longer has a being and so it could not be long, since it did not exist.

Therefore, let us not say, "The time that was past was long." For we cannot find anything in it that was long, since, as soon as time is past, it is no more.

Rather let us say, "The present was long," for while it was present, indeed it was long. For it had not then passed away, so as to cease to be; therefore, it still had a being that could be long. But as soon as it passed, it ceased to be long at that instant, because it ceased to be.

Therefore, let us see, O human soul, whether present time can be long, for to you is it given to realize and to measure the spaces of time. What will you answer me? Are the present hundred years a long time? First see whether a hundred years can be present. If the first of these years be now current, that one indeed is present, but the other ninety-nine are in the future, and therefore they do not yet exist. If the second year is in progress, then one year is already past, another is present, and the rest are all in the future. And in the same manner, if we suppose any year of that hundred to be present, all those before it will be in the past and those after it will be in the future. Therefore, a hundred years cannot be present.

Meanwhile, let us attempt to resolve whether at least the one year that is current can be present. If the first month is current, then the rest are in the future. If the second month is current, then the first is already past and the rest are still in the future. Therefore, the current year is not completely present, and if it is not completely present, then the year is not present. For the year consists of twelve months, and the month that is now current is present, all the rest being either in the past or in the future. Neither is the current month present, but one day only. If that day be the first, the rest are yet to come; if it be the last, the rest are in the past; if it be any of the intermediate days, then it is between the past and the future.

Behold how the present, which alone we found could be called long, is already contracted scarcely to the space of a day. Let us discuss that also, for not even so much as a single day is wholly present. It is composed of twenty-four hours of night and day, of which the first views the rest as in the future, and the last views them as in the past, while any intermediate hour sees the hours before it in the past, and those after it as in the future. And even that one hour passes away in fleeting moments, for whatsoever of it has fled is past, whatsoever remains is future.

Therefore, if any instant of time be conceived that cannot be divided up into the smallest particles of moments, this alone may be called the present. Such a moment flies at such a speed from the future into the past that it is not lengthened out by even an infinitesimal amount. For if once it be so lengthened out, it is divided into a past time and a future time, but as for the present time, it has no space.

Where then is that time which we may designate as long? Is it the future? We cannot say of it that it *is* long, because it does not yet exist. We say rather that it *will be* long. But when will it be long? If it will be long only then, at that time which is the future, it cannot be long, because as yet that which is to be long has no being at all. But it shall be long when it shall have begun to be, and so is no longer future but present, though indeed it may now be something and thus capable of being long; then the present cries out, in the words above, that it cannot be long.

CHAPTER 16 — Comparing Intervals of Time

AND yet, O Lord, we are aware of intervals of time, and we compare them, reasoning that some are longer and others shorter. We measure also how much this time or that is longer or shorter, and we say: This time is twice or three times as long, and that time is equal to, or just as long as, the other. But we measure time as it passes, and by observation we measure it.

As for times past that now are not, and times to come that as yet are not, who is able to measure them, unless perhaps someone will be so bold as to say that he can measure that which does not exist. While, therefore, time is passing, it can be perceived and measured, but once it has passed, it cannot be measured, because then it does not exist.

CHAPTER 17 — Past and Future Time

I ASK questions, Father. I do not affirm anything. O my God, rule and guide me. Who is there who will tell me that there are not three times, as we learned in boyhood, and as we afterward taught boys—the past, the present and the future—but that there is only a present time, because the other two do not exist? Or do these two perhaps also exist, but when the present comes into being from the future, it proceeds from some secret place, and when the past comes out of the present, it recedes into some hidden place?

For where have those who foretold the future seen it if as yet it does not exist? For that which does not exist cannot be seen. So also, those who describe past things could not indeed describe true things if they did not perceive them in their mind, and if these things did not exist at all, they could not be perceived. Therefore, past and future things really exist.

CHAPTER 18 — The Present Time

LET me seek further, *O Lord, my Hope* (Ps 71:5); do not allow my purpose to be turned aside! If past and future times do exist, I want to know where they are. But if I cannot as yet succeed, I still know this: that wherever they are they are not there as the future or the past but only as the present. For if they are there as future things, they are not yet there, and if they are there as past things, then they are no longer there.

Consequently, wherever and whatsoever they are, they do not exist except as present things. However, when past things are accurately related, they are not the past things themselves that are drawn out of the memory, but only such words as were conceived by their images that, like so many footprints, were fixed on the mind as they passed through the senses.

For example, my childhood, which is now no more, belongs to the past, which no longer exists.

But when I recall it and speak of it, I behold it in the present time, because it still remains in my memory.

Whether or not there is a like cause for also prophesying the future, namely, that the images of things that do not yet exist should be represented as if already existing, I confess to You, O my God, that I do not know. But this indeed I know, that we often think of future actions, and that this premeditation is in the present, but as for the action that we premeditate, it does not yet exist, because it is future. As soon as we shall have set upon our task and begun to do what we premeditated, then that action will exist, because it will no longer be future but present.

Whatever may be the secret of foreseeing future things, nothing can be seen except that which is present. But what now exists is not future but present. When, therefore, future things are said to be seen, what are actually seen are not the things themselves, which as yet do not exist, i.e., future things, but their causes perhaps, or signs, for these already exist. Therefore, they are not future but present to those who see them. And from these, future things are foretold, as the mind conceives them. These concepts again are beheld as present in the minds of those who foretell them.

Let the many things that we see provide an example of this. I see the dawn, and I foretell that the sun is about to rise. What I see is present; what I foresee is to come—not the sun that already exists, but the sunrise that is yet to come. But if I did not visualize the sunrise itself in my own mind, as I now do when I speak of it, I could not foretell it. Yet the dawn that I see in the sky is not the sunrise, although it precedes the sunrise, nor is it the image of the sunrise that is in my mind. However, both of them are seen as present, so that the other may be foretold as yet to come.

Therefore, future things do not yet exist, and if they do not yet exist, they are not yet, and if they are not yet, it is not possible for them to be seen. However, they can be foretold by means of present things that already exist and are seen.

CHAPTER 19 — A Plea for Enlightenment

BUT tell me, O Ruler of Your creatures, how is it that You teach souls those things that are to come? Already You have so taught Your Prophets. How is it that You teach future things, You to Whom nothing is future? Or, rather, do You teach present things about what lies ahead? For what does not exist certainly cannot be taught.

This method is far beyond the limits of my understanding. It is too incomprehensible for me, and I cannot attain such understanding. However, with Your help I shall be able to do so when You shall grant it, sweet Light of my hidden eyes.

CHAPTER 20 — Three Kinds of Time

THEREFORE, it is now clear and plain that neither the past nor the future exists. Nor may it properly be said that there are three times: past, present, and future. Perhaps it might properly be said: "There are three times: a present time of things past, a present time of things present, and a present time of future things." Indeed there are three such times as these in the mind, and I see them nowhere else.

The present time of past things is our memory, the present time of present things is our sight, the present time of future things is our expectation.

If we are permitted to speak thus, I do indeed see and I confess that there are three times. It may also be said: "There are three times: past, present, and future," according to the usual incorrect manner of speaking. I am not troubled at this, nor do I resist or argue about it, as long as it is understood that neither the past nor the future now exists. Indeed, there are few things that we speak of properly, and very many that we speak of improperly, but what we mean to say is understood.

CHAPTER 21 — The Measure of Time

AS I have just now said, we measure the times as they pass, so as to say that this time is twice as long as that, concerning those other parts of time that we are able to measure as they pass. Therefore, as I commented, we measure the times as they pass. And if anyone should ask me, "How do you know this?" I answer that I know it because we measure them, but we cannot measure those things that do not exist, and the past and future do not exist. But how do we measure the present if it has no space? We measure it, then, while it is passing; however, when it shall have passed, we cannot measure it, for there will then be nothing to be measured.

But from where does it come, and by what way, and where does it go, when it is being measured? From where? From the future? By what way? By the present? Where does it go? To the past? Therefore, it passed from that which does not yet exist, by way of that which has no space, into that which no longer exists.

Yet, what is it that we measure unless time is in some space? For do we not speak of single, double, triple, equal, and whatever else we say when speaking of time, except with reference to the duration of time. Therefore, in what space do we measure present time? In the future, from which it passes? But what does not exist cannot be measured. In the present, by which it is passing? But we cannot measure what has no space. In the past to which it passes? But neither can we measure what no longer exists.

CHAPTER 22 — Trying To Solve an Enigma

MY MIND yearns to understand this most entangled problem. In the Name of Christ, I beseech You, O good Father, my Lord and God, do not shut me off from knowledge of these ordinary and yet obscure things so that my mind may not penetrate them. Let them be revealed to me, O Lord, through the light of Your mercy.

Whom shall I ask about these things? To whom more fruitfully than to You shall I confess my ignorance? For to You these studies of mine—which burn so eagerly for the understanding of the Scriptures—are in no way troublesome.

Grant me that which I love, for I do love this, and even this love You have given to me. Grant this gift to me, O Father, You *Who truly know how to give good gifts to Your children* (Mt 7:11). Grant this, because *I have studied that I might know it, and it is a labor in my sight* (Ps 73:16), till such time as You shall open it.

I beseech You in the name of Christ, the Holy of Holies, let no man interrupt me. For I believed;

therefore have I spoken (Ps 116:2). This is my hope; for this do I live, that *I may see the delight of the Lord* (Ps 27:4). *Behold, You have made my days old* (Ps 39:6); they passed away and I know not how.

We speak of time and time, of times and times: "How long is it since he said this?" "How long is it since he did this?" "How long is it since I saw that?" "This syllable is twice the length of that other short syllable." We say and hear these things; we understand and are understood by others. They are the most ordinary and most common of words, yet they are much too obscure, and their meaning is still to be discovered.

CHAPTER 23 — Time as an Extension

A CERTAIN learned man once said that the movements of the sun, the moon, and the planets constituted time, but I disagreed. For why should not rather the movement of all bodies in general be time?

Supposing the celestial lights should cease, but some potter's wheel continued to turn, would there be no time whereby we might measure its rotations? Could we not say that some of its rotations ran at equal intervals, some faster and some slower, some longer and some shorter? Or while we were saying these things, would we not ourselves be speaking in time? Would there not be in our words some long syllables and some short, for the basic reason that some took a longer time to pronounce and some a shorter time?

Grant to men, O God, that in such a minor matter we may discern ideas that are common to small things as well as great things.

The stars and the heavenly lights coordinate *with signs and seasons, years and days* (Gn 1:14). They truly so function. However, just as I would not say that one revolution of that little wooden wheel is a day, neither should that learned man say that therefore there is no time at all.

I am trying to understand the force and nature of time, whereby we measure the movements of bodies, and say, for example, that this movement is twice as long as that other. A day means not only the time of the sun's stay above the earth, according to which account the day is one thing and the night another, but also the time of the whole circuit that the sun travels from east to east again, according to which account we say, "So many days have passed." For the days, reckoned with the nights, are always called so many days, and the spaces of the nights are not left out of the account.

Therefore, since a day constitutes the circular motion of the sun from east to east again, I ask whether the movement itself be the day, or the length of time in which that movement is completed, or both together?

If the first were a day, then it would still be a day, even though the sun should complete its course in a space of time as short as that of one hour. If the second, then it would not be a day if, between one sunrise and the next, there were but a space as short as that of one hour, for then the sun would have to go around twenty-four times to complete one day. If both together, then neither could it be called a day if the sun should make its whole circuit in the space of one hour, nor if, while the sun stood still, as much time should pass as that in which the sun normally takes to make its entire course from one morning to another.

Therefore, I will not ask now what it is that is called a day, but what time is, whereby we should say, on measuring the circuit of the sun, that it had gone around in half the required time, if it had completed the circuit in such a small space of time as twelve hours. Comparing both times, we should say that the latter is a single period of time, and the former is a double period of time, although the sun would run its course from east to east, sometimes in a single period and sometimes in a double period.

Therefore, let no man say to me that the movements of celestial bodies are periods of time, for we must remember that, upon the prayer of a certain man that he might be victorious in battle, the sun stood still but time went on. For in the space of time that was sufficient for him, the battle was fought and finished.

Thus I perceive that time is a kind of extension. But do I truly perceive this, or do I only seem to perceive it? You, Who are Light and Truth, will reveal this to me.

CHAPTER 24 — Time and Movement of Bodies

DO You wish me to agree with someone who says that time is the movement of a body? No, You would not. I understand that no body is moved except in time. You have said this. But that the very movement of a body constitutes time, I do not hear nor do You say it. For when a body moves, I measure by time how long it moved from the moment when it began to be moved until it ceased moving.

And if I did not see when it began to be moved, and it continues so that I cannot see when the movement stops, then I cannot measure it, except from the time when I began to see it until the time when I cease to do so.

If I look at it for a long time, I can only say that it is a long time, but I cannot say how long. For when we say how long a time is, we must do so by comparison—for example, that this is the same length as that or twice the length of that.

But if we were able to note the distances between those places from where and to where the whole body that is moved goes—or any of its parts if it moves on a wheel—then we can tell how much time the movement of the body or of any of its parts takes to go from this place to that.

Therefore, since the movement of a body is different from that by which we measure how long the movement takes, who cannot now see which of these two should be called time?

Although a body sometimes moves and sometimes stands still, we measure not only its motion by time, but also its rest.

We say, "It was at rest for as long as it moved," or, "It was at rest twice or three times as long as it moved," or any other space of time that we have measured or estimated, more or less, as we are accustomed. Therefore, time is not the movement of a body.

CHAPTER 25 — A Continuing Enigma

AND I confess to You, O Lord, that I do not yet know what time is, and again I confess to You, O Lord, that I know that I speak these things in time, and that, having spoken a long time, that very length of time is not long except by the passage of time.

But how do I come to know this, when I do not know what time is? Or is it, perhaps, that I do not know how to express what I know? To my shame I confess that I do not so much as know the extent of my own ignorance.

Behold, O my God, I stand before You and I do not lie; as my tongue speaks, so is my heart. *You light my lamp, O Lord. O my God, enlighten my darkness* (Ps 18:29).

CHAPTER 26 — Measuring Time

DOES not my soul truthfully confess to You that I do measure periods of time? Yes indeed, I measure them, O Lord my God, and yet I know not what I measure. I measure the movement of a body in time; do I not then measure time itself? Or could I indeed measure the movement of a body, how long it is, and how long a time it requires to come from this place to that, unless I could measure the time in which it is moved?

How, then, do I measure this time itself? Do we measure a longer time by a shorter one, as we measure the length of a beam by the length of a cubit?

In the same way we seem to measure the length of a long syllable by the length of a short one, and to say that it is twice as long. So, too, do we seem to measure the length of a poem by the number of verses, and the length of verses by the number of feet, and the length of feet by the number of syllables, and the length of long syllables by the number of shorter ones.

We do not measure a poem by the number of pages, for in that way we would measure space, not time; but when, as we pronounce them, the words pass by, we say, "It is a long poem because it is made up of so many verses; the verses are long because they are composed of so many feet; the feet are long because they include so many syllables; and it is a long syllable, for it is twice the length of a short one."

Yet, neither in this way is the measure of time comprehended, because it may so happen that a short verse that is pronounced slowly may take up a longer time than a longer verse that is pronounced hurriedly. The same is also true for a poem, for a foot, and for a syllable.

Therefore, it seems to me that time is nothing but an extension in length, but I do not know of what, and I marvel if it not be of the mind itself. Yet what, I beseech You, O my God, do I measure, when I say, either indefinitely, "This is a longer time than that," or more definitely, "This is twice as long as that"? I know well that it is time that I measure. However, I do not measure future time, because it does not yet exist; I do not measure the present, because it is not extended in any space; I do not measure the past, because that no longer exists. Therefore, what do I measure? Is it time as it passes, but is not yet past? This I have already said.

CHAPTER 27 — The Solution of the Question

PERSEVERE, O my soul! Press forward bravely! *God is our helper* (Ps 62:9). *He made us and not we ourselves* (Ps 100:3). Press forward where Truth now brightens like the dawn.

Suppose the voice of a body begins to sound. It sounds, is sounding still, then it sounds no more. Now there is silence, for that voice is past; it is a voice no longer.

Before it began to sound, this voice was to come, and so it could not then be measured since it did not exist; and now it cannot be measured because it no longer exists. But while it sounded, it could be measured because then indeed it did exist. Yet, even then, it did not stand still, but went on and passed. Could it then be more easily measured for that reason? For while passing by, it had to be stretched out into some other space of time by which it was measurable, since the present has no space.

If, therefore, it might be measured, let us suppose that another voice begins to sound, and sounds continually, without any interruption, in one even flow. Let us now measure it while it sounds, seeing that when it has ceased to sound, it will be past and will no longer be measurable. Let us then measure it and say how long it is. But it is still sounding, and it cannot be measured except from the instant when it began to sound, to the end when it ceased. For the intermediate interval is the space that we are to measure, from some beginning to some end.

Therefore, a voice that is not as yet ended cannot be measured, so that we can say with assurance how long or how short it is, nor can it be called equal to any other, or as much, or twice as much, or the like. However, as soon as it is ended, it will no longer exist.

How then can it be measured? Yet, for all this, we do measure periods of time, though neither those that do not yet exist, nor those that no longer exist, nor those that are not extended by some pause, nor yet those that have no ending. In other words, we measure neither future time nor past time nor present time nor passing time; and yet still we do measure time.

Deus Creator Omnium ("God, the Creator of us all"): this verse of eight syllables contains long and short syllables alternately. There are four short syllables: the first, third, fifth, and seventh, and these are single in relation to the four long syllables, which are the second, fourth, sixth, and eighth. Each long syllable is twice as long as each short syllable; I pronounce them and repeat them, and I find it to be so, as common sense dictates.

By common sense then, I measure a long syllable by a short one, and I find that it is twice as long. But when one syllable sounds after another, and if the first is short and the second is long, how shall I hold fast to the short one, and how shall I compare it to that long one when I measure it, so that I may find the long one to be twice as long as the short one?

For the long syllable does not begin to sound until the short one has ceased. I cannot measure the long one while it is present, since I do not measure it until it has ceased, and its passing marks its completion.

Therefore, what is it that I can measure? Where is the short syllable that I measure? Where is the long one that I measure? They have both sounded, have passed, and have fled away. They no longer exist. Yet I still measure them, and I answer with confidence—insofar as the experience of the senses may be trusted—that as to the length of time, one syllable is single and the other is double. Nor could I do this much unless they had already passed and ended. Therefore, I do not measure these sounds that no longer exist, but something in my own memory that remains fixed there.

It is in you, O my mind, that I measure time. Do not aggravate me with other concepts of time. Do not create problems with the multitude of your own impressions. It is in you, I say, that I measure time. The impression that things make on you as they pass by still remains, even when the things themselves are gone.

That present impression is what I measure, not the things that have passed whereby this impression was made. I measure this impression when I measure time. Therefore, either this is what time is, or else I do not measure time.

But how do we resolve the problem when we measure silence and we say that this particular silence lasted as long as that voice did? Do we not then stretch out our thought to the measure of a voice, as though it still sounded, so that we may be able to give some account of the intervals of silence in a given space of time? For while the voice and tongue are silent, we still go through poems and verses and any discourse in our thoughts, or any other dimensions of motions, and we pronounce what relation one had to the other, in relation to the length of time, no less than if we did repeat them verbally.

If a man should wish to utter a speech of some length, and should fix its length in his mind, this man has already spent a space of time in silence;

then, committing it to memory, he begins to utter that speech, which sounds until it reaches the length previously decided upon. Indeed it has sounded, and it will sound. For so much of it as was uttered has already sounded, and what remains will sound. And thus it passes on, as his present intention causes the future to become past, the future lessening and the past increasing, until, by the consumption of all that was future, everything is past.

CHAPTER 28 — The Three Acts of the Mind

BUT in what way is the future either diminished or consumed, since it does not yet exist? Or how is the past increased, which is now no longer? Only because in the mind, which does all this, there are three acts: it looks forward, it considers, and it remembers, so that the thing to which it looks forward passes through that which it considers into that which it remembers.

Who can deny that future things do not as yet exist? Yet already in the mind there is an expectation of future things. And who can deny that past things no longer exist? Yet there remains in the mind a memory of past things. And who can deny that the present has no space, since it passes away in a moment? But our attention continues, so that through it that which is present may become that which no longer exists.

Therefore, it is not future time that is long, for as yet it does not exist, but a long future is a long expectation of the future. Nor is past time, which does not exist, a long time, but a long past is a long memory of the past.

Suppose that I am about to recite a psalm that I know. Before I begin, my expectation is extended to the whole of it, but once I have begun, my memory also extends over as much as I recall from the past. Therefore, the life of this action is extended into my memory because of what I have said, and also into my expectation because of what I am about to repeat; yet my attention also is present there, whereby that which was future may be carried over so that it may become past.

The more this is done over and over again, by so much is my expectation shortened and my memory prolonged, until finally the whole of my expectation is consumed when that action is completed and the whole shall have passed over into my memory. And what is done in the entire psalm is done also in every single part of it and in every syllable. The same holds true in any longer action of which the psalm may be only a part.

Likewise this holds true for the whole life of a man, the parts of which contain all of the man's actions, and the same holds true throughout the history of the sons of men, of which the lives of all men are parts.

CHAPTER 29 — Christ Our Hope

BUT because *Your mercy is better than life* (Ps 63:4), behold, my life is but a distraction, and *Your right hand has held me up* (Ps 18:36) in my Lord, the Son of Man, the Mediator between You, the One, and us who are many and are led astray in many ways and in many things. It is *through Him that I may lay hold of that for which He has laid hold of me* (Phil 3:12), and may be gathered up from my former life, to follow the One, *forgetting what is behind* (Phil 3:13), not distracted by thoughts of future things and those that are transient, but extended to those things that are before.

Not distractedly but intently I *press on to the prize of my heavenly calling* (Phil 3:14) where *I may hear the voice of Your praise* (Ps 26:7) *and contemplate Your delights* (Ps 27:4) that neither come nor pass away.

However, at the moment *my life is wasted with grief* (Ps 31:11), and You, O Lord, my Comfort, my Father, are everlasting. But I am still confused about the problems of time, of whose order I still know nothing. My thoughts and the deepest recesses of my soul are torn asunder by tumultuous changes, until such time as I shall flow completely into You, purified and melted by the fire of Your love.

CHAPTER 30 — No Coeternal Time

AND now will I stand and be strengthened in You, in Your Truth that is my mold. Nor will I endure the questions of men who, through the disease that is their punishment, thirst for more than they can drink, and say, "What did God make before He made Heaven and earth?" or "What moved Him, then, to make anything, since He had never previously made anything?"

O Lord, give them grace to think well about what they say, and to realize that they cannot say "never" when there is no time. Therefore, when a man says that he "never" made anything, what else does he mean to say except that he did not make anything at any time?

Let them see, then, that there can be no time without creation, and let them cease to speak thus idly. Let them rather *strain forward to what is before* (Phil 3:13), and let them understand that You, the eternal Creator of all times, are before all times, and that no times are coeternal with You, nor is any creature such, even if there were a creature, prior to the creation of the world.

CHAPTER 31 — Divine and Human Knowledge

LORD, my God, how deep is the charm of Your secrets, and how far off have the consequences of my deep sins cast me? Heal my eyes, that I may take pleasure in Your light. Certainly, if there is a mind excelling with knowledge and foreknowledge to such an extent that all things past and future are known to it, as one psalm is known to me, without a doubt that mind is exceedingly admirable and amazing.

For from that mind, nothing in the past or in future ages is hidden, any more than anything is unknown to me as I sing that psalm about what and how much of it I had sung from the beginning, or about what still remains to be sung until the end.

But far be it that You, the Creator of the universe, Creator of both souls and bodies, far be it that You should know all things past or to come in such a way. You know them far more admirably and more mysteriously. For when a man sings what he knows, or hears a well-known song, his feelings vary and his senses are divided between the remembrance of those words that are past and an expectation of those that are to come. No such thing can happen to You Who are unchangeably eternal, that is, the eternal Creator of minds.

Therefore, just as in the Beginning You knew Heaven and earth without any change in Your knowledge, even so in the *Beginning did You make Heaven and earth* (Gn 1:1) without any change in Your activity. Let him who understands praise You, and let him who does not understand praise You also. Oh how exalted You are, and yet those who are humble in heart are Your dwelling place. For *You lift up all who are cast down* (Ps 146:8) and they can never fall, for You are their exaltation.

Book 12—The Meaning of Holy Scripture

St. Augustine discusses the meaning and interpretation of the words "Heaven" and "earth" as they are set forth in Holy Scripture. He weighs the different interpretations and then goes on to explain the sense and meaning of Holy Scripture.

CHAPTER 1 — The Words of Holy Scripture

MY HEART, O Lord, affected by the words of Holy Scripture, is deeply concerned about many matters as I survey this poverty of my life. For the most part, the poverty that constitutes man's understanding is camouflaged in copious language, for our inquiries speak more fluently than does finding the answers, our petitions take longer than obtaining what we request, and the hand that knocks has more work to do than the hand that receives.

Yet, we have a promise, and who shall destroy it? *If God is for us, who is against us?* (Rom 8:31). *Ask, and you shall receive; seek, and you shall find; knock, and it shall be opened to you. For everyone who asks receives; and he who seeks finds; and to him who knocks it shall be opened* (Mt 7:7-8). These are Your promises, and who fears to be deceived when the Truth itself promises?

CHAPTER 2 — The Heaven of Heavens

THE weakness of my tongue confesses to Your Highness that *You have created Heaven and earth* (Gn 1:1)—this Heaven that I see, and this earth that I tread upon, from which this other earth of my body is made that I bear with me. You made it. But where is that Heaven of heavens, O Lord, of which we have heard by the voice of Your psalm, *The Heaven of heavens is the Lord's, but the earth He has given to the children of men* (Ps 115:16)? Where are you, O Heaven that we do not see, in comparison with which all this that we see is simply earth?

For this corporeal whole, which is not whole everywhere, has retained its portion of beauty in these lower parts, even to this earth that is the lowest, but, in comparison with that Heaven of heavens, even this very heaven of our earth is but earth. Therefore, both these great bodies may not without reason be called earth, in comparison with the unknown Heaven that is the Lord's and not that of the sons of men.

CHAPTER 3 — Darkness over the Face of the Abyss

CERTAINLY this earth was invisible and without form (Gn 1:2), and I know not how deep the abyss was, upon which there was no light, because it had no form. Therefore, You commanded it to be written that *darkness was upon the face of the deep* (Gn 1:2). What else could this be other than the absence of light? For, had there been light, where should it be, unless above, rising aloft and illuminating?

Therefore, where there was yet no light, what could the presence of darkness signify but the absence of light? Moreover, darkness was above because light was not over it, just as there is silence where there is no sound. And what is silence anywhere except the absence of sound?

O Lord, have You not taught this soul that now confesses You? Have You not taught me, O Lord, that before You did separate and form this formless matter, there was nothing: neither color, nor shape, nor body, nor spirit? And yet there was not altogether nothing, for there was a certain formlessness, without any shape.

CHAPTER 4 — The Formless and Invisible Earth

WHAT then should it be called, and in what sense could it be conveyed to those of lesser intelligence, except by some ordinary word? And what is to be found among all parts of the world more similar to absolute formlessness than "earth" and "abyss"?

For they have less beauty because of their low degree than those other higher parts, which are all transparent and shining.

Therefore, why may I not conceive that the formlessness of matter, which You did create without beauty and yet made of it this beautiful world, was to be aptly conveyed to men by the name of earth, invisible and formless?

CHAPTER 5 — The Form of Matter:
Neither Intelligible Nor Sensible Form

WHEN thought seeks for something to which the senses may cling, it says, "It is not an intelligible form, as life or justice is, because it is the matter of bodies. Nor is it a sensible form, because in this invisible and formless matter there is nothing that may be seen or outwardly felt."

When man's thought says such things to itself, he may seek either to know it by being ignorant of it, or to be ignorant of it by knowing it.

CHAPTER 6 — Further Thoughts on Matter

BUT, O Lord, if I may confess with my tongue and my pen whatsoever You have taught me of this matter—having heard the name beforehand but not understanding it, since they who told me of it did not understand it themselves—I first conceived it as having an innumerable variety of forms; therefore, I did not conceive it at all.

My mind revealed certain ugly and horrible forms in considerable disarray, but yet forms they were. I called it formless, not because it lacked form, but because what it had was of such a kind that if it presented itself to me, my senses immediately would turn from it as unusual and absurd, something that would confound our weak human powers.

Nevertheless, that which I conceived as formless was not indeed deprived of all form, but only by comparison to the more beautiful forms, and right reason persuaded me that I must utterly deprive it of all remnants of form whatsoever if I wished to conceive of a matter that was totally formless. I could not do this. For I could more easily believe that it was totally formless than to conceive of something between form and nothing, neither formed nor nothing, formless and almost nothing.

My mind ceased to question my spirit anymore about this matter, seeing that it was full of images of formed bodies, which it varied and changed as it willed. I applied my mind to the bodies themselves, and I looked more deeply into their changeableness, as a result of which they cease to be what they were, and begin to be what they were not. And I suspected that this very change from one form to another was accomplished through something formless, not by way of nothing at all. This I desired to know, and not only to suspect it.

Although my will and pen might here confess to You everything that You untangled for me concerning this question, what reader will persevere so as to take it all in? Yet my heart shall not cease to give You honor, and to sing a canticle of praise for all those things that it is not able to express. For the changeableness of changeable things is itself capable of all those forms into which changeable things can be changed.

But what is it? Is it a soul? Is it a body? Is it any species of soul or body? If I could say, "It is something that is nothing," or, "It is and is not," I would say that this is accurate. Yet in some way it existed even then, since it could receive these visible and composite forms.

CHAPTER 7 — Creation out of Nothing

HOW and from where could this be but from You, from Whom are all things, insofar as they exist? The further a thing is from You, so much the more is it unlike You, for the distance is not of space. Therefore, You, O Lord—Who are not one thing in one place, and another elsewhere, but are the Selfsame, and the Selfsame, and the Selfsame, *Holy, Holy, Holy, Lord God Almighty* (Rv 4:8; cf. Is 6:3)—in the Beginning, which is of You, in Your Wisdom, which is born of You, You did make something, and that out of nothing.

For You made Heaven and earth, not of Your own substance, for then they should have been equal to Your only-begotten Son and consequently to Your own Self. Therefore, it would be unjust that anything should be equal to You that was not of You.

There was nothing else besides Yourself out of which You could make them, O God, One Trinity, and Triune Unity. Therefore, You did make Heaven and earth out of nothing, a great thing and a small thing, because You are omnipotent and good, to make all things good, even the great Heaven and the small earth.

You were and there was nothing else besides You out of which You made Heaven and earth: two things, one near You, the other almost nothing; one to which You alone would be higher, the other to which nothing would be inferior.

CHAPTER 8 — Heaven and Earth

*T*HE *Heaven of heavens is Yours, O Lord,* but the earth, *which You gave to the children of men* (Ps 115:16), to be seen and felt, was not then such as we now see and feel. For it was *invisible and without form,* and there was an abyss, over which there was no light; or *darkness was over the face of the deep* (Gn 1:2), that is, it was darker above the deep than in the deep.

The abyss of the visible waters has a light proper to its nature within its depths that in some manner is visible to the fish and other living things that creep in the bottom of the sea. However, that total abyss was almost nothing, since it was still altogether formless; nevertheless, it did exist, insofar as it was capable of being formed.

You, O Lord, did make the world out of formless matter, and it was out of nothing that You made those great works that we, the sons of men, admire.

Truly admirable is this material heaven, about which *firmament between water and water,* on the second day after the creation of light, You said, *Let it be made* (Gn 1:6), and it was made. And this firmament You called Heaven, that is, the Heaven over this earth and sea, which You created on the third day, by giving a visible form to that formless matter that You had created before all days. You had already made a Heaven before all days, but that was the Heaven of this Heaven, because in the beginning You made Heaven and earth.

This same earth, which You had made, was but formless matter, because it was invisible and formless, and darkness was over the deep. Out of this *invisible and formless earth,* out of this formlessness, this almost nothingness, You made all these things of which this changeable world consists.

Yet that of which it consists is not consistent, for mutability itself appears therein, and in it times can be perceived and measured. For periods of time result from the alteration of things, while the forms, whose matter is this visible earth already mentioned, are changed and turned about.

CHAPTER 9 — The Heaven of Heavens

THEREFORE, when Your Spirit, the Teacher of Your servant, recounts that in the beginning You made Heaven and earth, He speaks nothing of time and is silent as to days. Without a doubt the *Heaven of heavens* that *You created in the Beginning* is some form of intellectual creature that, although in no way coeternal with You, the Trinity, is still in some way a partaker of Your eternity. It strongly restrains its own mutability that is part of its nature because of the sweetness of joyfully contemplating You. Without any fall since its first creation, it adheres to You and has established itself beyond all the vicissitudes of time.

Neither is this very formlessness of the *earth invisible and without form* numbered among the days. For where there is no form or order, neither does anything come or pass away. Therefore, when this does not occur, there can be no days, nor any change indicating the duration of time.

CHAPTER 10 — Prayer To Understand the Scripture

LET Truth, the Light of my heart, and not my own darkness, speak to me. I turned aside to these material things and became darkened, but from there, even from there, I loved You. *I have gone astray* (Ps 119:176), *and I remembered You* (Jon 2:8). *I heard Your voice behind me* (Ez 3:12), calling me to return, though I could scarcely hear it amid the noise of sinners.

And now, behold, I return, panting and gasping to Your fountain. Let no one forbid me. I shall drink of this fountain and so I shall live. Let me not continue to live as I have lived, for I acknowledge that I have lived badly. To myself I was death, and in You do I live again. Speak to me, discourse with me. I have believed Your books, and their words are full of mystery.

CHAPTER 11 — God's Response

O LORD, now have You spoken with a strong voice into my interior ear, revealing that You are eternal, You Who *alone have immortality* (1 Tm 6:16), because You are not changed by any form or motion. Nor does Your will change with the times, for that which is now one thing, and now another, is not an immortal will. In Your sight, this is already clear to me. I beseech You that it may be made more and more apparent, and in its manifestation let me continue with sobriety under Your sheltering wings.

Likewise You have said to me, O Lord, with a strong voice in my interior ear, how You Yourself have made all those natures and substances that are not what You Yourself are, but that yet exist. You have revealed to me that whatever does not come from You does not exist, as is also true of the will that turns away from You Who are and to that which exists in a lesser way. For all such movement is transgression and sin, and no one's sin hurts You or disturbs the order of Your dominion, either in first or last things.

All this is now clear to me in Your sight, and I pray to You that it may be still more and more apparent, and in that manifestation let me continue with sobriety under Your wings.

You have spoken with a strong voice in my interior ear the truth that not even that creature is co-eternal with You whose delight You alone are, and who with a most persevering purity, deriving its sustenance from You, in no place and at no time has ever asserted its natural mutability. This is so even though being ever in Your presence, to Whom it clings with all its love, it has neither any expectation of the future, nor any remembrance of time past, and is neither altered by any change nor extended toward any temporal things.

O blessed creature, if such there be, who is blessed by adhering to Your blessedness, blessed in

You Who are the eternal Inhabitant and Illuminator thereof. I do not find what I can more worthily call the *Heaven of heavens, which is the Lord's* (Ps 115:16), than that house of Yours which contemplates Your delight, never deserting You for any other—one pure mind, most peacefully one, by the establishment of the peace of those holy spirits, the citizens of Your city that is in Heaven, far above those Heavenly places we see.

By this then may the soul, whose pilgrimage has been made long and far from You, understand that if now it thirsts after You, if now *its tears have become its bread, while it is daily said to it, "Where is Your God?"* (Ps 42:4), if it now *asks of You one thing and desires it, that it may dwell in Your house all the days of its life* (Ps 27:4)—and what is its life but You? And what are Your days but Your eternity, just as are *Your years, which fail not, because You are ever the same?* (Ps 102:28)—from all this can the soul, as far as it is able, understand how far beyond all times You are eternal.

For Your house, which at no time has wandered from You, although it is not coeternal with You yet inseparably and incessantly united to You, suffers not the least vicissitude of time. All this is now clear to me in Your sight, and I pray that it may become still more and more apparent, and in that manifestation let me continue with sobriety under Your wings.

Behold, I know not what formlessness there is in the changes of these last and lowest of Your creatures. And who will tell me, unless it be one who, in the emptiness of his heart, wanders about and tosses around the fancies of his own brain? Who then but such a one will tell me that, if all form was wasted and consumed and only that formlessness should remain, through which a thing was changed and turned from one figure into another, this still can show the changes of time? For certainly this could not be, because without a variety of movements there are no times, and there is no variety where there is no form.

CHAPTER 12 — Things Not Subject to Time

ALL these things being considered, O my God, insofar as You give me the power, insofar as You stir me up to knock, and insofar as You do open to me when I knock, I find two things, both of which You made, but without any relation to time, since neither is coeternal with You.

One of them is so formed that, without ever ceasing from its contemplation, without any interval of change, never changed although changeable in itself, it thoroughly enjoys Your eternity and immutability. The other is so formless that it cannot be changed from one form to another, whether of motion or of rest, whereby it might be subject to time.

However, You did not allow the second to remain formless, because *in the Beginning,* before all days, *You did create Heaven and earth* (Gn 1:1), these two things whereof I am speaking. *But the earth was invisible and formless, and darkness was over the deep* (Gn 1:2). By these words the idea of formlessness is conveyed by You to us so that by degrees this may be conceived by men who are not able to grasp a complete privation of all form in a thing that actually exists.

Out of this another Heaven might be made, together with a visible and ordered earth, and the beautiful waters, and whatsoever else in the constitution of this world we are told was made during those given days. And because they are of such a nature, the vicissitudes of time take place in them through the successive changes of movements and forms.

CHAPTER 13 — The Intellectual Heaven and the Formless Earth

IN THE meantime, O my God, this is what I think when I hear Your Scripture saying, *In the Beginning God made Heaven and earth, and the earth was invisible and without form, and darkness was upon the deep* (Gn 1:1-2), but not saying on what day You created these things. Meanwhile, I think it is said in this manner because of the Heaven of heavens—that intellectual Heaven, where the intelligence knows all at once and not by parts, not *through a mirror in an obscure manner,* but as a whole, *in full sight, face to face* (1 Cor 13:12), not first this thing and then that, but, as I have said, it knows all at once without any passage of time.

By earth is meant the invisible and formless earth, without any succession of time, that changes now to this thing and now to that, because where there is no form, there can be no variety of this and that.

Because of these two, one formed from the beginning and the other wholly formless—the one Heaven, that is, the Heaven of heavens, and the other earth, that is, an earth invisible and formless—because of these two, I, in the meantime, judge that Your Scripture says without any mention of days, "In the beginning God created Heaven and earth." For immediately it adds what earth it spoke of. And when it also states that on the second day a firmament was made and was called Heaven, it conveys what that Heaven was that before had been spoken of, without specifying a day.

CHAPTER 14 — The Depth of Holy Scripture

THE depth of Your words is marvelous. Behold, their surface is before us, delighting Your little children. Yet marvelous is their depth, O my God, marvelous is their depth. It is awesome to gaze upon that depth, but an awe dependent upon honor, an awe dependent upon love. I hate its enemies vehemently.

Oh that You would *slay them with a two-edged sword* (Ps 149:6), so that they would no longer be its enemies! For, thus do I love them, that they may die to themselves so that they may live for You. Yet, behold, there are others too who do not condemn but who praise the Book of Genesis: "The Spirit of God, Who wrote these words through His servant Moses, did not wish to have these words understood in this manner. He did not want them to be interpreted as you wish but rather as we say." To these I answer as follows, with You, O God of us all, as our judge.

CHAPTER 15 — Created and Uncreated Wisdom

WILL you say that those things are false that Truth with a loud voice has spoken to my interior ear concerning the true eternity of the Creator, namely, that His substance does not change in time, and that His will is in no way separate from His substance? Consequently, He does not will now one thing, now another, but that which He wills, He wills once and forever. He does not will again and then again, now in these things, now those. Nor does He will now what He would not will before, nor does He forebear to will now what He willed before. Such a will as this is changeable, and whatsoever is changeable is not eternal. But *our God is eternal* (Ps 48:15).

Again, Truth also speaks to my interior ear that the expectation of future things becomes insight once those things have come to pass, and that the same insight becomes memory when they have passed. Now every thought that thus varies is changeable, and nothing that is changeable is eternal. I gather up these things and put them together, and I find that my God, being an eternal God, did not establish His creation by any such new will, nor is His knowledge in any way subject to change.

What then will you say, you who object? Are these things false? "No," they say. What then? Is it false to say that every nature that is formed, and all matter that is capable of form, can have no being but from Him who is supremely good, because He supremely is? "Neither do we deny this," they say.

What then? Do you perhaps deny that there is a certain sublime creature who so chastely adheres to the true and truly eternal God that, although it is not coeternal with Him, it never loosens itself or falls away from Him because of any variety or change of time, but reposes in the most true contemplation of Him alone?

You, O God, show Yourself to him who loves You as much as You command, and it is enough for him. Therefore, he neither moves away from You nor toward himself. This is the house of God, of no corporeal bulk either earthly or celestial, but a spiritual house, a sharer in Your eternity, because it remains eternally without sin. *For You have established it forever and for ages of ages. You have made a decree, and it shall not pass away* (Ps 148:6). Yet it is not co-eternal with You, O God, because it is not without a beginning, since it was made.

Although we find no time before it, since *wisdom has been created before all things* (Sir 1:4), surely it is not that Wisdom that is absolutely equal and co-eternal with You, our God, His Father, by Whom all things were created, and in Whom, as the Beginning, You did create Heaven and earth. But I mean rather that created wisdom, the intellectual nature that, by contemplating the Light, is still light. For even this, though created, is also called wisdom.

There is as much difference between the Light that illuminates and the light that is illuminated as there is between the Wisdom that creates and the wisdom that is created, or again between the Righteousness that justifies and the righteousness that results from justification. For we have been called Your righteousness, as Your servant says, *that we might become the justice of God in Him* (2 Cor 5:21).

Therefore, a certain created wisdom was made before all things, the rational and intellectual mind of Your chaste city, *our mother, which is above and is free* (Gal 4:26) and *eternal in the heavens* (2 Cor 5:1). In what heavens, unless in those that praise You, the *Heaven of heavens?* For this also is that *Heaven of heavens, which is the Lord's* (Ps 115:16). And if we do not find time in it, since that which was created before all things precedes also the creation of time, yet the eternity of the Creator Himself lies before it. For, having been created by Him, it took its beginning from Him, although not in time, since time did not yet exist, but in its very creation.

It proceeds from You, our God, in such a way as to be wholly different from You, and not the Selfsame. Yet we not only find no time before it but not even in it, since it is proper to *look always upon Your face* (Mt 18:10), nor does it ever turn away. Therefore, it is not altered by any change. Yet of itself it has a capacity for change, raising the possibility that it might grow dark and cold, unless with so strong an affection it cleaves to You, so that like a perpetual moon it shines and glows from You.

O house, full of light and beauty, *I have loved your beauty, and the dwelling place of the glory of my Lord* (Ps 26:8), your Builder and Owner. Let my pilgrimage sigh after you. To Him Who made you I pray that He may possess me also in you, because He also has made me. *I have gone astray like a sheep that is lost* (Ps 119:176); yet upon the shoulders of my Shepherd your Builder, I hope one day to be brought back to You (cf. Lk 15:5).

What do you have to say to me, you to whom I speak as my opponents, you who believe that Moses was a holy servant of God, and that his books are the oracles of the Holy Spirit? Is not this the house of God, though not indeed coeternal with Him, yet after a fashion *eternal in the Heavens* (2 Cor 5:1), where in vain you seek the changes of time, because you will never find them there? It passes beyond all extension of space and all periods of time, for *its good is to adhere to God forever* (Ps 73:28). "It is so," they say.

What then is there of all that which *my heart has cried out to my God* (Ps 18:7), when it did inwardly *hear the voice of His praise* (Ps 26:8)? What is there that you charge to be false? Is it this, that the matter was formless, in which there was no order because there was no form? But where there is no order, there can be no change of time. And yet this "almost nothing," since it was not altogether nothing, must have been from Him, from Whom is whatever is, in whatever degree. "This too," they say, "we do not deny."

CHAPTER 16 — God the Arbiter

I DESIRE to confer a while in Your presence, O my God, with those who concede all these things to be true, which Your Truth affirms within me. As for those others, who deny what Your Truth affirms, let them bark and mutter to themselves as much as they will; I will try to persuade them to be quiet so that they may allow Your Word to enter into their hearts.

Should they be unwilling and reject me, I beseech You, O my God, *do not be silent to me* (Ps 28:1). Speak truly to my heart, for only You so speak. I will send them outside, blowing upon the dust and filling their eyes with dirt.

I myself will enter into my chamber, and there I will sing love songs to You, mourning with unutterable groanings on my pilgrimage, remembering Jerusalem, with my heart raised up toward it—Jerusalem, my country, Jerusalem, my mother, and You Yourself Who are its Ruler, the Light, Father, Teacher, Spouse, the pure and strong Delight, the lasting Joy, and all good things unspeakable, all of them together, because You alone are the One Supreme and true Good.

Nor will I turn away until You shall gather me up from this present state of distraction and disorder into the peace of that most dear Mother, where already are the *firstfruits of my spirit* (Rom 8:23) from which I am assured of the truth of these things, and until You shall conform me and confirm me in it for eternity, O my God, and my Mercy.

As for those who do not affirm as false those things that are true, and who honor Your Holy Scripture, which was delivered by holy Moses, placing it, as we do, at the pinnacle of authority that must be followed—to these, although they contradict me in some things, I answer: O our God, be the Judge between my confessions and their contradictions.

CHAPTER 17 — The Meaning of Heaven and Earth

FOR they say, "Although these things may be true, yet Moses did not mean those two when, by the revelation of the Spirit, he said, *In the Beginning God made Heaven and earth* (Gn 1:1). By the word *Heaven* he did not signify the spiritual and intellectual creature that ever contemplates the face of God, nor by the word *earth* did he mean formless matter." What then? "That man of God," they say, "both meant and in words declared what we affirm." But what is that?

They answer, "By the words *Heaven and earth,* He first signified the whole visible world universally and briefly so that by an enumeration of days He might express in detail those things that it pleased the Holy Spirit to express in such general terms.

For the people to whom he spoke were rude and carnal, so much so that he deemed it fit to mention to them only such works of God as were visible."

However, they agree that the invisible and formless earth and the dark abyss out of which, as is shown subsequently, all visible things that are known to us were all made and set in their order in those days, things that are known to all men, may not unfittingly be understood to be formless matter.

What now if another should say that this same formlessness and confused matter was meant at first by the words *Heaven* and *earth,* because out of it this visible world, with all those natures that so clearly appear therein and are often called by the words *Heaven* and *earth,* was made up and perfected? Or again, another may say that the invisible and visible natures were not improperly called *Heaven* and *earth,* and, consequently, that the whole of creation, which God by His Wisdom made in the Beginning, is comprehended by those two words.

However, all things are made out of nothing and not out of the substance of God—because they are not the same thing that God is, and in them all there is a mutability, whether they remain as the eternal house of God, or are changed, as the body and soul of man. Therefore, this common matter of all visible and invisible things, though as yet unformed but capable of receiving a form, out of which Heaven and earth were to be made, that is, both the invisible and the visible when they would be formed, was signified by those words, whereby derive the expressions "the earth invisible and without order" and "the darkness upon the face of the deep."

However, it was with this distinction, that "the earth invisible and without order" applies to corporeal matter before the quality of form was introduced, and "the darkness upon the face of the deep" applies to spiritual matter, before it underwent any restraint of its boundless flow, and before it was enlightened by Wisdom.

There is yet more for someone to say, if he wishes, namely, that when we read *In the Beginning God made Heaven and earth,* the words *Heaven* and *earth* do not signify those visible and invisible natures, already perfected and formed. Rather they signify a still unformed beginning of things, the matter capable of being formed and treated because in it were contained, in a confused manner not yet distinguished by forms and qualities, two things that now are arranged in order and called *Heaven* and *earth,* the one a spiritual and the other a corporeal creation.

CHAPTER 18 — No Falsity in Scripture

HAVING heard and weighed all these things, *I do not want to dispute, for that is useless, leading to the ruin of the listeners* (2 Tm 2:14). *But the Law is good to edify, if a man use it lawfully, for its purpose is charity, from a pure heart and a good conscience and unfeigned faith* (1 Tm 1:8, 5). And our Master well knew upon which *two commandments* He made *the whole Law and the Prophets depend* (Mt 22:40).

And what harm is it to me, O my God, *the Light of my inward eyes* (Ps 38:11) in secret, when I confess these things zealously to You, should different meanings be found out of these very words, all of which are yet true? What harm is it to me, I say, if I think that the writer meant otherwise than someone else thinks that he meant? Doubtless all of us who read strive to comprehend what was meant by the writer, and if we believe that he speaks the truth, we dare not believe him to have said anything that we either know or think to be false.

Therefore, since everyone tries to understand the Sacred Scriptures in the same sense that the writer intended, what harm is there if a man understands it as You, the Light of all true speaking minds, show him to be true, even if the author whom he reads did not understand this, seeing that he also understood a truth therein, but not this truth?

CHAPTER 19 — Many Things About Which All Agree

IT IS true, O Lord, that You have made Heaven and earth, and it is true that the *Beginning* is Your *Wisdom, in which You did create all things* (Ps 104:24). It is also true that this visible world is made up of two great parts, Heaven and earth, which in brief comprises all formed and created natures. It is true that every changeable thing brings to our attention a certain formlessness by which it receives a form and by which it is changed or transformed. It is true that a thing is not subject to time, which so adheres to the unchangeable Form that it is never changed, even though it is changeable in itself.

It is true that formlessness, which is almost nothing, cannot be subject to a succession of times. It is true that that which a thing is made of may, by an improper use of words, be called by the name of the thing made from it, so that the formlessness of which Heaven and earth were made might be called Heaven and earth. It is true that among all things which have form, there is nothing nearer to having no form than earth and the abyss. It is true that not only every created and formed thing but all that can be created and given form was created by You, *from Whom are all things* (1 Cor 8:6). It is true that whatever is formed out of that which is formless was formless before it was formed.

CHAPTER 20 — A Manner of Interpretation

OUT of all these truths, which are not doubted by those whose internal eye You have enabled to see all these things, and who believe steadfastly that Your servant Moses spoke in the Spirit of Truth—out of all these things one meaning is taken by a man who says, *"In the Beginning God made Heaven and earth,* that is, in His Word, coeternal with Himself, God made intelligible and sensible, or spiritual and corporeal, creation."

Another is taken by one who says, *"In the Beginning God made Heaven and earth,* that is, in His Word, coeternal with Himself, God made the whole mass of this corporeal world together with all those creatures, both seen and known, that are contained therein."* Another is taken by one who says, *"In the Beginning God made Heaven and earth,* that is, in His Word, coeternal with Himself, God made the formless matter of spiritual and corporeal creation."

He takes yet another meaning who says, *"In the Beginning God made Heaven and earth,* that is, in His Word, coeternal with Himself, God made the formless matter of corporeal creation in which Heaven and earth lay as yet confused, which we now see distinct and formed in the mass of this world." Lastly, he takes still another meaning who says, *"In the Beginning God made Heaven and earth,* that is, in the very first beginning of His making and working, God made the formless matter that in a confused manner contained both Heaven and earth in itself, out of which they were formed, and now appear and shine forth visibly, with all that is in them."

CHAPTER 21 — Further Explanations

L IKEWISE, in regard to the meaning of the following words, out of all those truths one meaning is taken by a man who says, *"But the earth was invisible and formless, and darkness was upon the face of the deep,* that is, this corporeal thing made by God was previously the formless matter of corporeal things, without order and without light."

He takes another meaning who says, *"But the earth was invisible and formless, and darkness was upon the face of the deep,* that is, this whole, which we now call Heaven and earth, was then a formless and dark matter, out of which were to be made the corporeal Heaven and the corporeal earth, together with all things contained therein, which are known to our corporeal senses."

He takes another meaning who says, *"But the earth was invisible and formless, and darkness was upon the face of the deep,* that is, this whole, which we now call Heaven and earth, was then but a formless and dark matter, out of which were to be made both the intelligible Heaven, elsewhere called the Heaven of heavens, and the earth, that is to say, the whole corporeal nature, under which name may be understood also this corporeal Heaven, namely, from which would be made all invisible and visible creation."

He takes another meaning who says, *"But the earth was invisible and formless, and darkness was upon the face of the deep,* that is, Scripture did not call that formlessness by the name of Heaven and earth, but that formlessness was already in being, which Moses called *the earth invisible and without order* and *the darkness upon the face of the deep,* of which he had said before that God had made Heaven and earth, that is, the spiritual and corporeal creation."

He takes another meaning who says, *"But the earth was invisible and formless, and darkness was upon the face of the deep,* that is, there was already a kind of formless matter of which Scripture says that God made Heaven and earth, namely, the whole corporeal mass of the world divided into those two great parts, the upper and the lower, with all the common and known creatures that are in them."

CHAPTER 22 — False Opinions About Creation

SOMEONE might try to object to these two last opinions thus: "If you will not grant that this formless matter is signified by the names of Heaven and earth, it must follow that there was something not made by God, out of which He made Heaven and earth. For Scripture has not told us that God made this matter, unless we should understand it as signified either by the name of *Heaven and earth,* or by that of *earth* alone, when it was said, *In the Beginning God made Heaven and earth.*

Therefore, in the words that follow: *But the earth was invisible and formless*—although He was pleased so to describe formless matter—we may understand no other matter but that which God made, as written above, *God made Heaven and earth.*"

The champions of these two opinions that we have put last, whether of one or of the other, either of them, when they hear these things, will answer and say: "We do not deny that this formless matter was made by God, from Whom come all things that are very good. For, as we affirm that what is created and formed is a greater good, so do we confess that what is made capable of creation and form is a lesser good, but even that is still good.

"We say, however, that Scripture has not said that God made this formless matter, just as it has not mentioned many other things, such as the Cherubim and Seraphim, and those others concerning which the Apostle distinctly speaks: *Thrones, Dominations, Principalities, and Powers* (Col 1:16), all of which it is clear that God made.

"Or if in the words *God made Heaven and earth* all things are included, what shall we say of the waters *upon which the Spirit of God moved* (Gn 1:2)? For if all things are understood as included in this word *earth,* how then can we call this formless matter by the name of earth, when we see that the waters are so beautiful? Or, if it be so taken, why then is it written that, out of that same formlessness, the firmament was made and was called *Heaven,* when yet it is not written that the waters were created? For those waters are still not formless and invisible that we see flowing in such a graceful manner.

"But if they then received their beauty when God said, *Let the waters that are under the firmament be gathered together into one place* (Gn 1:9), so that their gathering together should be their very formation, what shall be said of those waters that are above the firmament? For neither would things that are formless be worthy of so honorable a place, nor is it written by what word they were formed.

"Thus, if Genesis is silent as to anything that God has made—which neither a sound faith nor a well-grounded intellect will doubt that He did make—no sound knowledge will presume to affirm that those waters are coeternal with God, because while we find them mentioned in the Book of Genesis, we do not indeed find where or when they were made.

"Why, as Truth instructs us, should we not as well hold that formless matter—which Scripture calls *the earth invisible and without order and the darkness upon the face of the deep*—was created by God out of nothing, and, therefore, is not coeternal with Him, although in that narration it is not mentioned where it was made?"

CHAPTER 23 — The Interpretation of Holy Scripture

HAVING heard and considered these things according to weak abilities that I confess to You, O God, Who know it, I see that two kinds of disagreement may arise when anything is related in words by truthful narrators. One deals with the truth of the things themselves; the other concerns the intention of the person who speaks. For in one way we inquire about what is true concerning the process of creation, and, in the other way, what it is that Moses, that excellent revealer of Your faith, wished to make his hearer or his reader understand.

With regard to the first kind of objection, let all those depart from me who think they know as true what is indeed false. As for the other, let all those also depart from me who think that Moses spoke things that are false. Rather, in You, O Lord, let me be associated and rejoice with those who are nourished by Your Truth, in the breadth of charity. Let us approach together the words of Your Book, and seek therein for Your Will, through the will of Your servant, by whose pen You have given them to us.

CHAPTER 24 — The Full Meaning and Moses

BUT who among us shall be able to find out this true meaning, among so many truths that occur to those who look for it in words that are understood in different ways, so that we may confidently affirm that Moses thought this, and wishes that to be understood in that narration, with the same confidence that he can say that this meaning is true, or whether Moses thought this or something different? For behold, O my God, *I, Your servant* (Ps 116:16), in this book have vowed to offer to You the sacrifice of my confession, and pray that, by Your mercy, I may *fulfill my vows to You* (Ps 22:26).

Behold how confidently I affirm that, in the immutable Word, You did make all visible and invisible things. But can I with equal confidence affirm that Moses meant nothing else but this when he wrote, *In the Beginning God made Heaven and earth*? I do not clearly see whether this was in his mind when he wrote it, though in Your Truth I see this to be certain. For when he said, *In the Beginning*, he might have meant the very beginning of creation, and by *Heaven and earth* in this place he might not have intended any formed and perfected nature

whether spiritual or corporeal, but both of them
formless and not as yet formed.

I see that, whichever of the two had been said, it
might have been said truly. But which of the two he
had in mind when he said these words, I do not
clearly see. Whether either of these two meanings,
or any other truth that I have not yet mentioned,
was intended by that great man when he expressed
these words, I have not the slightest doubt that he
saw the true meaning and expressed it appropri-
ately.

CHAPTER 25 — The Law of Charity in Interpreting Scripture

LET no man, therefore, irritate me now by saying, "Moses did not mean what you say, but he
meant what I say." But if he should say to me,
"How do you know that Moses meant that, which
you deduct from his words?" I would take it calmly
and answer him perhaps as I have done before, or
somewhat more at length, if he proved to be stub-
born.

But when he says, "Moses did not mean what
you say, but what I say," yet does not deny that
what each of us says is true, then, O my God, O
Life of the poor, in whose bosom there is no contra-
diction, rain down Your consolations into my heart
so that I may patiently endure such talk.

They do not say such things to me because they
are men of God and have seen these things in the
heart of Your servant, but because they are proud.
They do not know the meaning of Moses but love
their own, and this, not because it is true, but because it is their own. Otherwise they would love the

truth as much as I love what they say when it is the truth, not because it is their opinion, but because it is true. Therefore, since it is true, it is not really theirs. However, if they love it because it is true, it becomes theirs and mine, as common to all lovers of Truth.

However, to contend that Moses did not mean what I say, but what they say, this I neither like nor love, because even if it should be so, yet it is the rashness not of knowledge but of boldness; it is born not of vision but of pride. Therefore, Your judgments, O Lord, are to be dreaded, because Your truth is neither mine, nor his, nor any man's, but it belongs to all of us, whom You call publicly to share in it, warning us in a dire manner not to regard it as our private property, lest we be deprived of it.

For whoever claims as his own what You appointed for the enjoyment of all, and would have only as his own what belongs to all, is driven forth from what is common to all to what is indeed his own, that is, from the truth to a lie. For he *who speaks a lie speaks it of his own* (Jn 8:44).

Hearken, O most excellent Judge, O God, Truth itself, hearken to what I am about to say to this objector, hearken. For I speak before You and before my brethren, who make *right use of Your Law with the motive of charity* (1 Tm 1:8). Hearken and mark what I say to him, if it be pleasing to You to do so.

For these are the brotherly and peaceful words I will say to him: "Suppose that both of us see that what you say is true, and both of us see that what I say is true, where, tell me, do we see it? Neither do I see it in you nor you in me, but both of us see it in unchangeable Truth itself, which is above both our minds.

"Therefore, seeing that we do not contend about the very light of the Lord our God, why do we contend about the very thoughts of our neighbor, into which we cannot see as clearly as we can into the unchangeable Truth? For if Moses himself had appeared to us and said, 'I meant this,' even then we would not see it, but we would believe it. *Let us then not be puffed up one against another, transgressing what is written* (1 Cor 4:6). Let us love *the Lord our God with our whole heart, with our whole soul, and with our whole mind, and our neighbor as ourselves* (Mt 22:37, 39). For unless we believe that, in accordance with these two precepts of charity, Moses meant whatever in these books he did mean, we make God a liar, judging otherwise of His servant's mind than He has taught us.

"Therefore, now see how foolish this is, in such an abundance of true meanings that can be drawn out of these words, to affirm rashly which of the two Moses particularly intended, and thereby, with pernicious strife, to offend that very charity, by reason of which He spoke, whose words we try to explain."

CHAPTER 26 — The Style of Holy Scripture

AND yet, O my God, the Exaltation of my humility and the Rest from my labors, You Who hear my confessions and *forgive my sins* (Mt 6:15), since You command me *to love my neighbor as myself* (Mt 22:39), I cannot believe that You gave to Moses, Your most faithful servant, a lesser gift than I myself should have desired and wished to receive from You if I had been born at the same time as he, and if You had established me in the same position, so that those books might be distributed through the service of my heart and tongue, which for so long afterward were to profit all people, and from so great a height of authority were to surmount all false and proud opinions throughout the entire world.

Indeed, had I been Moses, I should have wished—for all of us are from the same dust, and *what is man that You are mindful of him?* (Ps 8:5)—I should have wished, had I been what he was, and had I been enjoined by You to write the Book of Genesis, for such a gift of eloquence and stylistic ability to be given to me that even those who cannot as yet understand in what manner God creates would not reject my words as being too hard for them to understand.

In the same way, I should have wished that those who are already able to do this might not find passed over in those few words of Your servant whatever true opinion they had arrived at by their own thinking, and that if any other man should have discovered some further meaning by the light of truth it should not fail to be found in those same words.

CHAPTER 27 —The Understanding of Holy Scripture

THE situation is similar to that of a fountain that in a limited space is more plentiful and supplies a tide for many streams over larger spaces than any one of those single streams that, after traversing a long distance, is derived therefrom and flows through many regions. In the same way, the narration of the messenger of Your words, which was to be of service to many future commentators, delivers the clear streams of truth in concise language. From there every man may draw for himself such truth as he can—some one truth, some another—by further discourse in greater depth.

When they read or hear these words, some people think that God—like a man or even some huge bulk of immense power—did, by some new and sudden decision, *create Heaven and earth* outside Himself and somewhat at a distance from Himself, as two great bodies above and below, wherein all things were to be contained. And when they hear, *God said, Let it be made, and it was made,* they think that these words had a beginning and an end, words that sound in time and then pass away. After this they believe that there came into being that which was commanded to do so, and any other similar thoughts that their human intelligence causes them to imagine.

Being like infants, while their weakness is carried in this humble manner of speech as in their mother's bosom, their faith is wholesomely built up, whereby they believe and are certain that God made all those natures that their senses everywhere discern in such admirable variety. But if anyone, despising these words as if they were trivial, shall with a foolish pride thrust himself out of the cradle wherein he was nursed, he will, alas, have a miserable fall.

O Lord, have mercy, lest those who pass up and down on the way should trample upon that fledgling bird. *Send Your Angel* (2 Mc 15:23) to lodge it in the nest again, that it may live until it can fly.

CHAPTER 28 — More Opinions About
Understanding the Scriptures

BUT others, to whom these words are no longer a nest but a grove of trees, see the fruits lying hidden in the leaves, and they flutter about with joy, and with merry chirping they pluck them. For they see, when they read or hear these words, O God, that all past and future times are surpassed by Your eternal and changeless abiding, and yet that there is no temporal creature that You did not make. Your Will, because it is one with Yourself, is by no means changed, or other than it was before, yet You have made all things through it.

Nor did You form them out of Yourself, in Your own likeness, which is the form of all things, but out of nothing, in a form utterly unlike Yourself, which might afterward be formed in Your likeness, each having recourse to You, the One, according to the capacity appointed to it, so far as is given to each thing, according to its kind.

All of them were made very good, whether they remained near You, or, being removed from You according to their degrees to further distances in time or place, they were to make or to suffer beautiful variations. These things they see, and they rejoice in the light of Your Truth, to the small degree they may here do so.

Another of them, turning his attention to that which is said, *"In the Beginning God made Heaven and earth,"* thinks that *Beginning* means Wisdom, *because it also speaks to us.*

Another man marks those same words, and by *Beginning* he understands the commencement of things created, thus taking *In the Beginning He made* as if it meant, *He at first made.*

And among those who understand *In the Beginning* to mean, *In Your Wisdom You did make Heaven and earth,* one thinks that the matter out of which Heaven and earth were to be created is called *Heaven* and *earth;* another, that they were already distinct and formed natures; another, that *Heaven* means a formed and spiritual nature, and *earth* means a formless and corporeal matter.

They again who understand *Heaven and earth* to be matter as yet unformed, out of which Heaven and earth were to be formed, do not yet agree as to one meaning only. But one holds that it is the matter out of which both intelligent and sensible creation were to be produced; another holds that it was only the matter out of which this corporeal mass was to be produced, containing in its vast bosom all those natures which are visible and prepared.

Neither do they agree who believe that the creatures already ordered are in this place called *Heaven and earth;* one thinks that both the invisible and the visible are comprehended, while the other thinks that it is the visible only, in which we admire the luminous Heaven and earth covered in darkness and all those things contained therein.

CHAPTER 29 — The Different Ways in Which One Thing May Be Said To Be Before Another

BUT he who thinks that *In the Beginning He made* means *He at first made* can only understand by *Heaven and earth* the matter of *Heaven and earth,* namely, of universal creation, that is, the whole intelligible and corporeal creation. For if he wishes to interpret by this that the entire universe was already formed, he might justly be asked this question: "If God made this first, what did He make afterward?" And since after the whole universe he will find nothing, therefore he will be asked another question to which he must reluctantly reply: "How could it be first if there is nothing afterward?"

However, if he asserts that at first it was formless and then was formed, his stance can be defended if he is able to discern the distinction between priority in eternity, in time, in choice, and in origin: priority in eternity, as God precedes all things; in time, as the flower precedes the fruit; in choice, as the fruit precedes the flower; in origin, as the sound precedes the song.

Of these four, the first and last that I have mentioned are understood with extreme difficulty, but the middle two with great facility. For it is an unusual and sublime concept, O Lord, to behold Your immutable eternity creating changeable things, and these must therefore be before them. Moreover, who is so acute in intelligence as to be able to discern without great concentration how sound may precede a song? The solution is that a song is a formed sound, and although a thing not formed may exist, that which does not exist cannot be formed?

Thus, matter is prior to the thing that is made of it, not because it makes it, for it is itself made, nor is it prior to it by any interval of time. For we do not first utter formless sounds without singing, and then later adapt or shape them into a song, as we shape wood into a chest, or silver into a cup. Such materials, even in time, precede the forms of the things that are made of them, but in singing this is not so.

When one sings, the sound of the song is heard; there is not first a formless sound that afterward is shaped into a song. For as soon as each sound is heard, it passes away, nor can you find anything of it that you may collect and compose into a song.

Therefore, the song has its being in its sound, and this sound is its matter. Accordingly, the sound is formed that it may be a song. Hence, as I said, the matter of the sound is prior to the form of the song.

It is not prior through any power that it has to make a song, nor is the sound in any way the singer who sings, but it is furnished out of the body for the singer's mind to make a song of it. Nor is it prior in respect to time, for it is uttered together with the singing. Nor is it prior by choice, for a sound is not better than a song, since a song is not only a sound, but a beautiful sound. However, it is prior in point of origin, because the song is not formed to cause it to become sound, but the sound receives form to become a song.

By this example, let him who is able to do so understand how the matter of things was first made and called *Heaven and earth*, because Heaven and earth were made out of it. Yet, it was not made first in time, because the form of things is what gives rise to time. That matter was formless, though now it is in time an object to be perceived together with its form. Nor can anything be said of that matter, except that it is prior in time.

In value it is to be ranked lower, because things that are formed are superior to things that are formless. It is preceded by the eternity of the Creator, so that out of nothing might be made something.

CHAPTER 30 — The Virtue of Charity in All Controversies

IN THIS diversity of true opinions, let Truth itself beget harmony, and *may our God have mercy on us* (Ps 67:1), so that we may *use the Law legitimately* (1 Tm 1:8), in accordance with pure charity, which is the end of the Commandment.

In accord with this pure charity, should anyone ask me which of all these interpretations Moses, Your servant, intended, my reply would not be suitable for my confessions if I should not confess to You that I do not know.

Yet I do know that all these interpretations are true, excepting only those carnal ones, of which I have already said as much as seemed necessary.

However, the words of Your Book, expressing lofty and abundant concepts in humility and brevity, do not terrify Your little ones who have fervent hope. Let all of us whom I believe to both see and speak the truth in those words *love one another* (1 Jn 4:11), and together let us love You, our God, the Fountain of truth, if we thirst for truth and not for vanity.

In this way let us honor Moses, Your servant, the dispenser of Your Scripture who was filled with Your Spirit, that when by Your revelation he wrote these things, we may believe him to have intended whatever excels in them both in the light of truth and in their fruitfulness for our profit.

CHAPTER 31 — Many True Meanings

THEREFORE, when one shall say, "Moses meant what I say," and another, "No, he meant what I say," I think that I speak with greater piety when I suggest: "Why not rather as you both say, if both are true?" And if there be a third, a fourth, or any other truth that someone may discern in these words, why may we not believe that Moses intended them all?

For through his ministry the one God has adapted Holy Scripture to the minds of many, and those were to discover in it true but different meanings. Certainly—and I declare this fearlessly from my heart—if I were to write anything that should have supreme authority, I would rather write in a manner that my words might express in them any truth whatsoever that each person could gather from them in these matters, rather than to express one meaning only in so clear a fashion as to exclude the rest, which not being false could not harm me.

Therefore, I will not be so rash, O my God, as to believe that Moses did not deserve this much from You. When he wrote these words he perceived and meant whatsoever we could find true in them, and whatsoever else we could not find in them, or have not yet been able to find, although it still can be found in them.

CHAPTER 32 — God, Guide to the Truth

FINALLY, O Lord, You Who are God and not flesh and blood, even if a man should not see all that is there, could any part of that be concealed from *Your good Spirit, Who shall lead me into the right land* (Ps 143:10), which You Yourself by these words were to reveal to the future readers, even though he by whom they were spoken might perhaps have perceived but one out of many true meanings?

Granted that this is so, let the meaning that he saw be more excellent than the rest, but, O Lord, either reveal that meaning to us, or any other true meaning that may be pleasing to You. In this way whether You reveal to us the same meaning as You showed to Your servant or any other by using the same words, it will still be You Yourself Who feed us, and not error deceiving us.

Behold, O Lord my God, I beseech You, how much we have written on these few words, how much! What strength of ours and what amount of time would be required to deal with all Your books in this fashion? Let me therefore confess to You in a briefer manner and select out one true meaning, certain and good, with which You shall inspire me, although many meanings occur to me where so many are possible.

Let my confessions be guided by this rule, that if I should say what Your servant meant, that will be not only good but best, for that is the thing for which I must strive. However, if I cannot attain this goal, then let me say what Your Truth willed to tell me by his words, that Truth which also revealed to him what it willed.

Book 13—Total Dependence on God

St. Augustine concludes that all things depend upon God. This book treats of the Blessed Trinity, the virtues of faith, hope, and charity, grace, the Gospel, spirituality, the fruits of the earth, the Sabbath, and eternity.

CHAPTER 1 — God's Independence of Us

I CALL upon You, *O my God and my Mercy* (Ps 59:18), Who created me and did not forget me, though I had forgotten You. I call You into my soul, which You prepared for Your own reception by inspiring me with this desire.

Do not forsake me now when I call upon You. Previously, when I called upon You, You anticipated my prayer and often in many different ways You encouraged me so that I would hear You from afar and be converted to You, calling upon You Who kept calling to me.

For You, O Lord, destroyed all my evil dealings, lest otherwise You should have been obliged to punish me for the works of my hands whereby I fell away from You, and You anticipated all my good deeds so that You might make a recompense to Your own hands whereby You did make me.

For before I was, You were, nor was I anything to which You might bestow existence. Yet now, behold, I am, because of Your goodness, which anticipated all this by which You have made me to be, and also all that out of which I was made. For neither had You any need of me, nor am I so good that I might thereby help You, O Lord, my God. I do not serve You in any manner, as if to save You from weariness in Your labor, or as if Your power would be less unless I assisted You.

Nor do I so cultivate You as a man does his land, as if You could not yield any fruit unless I tilled You. But I serve You and worship You, so that all may be well with me in Your regard, for from You it comes to pass that I have a being capable of achieving happiness.

CHAPTER 2 — God, Source of All Things

FOR Your creature subsists out of the fullness of Your goodness, so that a good that in no way benefits You, and is not of You in such a manner as to be equal to You, might yet not be found wanting, since it could be made by You. For what could that *Heaven and earth,* which You made *in the Beginning,* merit of You?

Let those spiritual and corporeal natures that You made in Your Wisdom say what they deserved of You, so that everything that was inchoate and formless might in its own kind depend upon Your Wisdom, whether it was spiritual or corporeal, ready to fall away into an immoderate excess and an extreme unlikeness to You—the spiritual, though formless, superior to the corporeal, though formed, and the corporeal, though formless, more excellent than if it were wholly nothing—and thus, being formless, might so depend upon Your Word, unless by the same Word they were brought back to Your Unity, and so were formed and made to be very good by You the one sovereign Good. How could they deserve of You to be even formless, inasmuch as they would not have even existed, except for You?

What did that corporeal matter deserve of You that it should be made *invisible and without form,* seeing that it would not have existed even thus if not for You? Therefore, seeing that it did not exist, it could not deserve to be made.

Or what could that inchoate spiritual creation deserve of You, being completely dark like an abyss, but totally unlike You, unless it had been converted to that same Word by which it was made, and been enlightened by You and had become light—although not in any way equal to the form equal to You, yet in conformity to the form that is Your equal?

In a body, to exist is not the same thing as to be beautiful; otherwise it could not exist devoid of beauty. By the same token, for a created spirit, to live is not the same thing as to live wisely; otherwise it would be unchangeably wise. But *it is good for it always to adhere to You* (Ps 73:28), lest by turning from You it lose that light which it gets by turning to You, and so might fall back again into a life similar to that dark abyss.

For we also, who as far as the soul is concerned are a spiritual creation, having turned away from You our Light, were once darkness in that life, and we still labor in the relics of our old obscurity, until we are made *Your justice, similar to the mountains of God* in Your Only-begotten Son. For we have been *Your judgments that are like a great deep* (Ps 36:7).

CHAPTER 3 — God, Source of Happiness

BUT what You did say at the beginning of creation, *Let there be light, and there was light* (Gn 1:3), I understand as properly applicable to a spiritual creature, because there was already a kind of life capable of being illumined by You. But as it was in no way deserving to be enlightened, so neither, when it existed, did it deserve of You to be enlightened. Its formlessness would not have pleased You unless it could become light, and it became light not merely by existing, but by turning toward that illuminating light and adhering to it.

Therefore, whatsoever lives at all, and whatsoever lives happily, can be attributed solely to Your grace. By a change for the better, it has been converted into that which can never be changed either for better or for worse.

You alone have Being, because You alone simply are. For with You, to live and to live happily are to live in blessedness, because You are Your own Blessedness.

CHAPTER 4 — The Need of Creatures for God

WHAT, therefore, could have been wanting to Your goodness that You Yourself are, although all these things had either never existed or had remained formless? You did not make these things out of any need, but out of the fullness of Your goodness, restraining them and forming them, although Your joy was not increased thereby.

You are perfect and their imperfection is displeasing to You. Therefore, they were perfected by You and thereby became pleasing to You, but not as if You were imperfect and needed to be perfected by their perfection.

Your good Spirit indeed *moved over the waters* (Gn 1:2), but was not borne up by them as if resting upon them. For those on whom Your good Spirit is said to rest, He makes them to rest in Himself. But Your incorruptible and unchangeable Will,

itself all-sufficient in itself, *was borne over* the life
that You had made.

In regard to that life, to live and to live happily
are not one and the same, for that also may be said
to live which flows in its own darkness. Yet it is possible for this life to be turned toward Him by
Whom it was made, and to live more and more by
the Fountain of life, and in His light, and to be perfected, enlightened, and made happy.

CHAPTER 5 — The Blessed Trinity

BEHOLD, the Trinity appears to me as an
enigma, which You are, O my God, because
You, O Father, in the Beginning of our Wisdom,
which is Your Wisdom, born of You, equal to and
coeternal with You, that is, Your Son, *did create
Heaven and earth.*

We have said much already of the Heaven of
heavens, of the invisible and formless earth, and of
the darksome abyss, according to the unstable de-
fects of its spiritual formlessness, unless it had been
turned toward Him, from Whom comes such life as
it already had, and by Whose illumination it became a beautiful life and the Heaven of heavens
that afterward was set between water and water.

By the name of God Who made all these things,
I now recognized the Father, and by the name of
Beginning I recognized the Son, in Whom He
made these things. And believing, as I did believe,
that my God was the Trinity, I searched His holy
words, and behold, Your *Spirit moved over the
waters.* Behold the Trinity, my God, the Father, the
Son, and the Holy Spirit, the Creator of all creatures!

CHAPTER 6 — The Spirit Moving Over the Waters

BUT what was the cause, O Light that speaks the Truth? To You do I lift up my heart, lest it teach me vanities. Disperse its darkness, and tell me, I beseech You by charity our mother, tell me why, after naming Heaven, the invisible and form-less earth, and *the darkness upon the deep,* Your Scriptures should then mention Your Spirit?

Was it because Your Spirit had to be shown as being borne over, and because this could not be said unless mention were first made of that over which Your Spirit might be understood to have been borne? For neither was He borne over the Father or the Son, nor could He rightly be said to be borne over, if He were borne above nothing.

First, therefore, that over which He might be borne had to be mentioned, and then He Whom it was not fitting to mention otherwise than to say He was borne above. But why was it unfitting that He not be mentioned otherwise than by saying that He was borne above?

CHAPTER 7 — The Divine Spirit of Love

FROM hence, then, let him who can do so fol-low Your Apostle with his understanding where he asserts that *Your charity is poured forth in our hearts by the Holy Spirit Who has been given to us* (Rom 5:5), and where, *concerning spiritual gifts* (1 Cor 12:1), He teaches and *shows us a more excellent way* (1 Cor 12:31) of charity, and where *he bows his knee to You for us* (Eph 3:14), so that we may *know the supereminent knowledge of the love of Christ* (Eph 3:19). And, therefore, from the beginning was He supereminently *borne over the waters.*

To whom shall I say this? How shall I speak of the weight of sinful desires dragging us downward into the steep abyss, and of the uplifting of charity through Your Spirit Who was borne above the waters? To whom shall I relate this? In what language shall I utter it? For there are places into which we are plunged and from which we emerge. What can be more like them, and yet what is more unlike them? They are affections, they are loves—the uncleanness of our spirit flowing away downward with a love that brings naught but care.

But here too is the sanctity of Your Spirit, raising us upward by a love that is free from care, so that we may have our hearts uplifted to You, where Your Spirit is *borne over the waters,* and may arrive to that supereminent repose, when *our souls shall have passed through the waters that yield no support* (Ps 124:5).

CHAPTER 8 —The Fall of Angels and of Man

THE angels fell, and the soul of man also fell, pointing out the abyss of all spiritual creation in that dark depth if in the Beginning You had not said, *"Let there be light," and there was light* (Gn 1:3), and if every obedient intelligence of Your celestial city had not adhered to You and rested in Your Spirit, which unchangeably moves all things changeable. Otherwise even the *Heaven of heavens* itself would have become an abyss of darkness, but *now it is light in the Lord* (Eph 5:8).

Even in that miserable restlessness of those fallen spirits, after being stripped of the vestments of Your light and discovering their own darkness, You sufficiently show how noble You made the rational crea-

ture. For no other being that is less than You suffices to give it a blessed rest; wherefore it does not
suffice for itself. *For You, O our God, will enlighten
our darkness* (Ps 18:29). From You shall arise our
garment of light, and then *shall our darkness be as
the noonday* (Is 58:10).

Give Yourself to me, O my God! Restore Yourself to me! Behold, I love You, and if it is too little,
let me love You more. I cannot measure out my
love, enabling me to know what is yet lacking in it
to make it enough, so that my life may run to Your
embrace and never turn away until it be hidden *in
the secret place of Your face* (Ps 31:21).

This only I know: that it is never well with me
except when I am with You—not only outside myself but also within myself—and that all abundance
that is not my God is only poverty to me.

CHAPTER 9 — Why the Holy Spirit Alone Moved Over the Water

BUT did not the Father and Son also *move over
the waters*? For if we understand it as of a body
moving in space, then neither was the Holy Spirit
so borne. But if the supereminence of the unchangeable Divinity over all changeable things is
understood, then the Father, the Son, and the Holy
Spirit moved over the waters.

Why, therefore, is this said of Your Spirit only?
Why has a place where He might be, but which is
not a place, been affirmed only of Him, of Whom
alone it was said that *He is Your Gift* (Acts 2:38)?

In Your Gift we rest; there do we find joy in You.
Our rest is our peace. Love raises us up, and Your
good Spirit lifts up our lowliness *from the gates of*

death (Ps 9:14). In Your goodwill is our *peace*. The body tends toward its own place by its own weight. Weight does not tend downward only, but to its own proper place. Fire tends upward, a stone falls downward. They are driven by their own weights and seek their proper places.

When oil is poured under water it rises to the surface; if the water is poured upon oil, it sinks to the bottom. They are driven by their own weights, they seek their proper places. Things that are out of their proper place are restless; once they are placed in due order, they are at rest.

My weight is my love, and wherever I am borne, my love carries me there. By Your Gift we are kindled and lifted up. We burn within and we go forward. *We ascend in our heart* (Ps 84:6) and sing *a gradual psalm* (Ps 120:1). With that fire, that good fire of Yours, we burn within and we go upward toward the peace of Jerusalem; for *I rejoiced in those who said to me, "We will go up to the house of the Lord"* (Ps 122:1). There shall Your goodwill establish us, so that we may desire nothing else but to *remain there forever* (Ps 61:8).

CHAPTER 10 — The Excellence of the Angels

O HAPPY creature that has known no other state, though it would have been different from what it is unless, by Your Gift that moves over every changeable thing, it was lifted up as soon as it was created, with no interval of time intervening, by Your call whereby You said, *Let there be light, and there was light* (Gn 1:3).

However, there is a distinction of time in us, because we were first darkness and then were made light, but of that it was said only what it would have been if it had not been made light. And it was said as if it had been fluctuating and dark at first, so that it might appear that it was made to be otherwise, namely, that by being converted to the Light that never fails, it also might become itself Light.

Let him who can do so understand this; let him who cannot do so ask You. Why should he trouble me about it as if I could *enlighten every man who comes into this world* (Jn 1:9)?

CHAPTER 11 — To Be, To Know, To Will

WHO of us can understand the omnipotent Trinity? Who among us does not speak of it, if indeed it be the Trinity of which he speaks? Rare is the soul that, when speaking about the Trinity, knows what it says. Men debate and quarrel about it, yet no one sees that vision unless he is in peace.

It is my wish that men will reflect within themselves on three things. These three are far different from that one Trinity, but I mention them in the hope that they may consider them, weigh them, and perceive how greatly different they are. The three things of which I speak are: to be, to know, and to will.

Indeed, I am, I know, I will. I am a being who knows and wills. I know that I am and that I will, and I will to be and to know.

Therefore, let him who can do so see how life is inseparable in these three: one life, one mind, one essence, and, finally, how inseparable is the distinction, and yet there is a distinction. Every man stands face to face with himself. Let him look at himself and see, and let him tell me.

However, when he has discovered and said something about these things, he must not think that he has found out that unchangeable Being which is above all these things—that Being which is unchangeable, and knows unchangeably, and wills unchangeably.

As to whether there is a Trinity also because of these three acts, or whether all three acts are in each Person so that all three belong to each Person, or whether both concepts are equally true, so that the Selfsame exists unchangeably in its superabundant unity, in an admirable manner both simple and multiple, with an infinite end in and for itself, whereby it is, and is known to itself, and suffices to itself—who can easily conceive this? Who can in any way express it? Who can rashly pronounce an opinion on it?

CHAPTER 12 — Converted through the Spirit

PROCEED with your confession, O my faith. Say to your Lord God: *Holy, Holy, Holy, O Lord my God* (Is 6:3). *We have been baptized in Your Name* (1 Cor 1:15), O Father, Son, and Holy Spirit, and in Your Name we baptize others, O Father, Son, and Holy Spirit.

For among us also, in His Christ, did *God create Heaven and earth,* the spiritual and carnal members of His Church. And our *earth* also, before it received the form of doctrine, was *invisible and formless,* and we were beclouded by the darkness of ignorance. For You *have corrected man for his iniquity* (Ps 39:12), and *Your judgments are a great deep* (Ps 36:7).

But because Your Spirit moved over the waters, Your mercy did not forsake our misery, and You said, *"Let there be light! (Gn 1:3). Repent, for the Kingdom of Heaven is at hand (Mt 3:2).* Repent! Let there be light!" And because our soul was troubled within us, we *remembered You, O Lord, from the land of Jordan, and out of that mountain* (Ps 42:7), which was equal to You, but which became little for our sakes.

Our darkness displeased us, and we turned to You and there was light. And behold *we were once darkness, but we are now light in the Lord* (Eph 5:8).

CHAPTER 13 — Thirst for God

BUT as yet *we walk by faith and not by sight* (2 Cor 5:7), *for we are saved by hope, but hope that is seen is not hope* (Rom 8:24). As yet *deep calls unto deep,* but now *at the voice of Your floodgates* (Ps 42:8). And yet, even he who said, *I could not speak to You as to spiritual men, but only as carnal* (1 Cor 3:1), even he as yet does not *think himself to have laid hold of it, but forgetting what is behind and reaching forth to what is before* (Phil 3:13), he *groans, being burdened* (2 Cor 5:4), and his soul thirsts *after the living God, as the deer after the fountains of water,* and says: *When shall I come?* (Ps 42:2-3).

Desiring to be clothed with that dwelling of ours which is from Heaven (2 Cor 5:2), he calls upon the lower abyss, saying, *Be not conformed to this world, but be transformed in the renewing of your mind* (Rom 12:2). And *do not become children in mind, but in malice be children, that in understanding you may be perfect* (1 Cor 14:20). And again, *O foolish Galatians, who has bewitched you?* (Gal 3:1).

But now he no longer speaks in his own voice, but in You Who sent Your Spirit *from on high* (Wis

9:17), through Him Who ascended on high, and *opened the floodgates* (Mal 3:10) of His gifts in order that the force of His *streams might gladden the city of God* (Ps 46:5). For the *friend of the bridegroom* (Jn 3:29) sighs for him, *having now the firstfruits of the Spirit* stored up by union with Christ, *yet still groaning within himself, waiting for the adoption, the redemption of his body* (Rom 8:23).

To him he sighs, for he is a member of the Bride; for him is he zealous, for he is the *friend of the Bridegroom;* for him is he zealous, not for himself. For in *the voice of Your floodgates* (Ps 42:8), not in his own voice, he calls upon that other *abyss*, of which, since he is zealous, he fears, *lest as the serpent deceived Eve through his subtlety*, so *their minds should be corrupted from the purity that is in our Bridegroom, Your only Son* (2 Cor 11:3).

Oh what a light of beauty that will be, *when we shall see Him as He is* (1 Jn 3:2), and those tears shall pass away, which have been my bread day and night, while it is said to me daily, *Where is your God?* (Ps 42:4).

CHAPTER 14 — Hope and Perseverance

AND I say, "Where are You, my God?" Behold, here You are! *In You do I breathe a little* (Jb 32:20), when *I pour out my soul upon myself in a voice of joy and praise, the sound of one who is feasting* (Ps 42:5). And yet it is still sad, because it falls back again and becomes an abyss, or rather because it perceives itself still to be so.

My faith, which You have kindled in this night to be a light before my feet, says to it: *"Why are you sad, O my soul, and why do you trouble me? Hope in* the Lord (Ps 42:6); His Word is *a lamp to your feet"* (Ps 119:105). Hope and persevere, until the night that is the mother of the wicked passes, *until the wrath* of the Lord *passes* (Is 26:20)—of which *wrath* we also were once *children* (Eph 2:3), *for we were previously darkness* (Eph 5:8), the remains whereof we still bear *in our body, dead by reason of sin* (Rom 8:10)—*until the day breaks and the shadows retire* (Song 2:17).

Hope in the Lord (Ps 42:6). *In the morning l will stand and see* (Ps 5:4). I will praise You forever. *In the morning l will stand and will see* (Ps 5:4) *the salvation of my countenance, my God* (Ps 42:6), *Who also shall bring to life our mortal bodies, because of that Spirit Who dwells in us* (Rom 8:11), because in mercy He was borne over our dark and fluid inner being.

There we also have received a pledge on this pilgrimage of ours that we are now light, for *we are still saved by hope* (Rom 8:24) and are children of light and children of the day, *not children of the night, nor of darkness* (1 Thes 5:5), which formerly we were.

Between them and us, in this still uncertain state of human knowledge, only You can distinguish, *You Who prove hearts* (1 Thes 2:4) *and call the light "day" and the darkness "night"* (Gn 1:5). For who can truly discern what we are but You? And *what have we that we have not received from You* (1 Cor 4:7), vessels unto honor from that same lump from *which others also have been made unto dishonor* (Rom 9:21)?

CHAPTER 15 — The Eminence of Holy Scripture

WHO but You, our God, made that firmament of authority over us in Your divine Scripture?

For *the Heavens shall be folded up like a scroll* (Is 34:4), and now *they are extended over us like a skin* (Ps 104:2). For Your divine Scripture possesses a more sublime authority, since those mortals have died through whom You presented it to us. And You know, O Lord, You know how You *clothed men with skins* (Gn 3:21) when by sin they had become subject to death.

For this reason You have *stretched out, like a skin, the firmament of Your book,* that is, Your words, which so well agree with one another, and which, by the ministry of mortal men, You have placed over us. For by their very death, that solid firmament of authority, which was set forth by them in Your words, was sublimely placed over all things that are now under it, which, while they were living, had not extended so high. You had not as yet stretched out the Heavens like a skin; You had not as yet spread throughout the world the glory of their death.

O Lord, let us *look upon the Heavens, the work of Your fingers* (Ps 8:4). Clear away that cloud from our eyes with which You covered them. There is Your testimony, which *gives wisdom to the little ones* (Ps 19:8). *Perfect, O my God, Your praise out of the mouths of babes and infants* (Ps 8:3). For we do not know of any other books that so destroy pride, that so destroy *the enemy and the defender* (Ps 8:3), who by defending his own sins resists Your reconciliation.

O Lord, I do not know any other words so pure that so persuade me to make my confession and to bend my neck to Your yoke and that invite me to serve You without complaint. Grant, O good Father, that I may understand these things! Grant this to me who am subjected to them, since You have established them for those who have been subjected to them.

There are also other waters above this firmament, I believe, immortal and free from all earthly corruption. *Let them praise Your Name* (Ps 148:5). Let that supercelestial people, the angels, praise You, they who have no need to gaze up at this firmament, or, by reading, to know Your Word. For they *always see Your face* (Mt 18:10), and therein they read, without syllables spoken in time, what Your eternal Will ordains.

They read, they choose, they love. They are always reading, and what they read never passes away, for by choosing and by loving, they read the unchangeableness of Your counsels. Never is their book closed, nor their scroll rolled up, because You Yourself are this to them, and are so eternally. For You have established them above this firmament, which You have settled over the infirmity of the people below, where they might look up and come to know Your mercy, which declares You in time, Who made times.

Your mercy, O Lord, is in the Heavens, and Your truth reaches to the clouds (Ps 36:6). The clouds pass away, but the Heavens remain. The preachers of Your Word pass on, out of this life into the other, but Your Scripture is established over Your people, even to the end of the world. *Heaven and earth shall pass away, but Your Words shall not pass away* (Mt 24:35), because the skin shall be rolled together, and the grass over which it was spread shall with its glory pass away, but *Your Word remains forever* (Is 40:8).

That Word appears to us in the dark image of the clouds and in the mirror of the Heavens, not as it is, because though we also are the well-beloved of Your Son *it has not yet appeared what we shall be* (1 Jn 3:2). He has seen us through the lattice of our flesh, and He spoke tenderly and inflamed us, and *we followed His scent* (Song 1:3). But *when He shall appear, then shall we be like Him, for we shall see Him as He is* (1 Jn 3:2). As He is, O Lord, shall we see Him, though as yet that privilege has not been granted to us.

CHAPTER 16 —The Immutability of God

NO one but You can know You fully as You are, for You are unchangeable, and You know unchangeably and will unchangeably. Your essence knows and wills unchangeably, and Your knowledge is and wills unchangeably, and Your will is and knows unchangeably. Neither is it proper in Your eyes that in the same way that the unchangeable Light knows itself, so should it be known by the changeable being enlightened by it.

Therefore, *my soul is like earth without water to You* (Ps 143:6). For just as it cannot of itself enlighten itself, so neither can it of itself satiate itself. *For with You is the fountain of life, and in Your light we shall see light* (Ps 36:10).

CHAPTER 17 — The Arid Soul

WHO gathered together the embittered [against God] into one society? They all have one end in mind: temporal and earthly happiness. For this end they do all things, although they waver back and forth with an innumerable variety of anxieties. Who was it, O Lord, but You Who said: *Let the wa-*

ters be gathered together into one place, and let the dry land appear (Gn 1:9), which thirsts after You. *The sea also is Yours, and You have made it, and Your hands formed the dry land* (Ps 95:5).

For not the bitterness of men's wills but the gathering together of the waters is called sea. You also restrain the wicked desires of men's souls and establish their boundaries specifying how far the waters may be allowed to go, so that their waves may break upon one another. Thus do You make the sea by the order of Your dominion over all things.

But as for the souls that thirst after You and appear before You—being separated from the company of the sea by another boundary—You water them by a sweet and hidden spring so that the *earth may bring forth its fruit* (Ps 67:7). And at Your command, O Lord God, our soul brings forth its works of mercy *according to their kind.* (Gn 1:11) Loving our neighbor in relieving his bodily needs *has seed in itself according to its likeness* (Gn 1:12).

Out of consideration of our own infirmity, we take pity on those who are in need, assisting them, as we ourselves should desire to be assisted if we were in the same necessity. And the help we give is not only in slight things, as in the *herb-bearing seed,* but also in offering the protection of our aid with all our strength, like the *fruit-bearing tree* (Gn 1:12), that is, striving to rescue out of the hand of the strong man one who suffers injury, and giving him shelter and protection by the strong arm of just judgment.

CHAPTER 18 — The Works of Creation

THUS, O Lord, thus I beseech You: let there spring forth, as already You do in giving cheerfulness and strength—in the same way let truth *spring out of the earth and justice look down from Heaven* (Ps 85:12), *and let there be lights in the firmament* (Gn 1:14). *Let us break our bread with the hungry, and bring into our house the poor and the homeless. Let us clothe the naked, and despise not those of our own flesh* (Is 58:7). By such fruits that spring out of the earth, see how good it is.

Let this temporary *light* of ours *shine forth* (Is 58:8), so that passing on from this fruitfulness of action to the delights of contemplation, holding on high the Word of Life, we may appear *like lights in the world* (Phil 2:15), cleaving fast to the firmament of Your Scripture.

For therein You make it plain to us that we are enabled to distinguish between intellectual and sensible things, such *as between the day and the night* (Gn 1:14), or between souls interested in intellectual things as opposed to those interested in sensible things, so that now not only You in Your hidden judgment—as before when the firmament was made—*may distinguish between the light and the darkness* (Gn 1:18), but also Your spiritual children, settled and distinguished from one another in the same firmament—now that Your grace has been manifested throughout the world—may shine upon the earth, and distinguish between day and night, and mark off the seasons.

For old things have passed away, and behold all things are made new (2 Cor 5:17); and *our salvation is nearer than when we believed. The night is far spent and the day is at hand* (Rom 13:11-12), and *You will bless the crown of Your year* (Ps 65:12), *sending laborers into Your harvest* (Mt 9:38) in which *others have labored* (Jn 4:38), and *sending them also* into another field, whose harvest shall be in the end.

Thus, You grant the prayers of him who asks and bless the years of the just, *but You are the Selfsame, and in Your years, which fail not* (Ps 102:28), You prepare a granary for the years that pass. In Your eternal design, You poured the good things of Heaven upon the earth in their proper seasons.

For indeed, *to one through the Spirit is given the utterance of wisdom* (1 Cor 12:7-8), a greater light for the use of those who are delighted by the light of clear truth as the guiding rule of the day; *to another is given the utterance of knowledge according to the same Spirit,* as a lesser light; *to another, faith; to another, the gift of healing; to another, the working of miracles; to another, prophecy; to another, distinguishing of spirits; to another, different kinds of tongues.* And all of these are like stars. For *all these are the work* of the one and same Spirit, Who *allots to everyone according as He Wills* (1 Cor 12:8-10), and causes these stars to shine for the benefit of all.

But the *word of knowledge* in which *all mysteries* are contained, which are changed with the season like *the moon,* and those other manifest gifts, which are afterward reckoned like the stars—insofar as they fall short of the *brightness of wisdom,* in which the aforesaid day rejoices—are only for the beginning of the night. For they are necessary to such as those to whom Your most prudent servant *could not speak as to spiritual men, but only as carnal* (1 Cor 3:1), even he who speaks *wisdom among the perfect* (1 Cor 2:6).

But the natural man, being as yet only a little one in Christ, must be nourished with milk until he is sufficiently strengthened to eat solid food and may fix his eye upon the sun. Let him not have his night utterly dark, but let him be content with the light of the moon and the stars.

These things, O God, You reveal to us with wisdom in Your book, Your firmament, so that in wondrous contemplation we may distinguish all these things, although as yet only *in signs, and in times, and in days, and in years* (Gn 1:14).

CHAPTER 19 — All Christians Exhorted to Virtue

BUT first, *wash yourselves and be clean; take away the evil from your souls, and from my eyes* (Is 1:16), so that the dry land may appear. *Learn to do well, judge the fatherless, defend the widower* (Is 1:17). that the earth may bring forth the green herb and the fruit-bearing tree. *Come, let us reason together, says the Lord* (Is 1:18), that there may be *lights in the firmament of Heaven, and they may shine upon the earth* (Gn 1:14-15).

That rich man asked the good Master what he should do to attain eternal life. The good Master, whom the rich man conceived to be no more than a man—although He is good because He is God— answers him that *if he would enter into eternal life, he must keep the commandments.* He must put away the bitterness of malice and wickedness, *not kill, not commit adultery, not steal, not bear false witness* (Mt 19:17-20), so that the dry land may appear and bring forth the honoring of mother and father, and the love of neighbor. And the rich young man answers: "I have done all these things."

Therefore, from where do so many thorns come if the earth is fruitful? Go and root up those woody roots of avarice. *Sell what you have,* and be filled with fruits by giving to the poor, and *you shall have treasure in Heaven* (Mt 19:21). And *if you wish to be perfect, follow the Lord,* being in the company of those among whom He speaks wisdom, Who knows well what He distributes to the day and to the night, so that you may also come to know it, and that for you also there may be lights in the firmament of Heaven. But this will never occur unless your *heart is there* (Mt 6:21), nor will that occur either unless *your treasure is there also,* as you have heard the good Master say. But that barren earth was sad, and *the thorns choked the word* (Mt 13:7).

But you, *O chosen generation* (1 Pt 2:9), you *weak things of the world* (1 Cor 1:27), who have *forsaken all things to follow the Lord* (Mk 10:28), go after Him and *confound the mighty* (1 Cor 1:27). Go after Him, *O beautiful feet* (Rom 10:15), and shine in the *firmament,* that the *heavens may declare His glory* (Ps 18:2), dividing the light of the perfect, though not such as the angels are, and the darkness of the little ones, who yet are not to be despised. Shine over the whole earth, and let *the day,* made light by the sun, utter to day the *word of wisdom, and let the night,* made light by the *moon, show to night the word of knowledge* (Ps 18:1-4).

The moon and the stars shine by night; yet the night does not obscure them because they give it light according to its degree. For behold, it is as by the very command of God saying, *Let there be lights in the firmament of Heaven* (Gn 1:14), and *suddenly there came a sound from Heaven, as of a violent wind blowing, and there appeared parted tongues as of fire, which settled upon each of them* (Acts 2:2-3). And they became *lights in the firmament of Heaven, having the word of life* (Phil 2:15-16). Run everywhere, holy fires, glorious fires, for you are the light of the world, nor are you *put under a bushel* (Mt 5:14-15). He to whom you cleaved is exalted, and He has exalted you. Go forth and make this known to all nations.

CHAPTER 20 — The Creation of Spiritual Things

LET the sea also conceive and *bring forth* your works, and *let the waters bring forth the creeping creature having life* (Gn 1:20). By *separating the precious from the vile, you have been made the mouth of God* (Jer 15:19), by which He said, *Let the waters bring forth, not the living creatures that the earth brings forth, but the creeping creatures having life, and the fowls that fly above the earth* (Gn 1:20-21).

Your mysteries, O God, by the ministry of Your Saints, have overcome the waves of temptation in this world to sanctify the nations in Your Name through Baptism. And among these deeds great miracles were wrought, like the *great whales* (Gn 1:21), and the voices of Your messengers flying above the earth, in the firmament of Your Book, established over them as the authority under which they might fly wherever they want. For *there is no speech nor language where their voices are not heard, since their sound has gone forth into all the earth, and their words to the end of the world* (Ps 18:4-5), because You, O Lord, by Your blessing have multiplied them.

Do I lie, or do I inadvertently confuse matters by failing to distinguish between the clear knowledge of these things in *the firmament of Heaven* and those corporeal works in the turbulent sea and under the *firmament of Heaven*? Our knowledge of some things is firm and complete and not subject to change in future generations, such as are the lights of wisdom and knowledge. Yet even among these the corporeal operations are different and varied, and with one thing growing out of another, they are multiplied by Your blessing, O God.

You have consoled us for the frailty of our bodily senses, so that in the knowledge of our minds one thing may be pictured and expressed in many ways by the motions of the body. These things have the waters brought forth, but in Your Word. The needs of the people estranged from Your eternal truth have produced them, but in Your Gospel. For those waters cast them out, the bitter weakness of which was the reason why they were sent forth in Your Word.

Now all things are beautiful because You have made them, but You Who made them all are inexpressibly more beautiful. If Adam had not fallen, this bitterness of the sea would not have flowed out from his loins, that is, this human race, so profoundly curious, so tempestuously proud, so restlessly tossing up and down. Then there would have been no need for Your dispensers to work their mystical words and deeds in many waters in a corporeal and sensible manner.

Thus do I now understand why those curious creeping and flying creatures, by which men subject to corporeal rites were taught and initiated, would not progress further unless their soul advanced to a higher spiritual level, and unless after that progress it began to tend toward perfection.

CHAPTER 21 — The Operation of God's Grace

THUS, in Your Word, not the depth of the sea, but the earth itself—once it is separated from the bitterness of the waters—brings forth not creeping and flying creatures *that have life,* but *a living soul* (Gn 1:24). For now it has no need of Baptism as the heathens did and as it also had when it was yet covered by the waters. For there is no *other entrance into the Kingdom of Heaven* (Jn 3:5), since You instituted this to be the entrance, nor is there any need for great miracles whereby faith may be encouraged. It is not such that unless it sees *signs and wonders it will not believe* (Jn 4:48), for now the faithful earth is distinct from the waters of the sea that are made bitter by infidelity, and *tongues are intended for a sign not to believers but to unbelievers* (1 Cor 14:22).

Neither has the earth, which You have *founded upon the waters* (Ps 136:6), any need of the *flying creature* that by Your Word the *waters produced.* Send Your Word into it by Your messengers, for we indeed recount their works, but You are the One Who works in them, as a result of which they labor and bring forth a *living soul.* The earth produces it because the earth is the cause enabling them to produce these things in the soul, just as the sea was the cause enabling them to produce the *creeping creatures that have life and the birds that fly under the firmament of Heaven.*

Of these this earth now has no need, although it feeds on that Fish [i.e., Jesus Christ, Son of God, Savior] which was drawn from the deep and placed upon the *table* that *You have prepared in the presence* (Ps 23:5) of those who believe. Therefore, He was drawn out of the deep so that He might nourish the barren land, and the *birds,* though bred in the sea, are yet *multiplied upon the earth.*

The infidelity of men was the cause of the first preachings of the Evangelists, yet by them the faithful are also exhorted and blessed daily in many ways. But *the living soul* takes its beginning from *the earth;* for to the faithful only is it profitable to refrain from *loving this world* (Jas 4:4), so that their soul may live to You, which was *dead while it lived in pleasures* (1 Tm 5:6), in such pleasures, O Lord, as bring death. For You, O Lord, are the life-giving delight of the pure in heart.

Now, therefore, let Your ministers work upon the earth, not as upon the waters of infidelity by preaching and speaking by miracles, mysteries, and mystical words, wherein ignorance, the mother of wonder, might be attentive because of fear of those hidden wonders. This is the entrance into faith for the sons of Adam who have forgotten You, while *they hide themselves from Your Face* (Gn 3:8), and become an abyss. But let Your ministers work now as upon the dry land, separated from the whirlpools of the abyss, and let them be a *model to the faithful* (1 Thes 1:7) by living before them and inspiring them to imitation. For thus do men listen not only as something to hear, but as something to do.

Seek the Lord, and your soul shall live (Ps 69:33), so that the earth may bring forth the living soul. *Be not conformed to the world* (Rom 12:2), but keep yourselves from it; the soul lives by avoiding those desires that bring death.

Refrain yourselves from succumbing to the uncontrolled wildness of pride, from the sluggish pleasure of lust, and from *the false name of knowledge* (1

Tm 6:20), so that the wild beasts may become tame, the cattle broken to the yoke, and the serpents made harmless. Allegorically these are the passions of the soul. However, the arrogance of pride, the delight of lust, and the poison of curiosity are the motions of a dead soul. For the soul dies not so as to lose all motion, but it dies by forsaking the fountain of life, and thus is taken up with this transitory world and is conformed to it

But Your Word, O God, is the fountain of eternal life, and it does not pass away Therefore, this departure of the soul is forbidden by Your Word, when it is said to us, *Be not conformed to this world,* so that *the earth* may bring forth a living soul in the fountain of life, i.e., a soul made continent in Your Word revealed through the Evangelists, by *imitating the followers* of Your Christ. For this is indeed to be *according to its kind* (Gn 1:14), because the desire of a man is to imitate his friend. *Become like me,* says the Apostle, *because I also am like you* (Gal 4:12).

Thus in this living soul there shall be good beasts, meek in their conduct. For You have commanded, *Do your works in meekness, and you shall be loved by all men* (Sir 3:17). And *good cattle* shall there be in it likewise, which *if they eat shall not have any advantage, nor if they do not eat shall they suffer any loss* (1 Cor 8:8). And *serpents* also will be good, not poisonous to do harm, but wise in watchfulness, and making only such a search into this temporal nature as may be necessary so that eternity may be clearly seen, *being understood by the things that are made* (Rom 1:20). For these beasts are then obedient to reason when, being restrained from their deadly course, they live and are good.

CHAPTER 22 — Regeneration and the Creation of Man

FOR behold, O Lord, our God and our Creator, when our affections have been restrained from the love of the world, whereby we were dying through our evil living, and we have begun to be a living soul through good living, and when the Word that You spoke by Your Apostle shall have been accomplished in us, namely, *Do not be conformed to this world,* there shall come to pass that which You immediately added, saying, *But be transformed in the newness of your mind* (Rom 12:2).

No longer are we to live *according to our kind,* following our neighbor who has gone before us, nor to live according to the example of some better man. For You did not say, "Let man be made according to his kind," but *Let us make man to our image and likeness* (Gn 1:26), so that we *may prove what Your will is* (Rom 12:2).

It was for this purpose that that dispenser of Yours—who *by the Gospel begot* children (1 Cor 4:15), so that he might not have them remain always *children* whom he would *feed with milk* (1 Cor 3:2), and *cherish as a nurse* (1 Thes 2:7)—said: *Be transformed in the newness of your mind, that you may prove what is the good and acceptable and perfect will of God* (Rom 12:2).

Therefore, You do not say, "Let man be made," but *Let us make man.* Nor do You say, "according to his kind," but *to Our image and likeness.* For *someone who is renewed in mind and perceives and understands* Your truth does not need the direction of any other man to teach him to imitate his own kind. By Your direction he proves what is Your Will, *what is the good, the acceptable, and the perfect.* And You teach him, for he now has the capacity to establish the Trinity of the Unity, or the Unity of the Trinity.

Therefore, to that which is said in the plural, *Let Us make man,* there is added in the singular, *and God made man.* And to that said in the plural, *to Our image,* there is added in the singular, *to the image of God.* Thus is *man renewed in the knowledge of God, according to the image of his Creator* (Col 3:10), and being made *spiritual, he judges all things,* i.e., all things that are to be judged, but *he himself is judged by no man* (1 Cor 2:15).

CHAPTER 23 — The Spiritual Man

BY THE words *he judges all things* is meant that he has *dominion over the fish of the sea, and over the birds of the air, and over all cattle and wild beasts, and over all the earth, and over every creeping creature that moves upon the earth* (Gn 1:26). For this he does by the understanding of his mind, whereby he *perceives the things that are of the Spirit of God* (1 Cor 2:14); otherwise, *man, when he was placed in honor, did not understand; he has been compared to senseless beasts, and made like them* (Ps 49:13).

Therefore, in Your Church, O our God, *according to the grace that You have given to it* (Rom 12:6), *we are Your workmanship created in good works* (Eph 2:10), not only those who spiritually preside, but those also who are spiritually subject—for in this sense did You *make man male and female* (Gn 1:27), in Your spiritual grace, where according to the sex of body *there is neither male nor female,* just as there is *neither Jew nor Greek, neither slave nor free* (Gal 3:28).

Therefore, spiritual persons, whether they preside or obey, do judge spiritually. They do so not concerning that spiritual knowledge *which shines in the firmament*—for they ought not to judge of an authority so supreme—nor yet concerning Your Book—even if there is something in it which is not clear. For we submit our understanding to it, and are certain that even those things that are beyond our understanding are yet rightly and truly spoken.

Thus man, although now *spiritual and renewed in the knowledge of God, according to the image of his Creator* (Col 3:10), ought to be a *doer of the Law, not a judge* (Jas 4:11). Neither may he take it upon himself to judge concerning the distinction between spiritual and carnal men, who are known to Your eyes, O our God, but have not become known to us by their deeds, so that *by their fruits we might know them* (Mt 7:20). But You, O Lord, already know them, and You have already separated and called them in secret before the firmament was made.

Nor does any man, even though spiritual, judge the troubled people of this world, *for what has he to do in judging those outside* (1 Cor 5:12), being ignorant of those who will emerge from that state into the sweetness of Your grace, and those who will remain in the perpetual bitterness of impiety?

Therefore, man, whom You have *made to Your own image,* has not received dominion over the lights of Heaven, nor over that hidden Heaven itself, nor over day and night, which You called into existence before the foundation of the heavens, nor over the gathering together of the waters, which is the sea. However, he has received *dominion over the fish of the sea, and the birds of the air, and over all cattle, and the whole earth, and every creeping creature that moves upon the earth* (Gn 1:26).

For he judges and approves what is right, but he disapproves of what he finds wrong, whether it be in the celebration of that Sacrament by which are initiated those whom Your mercy seeks out in many waters [i.e., Baptism]; or in that other, wherein is presented that Fish which, being taken out of the deep, the devout earth feeds upon [i.e., the Eucharist]; or in the symbols and the utterance of words, subject to the authority of Your Book, which fly about like birds under the firmament, by interpreting, expounding, discoursing, disputing, blessing and calling upon You, with the accompanying signs bursting from the mouth and sounding forth, so that all the people may answer, "Amen."

The physical expression of those words is caused by the abyss of this world and the blindness of our flesh that cannot see thoughts. Therefore, one must convey ideas by speaking into the ears. Thus although *birds are multiplied upon the earth*, they have their origin from the waters.

The spiritual man also judges by approving what is right, and by disapproving that which he finds to be evil in the deeds and in the moral life of the faithful—in their alms, as it were, *the earth bringing forth fruit.* He passes judgment on the living soul, whose passions are lessened by chastity, by fasting, and by pious meditations on all those things that are perceived bodily by the senses. It can be said that he is to judge all those things in which he has also the power of correction.

CHAPTER 24 — Increase and Multiply

BUT what is this, and what kind of a mystery is it? Behold, O Lord, You *bless mankind* so that it may *increase and multiply, and fill the earth* (Gn 1:28). Do You not herein intend some special meaning for us? Why do You not likewise bless the light, which You have called day, or the firmament of Heaven, or the lights, or the stars, or the earth, or the sea?

I might say, O God, that You Who created us in Your own image, I might say that it was Your will to impart this blessing solely to man, if You had not in the same way blessed the fish and the whales, so that they *should increase and multiply and fill the waters of the sea,* and the birds, *that they should be multiplied upon the earth.* I might also say that this blessing belonged to such creatures as are propagated by generation between themselves, if I had found it also imparted to trees, and plants, and beasts of the earth. But neither to the plants, nor to trees, nor to beasts, nor to serpents is it said, *Increase and multiply,* although all these do by generation increase and preserve their kind.

What, then, shall I say, O Truth, my Light? Shall I say that it was spoken idly, or vainly? Not so, O Father of mercy! Far be it from a minister of Your Word to say such things. And if I do not understand what is meant by that passage, let those who are better, i.e., with greater understanding than I, make better use of it, according as You, O my God, have enabled each one to understand.

However, let my confession also be pleasing in Your sight, in which I confess to You, O Lord, that I believe that You did not speak thus to me in vain. Nor will I conceal what occurred to me as a result of reading it. For it is true, nor do I see what should hinder me from understanding the figurative words of Your books.

I know that a thing may be signified in many ways by the body that is understood in one way by the mind, and that a thing may also be understood in many ways by the mind that is signified in but one way by the body. Behold how the sincere love of God and of our neighbor is corporeally expressed in many religious rites, and in countless languages, and in each language by innumerable modes of expression. Thus do the offspring of the waters *increase and multiply*.

Let those who read these words observe this. Behold what the Scripture expresses and the voice pronounces in one way only. Is not the statement *In the Beginning God created Heaven and earth* understood in many ways, the result not of any fallacy of error, but of different kinds of true interpretations? Thus do the offspring of man increase and multiply.

If, therefore, we conceive of the natures of things, not allegorically but properly, then the words *Increase and multiply* can be applied to all things that are begotten of seed. But if we consider these words as spoken figuratively—and this I rather think to be the intention of Scripture, which does not apply this blessing in vain to the offspring of creatures of the sea and of men alone—then indeed we find multitudes in many other creatures as well.

We find it among both spiritual and corporeal creatures, as in *Heaven and earth*; and among both just and wicked souls, as in *light and darkness*; and among holy authors by whom the Law has been administered to us, as in the firmament that is settled between the waters and the waters; and in the company of embittered people, as in *the sea*; and in the zeal of pious souls, as on the *dry land*; and in the works of mercy performed in this present life, as in the *herbs bearing seed* and in *trees bearing fruit*; and among spiritual gifts set forth for edification, as in the *lights of Heaven*; and among passions subdued to temperance, as in the living soul.

In all these examples we meet with multitudes, fertility, and increase. However, in regard to what may increase and multiply, so that one thing may be expressed in many ways and a single statement may be understood in many ways, this occurs only in signs that are corporeally expressed and in things that are conceived in the intellect. Corporeally expressed signs are the generations of the waters, necessarily occasioned by the depth of the flesh, and things that are conceived in the intellect are human generations, on account of the fruitfulness of reason.

That is the reason we believe, O Lord, that the words *Increase and multiply* have been said to both these kinds. For in this blessing I am convinced that a power and a faculty were granted to us by You, both to express in many ways what we understand in but one and to understand in many ways what we read to be expressed in but one way, and that obscurely. Thus are the waters of the sea filled, which are not moved except by various signs. And thus with human offspring is the earth also filled, whose dryness appears in its thirst for You, and over which reason rules.

CHAPTER 25 — The Fruits of the Earth

I ALSO wish to reveal, O Lord my God, what the following words of Your Scripture tell me. I shall speak out, and I shall not fear. For I shall say the truth, inspired by You to speak those words You have willed me to say. For I believe that I could not speak the truth unless by Your inspiration, since You are the Truth, *but every man is a liar* (Ps 116:11). Thus, he who *speaks a lie speaks of his own* (Jn 8:44). Therefore, I must speak out of Your gift so that I may speak the truth.

Behold, You have given us for food *every herb-bearing seed upon the earth, and all trees* that have in themselves fruit of their *own seed* (Gn 1:29). Not only to us have You given these, but also *to all the birds of the air, and to the beasts of the earth, and to all creeping things* (Gn 1:30), but You have not given them to the fish and to the great whales.

Now we have said already that by these fruits of the earth, the works of mercy were signified and figured allegorically, which are provided out of a fruitful earth for the necessities of this life. Such an earth as this was the devout Onesiphorus, on whose house You bestowed mercy, because he often refreshed Paul, *and was not ashamed of his chains* (2 Tm 1:16). The brethren also did this, and they also brought such fruit, for those who came *from Macedonia supplied what was wanting to him* (2 Cor 11:9).

Note, however, how he grieved for certain *trees* that did not bear the fruit that was due to him, where he says: *At my first answer no man stood with me, but all forsook me; may it not be laid to their charge* (2 Tm 4:16). For those fruits are due to those who minister spiritual doctrine to us out of their understanding of the divine mysteries. They are owed to them as men, and they are also owed to them as the living soul, for they offer themselves as models for imitation in all forms of continence. Also they are due to them as flying creatures for their blessings that are multiplied upon the earth, because *their sound has gone forth into all the earth* (Ps 19:5).

CHAPTER 26 — The Works of Mercy

THEY are fed with these fruits who delight in them, *but those whose god is their belly do not delight in them* (Phil 3:19). In regard to those who offer these things, the fruit is not in what they give but in what spirit they give them. Therefore, I plainly see why he *who served God and not his own belly* (Rom 16:18) rejoiced, and I greatly rejoice with him. For he had *received* from the *Philippians* what they had sent to him by Epaphroditus, and I understand why he rejoiced. He was nourished upon that in which he rejoiced, for, speaking of it truthfully, he said, *I rejoiced in the Lord exceedingly, that now at length your thought for me has flourished again, as you did also think, but you had grown weary* (Phil 4:10).

These Philippians then had grown faint by long weariness, and even, as it were, had withered away from bearing this fruit of a good work, and now he rejoices, but not for himself because they relieved his necessities, but rather for them because they had begun to once again flourish. Therefore, he says afterward: *Not that I speak because I was in want. For I have learned to be self-sufficing in whatever circumstances I am. I know how to live humbly and I know how to live in abundance. I have been schooled to every place and every condition, how to be filled and how to be hungry, to have abundance and to suffer want. I can do all things in Him Who strengthens me* (Phil 4:11-13).

Why are you so joyful, O great Paul? Why are you so glad? Whence are you fed, O man, *renewed in the knowledge of God, according to the image of the Creator* (Col 3:10), O living soul, of so great continence, O tongue that is a flying bird, speaking mysterious things? For to such creatures is this food due.

What is it that feeds you? Joy! Hear what follows: *Still you have done well, by sharing in my affliction* (Phil 4:14). For this is he glad, upon this does he feed, because they had done well and not because his need was erased by them. He says to You, *When I was in distress, You did enlarge me* (Ps 4:2), because he knew how to abound, and how to suffer want, in You Who did strengthen him. For he tells the Philippians, *You yourselves also know that in the first days of the Gospel, when I left Macedonia, no church communicated with me in the matter of giving and receiving, but you only. For even in Thessalonica, you sent once and then again something for my need* (Phil 4:15-16). He now rejoices that they have returned to these good works, and he is glad that they have flourished again, like a fruitful field that recovers its fertility.

But was it on account of his own needs that he said, *You sent something for my needs?* Does he rejoice for that? No, not for that. But how do we know this? Because he himself says in the following words, *not because I am eager for a gift, but I seek the fruit* (Phil 4:17). A gift is the thing itself given by one who provides us with necessities such as money, food, drink, clothes, lodging, and assistance. But the fruit is the good and right will of the giver.

For the good Master did not only say, *He who receives a prophet,* but added, *in the name of a prophet;* nor did He only say, *He who receives a just man,* but added, *in the name of a just man.* One indeed shall receive a prophet's reward, and the other a just man's reward. Nor does He only say, *Whoever gives to one of these little ones a cup of cold water to drink,* but adds, *in the name of a disciple.* Then He concludes, *Amen, I say to you, he shall not lose his reward* (Mt 10:41-42).

The gift is to receive a prophet, to receive a just man, to give a cup of cold water to a disciple. The fruit is to do this in the name of a prophet, in the name of a just man, in the name of a disciple. With fruit was Elijah fed by the widow, who knew that she was feeding a man of God, and fed him because of that, but by the raven he was fed with a gift. Nor was the spirit of Elijah so fed, but the body only, which also might have perished for want of food.

CHAPTER 27 —The Fish and the Whales

THEREFORE, I will speak what is true in Your sight, O Lord. Unlearned persons and infidels need the initiation of the first Sacraments and the mighty works of miracles to win them to the Faith, and they are signified by the names of fish and whales. These persons may offer Your servants bodily refreshment or otherwise aid them with something that is necessary for this present life. But since they do not know why they do this or what purpose it serves, they do not truly feed these servants, nor are Your children truly fed by them. For neither do the givers do these things with a holy and a right intention, nor do the recipients rejoice at their gifts, since as yet they do not see the fruit.

Thus, the mind is fed upon that in which it rejoices. Therefore, do not the fish and the whales feed on such *meats* that the earth does not produce until after it is divided and set apart from the bitterness of the waters of the sea?

CHAPTER 28 — The Goodness of All Creation

AND You, O God, *saw everything that You had made, and it was very good* (Gn 1:31). For we also have seen these things, and behold, they are all very good. Of Your several kinds of works, when You had said, "Let them be made," and they were made, this one and that one, You saw that it was good. Seven times have I enumerated where it is written how You saw that what You made was good. And this is the eighth, that You saw all that You had made, and behold, they were not only good, but even very good, as now being renewed all together. Taken individually they were only good, but taken together they were not only good but very good.

In this way all bodies are said to be beautiful, for a body that is made up of beautiful members is far more beautiful than those very members are, when taken by themselves. By their well-ordered arrangement the entire being is perfect, composed of members that, taken individually, are beautiful.

CHAPTER 29 — In Time and Outside Time

AND I looked carefully so that I might be completely certain whether it was seven or eight times that You saw that Your works were good when they pleased You. And in Your seeing I found no record of any time at all whereby I might understand just how many times You saw the things You had made.

And I said, "Lord, is not this Your Scripture true, since You Yourself are true and, being Truth Itself, uttered it? Why then do You say to me that in Your seeing there is no time? Yet, Your Scripture tells me that You examined what You had made each day and saw that it was good. When I counted the times, I found how often this was."

To this You replied that You are my God, and with a strong voice You spoke to Your servant in his interior ear, breaking through my deafness and crying out: "O man, it is true that what My Scripture says, I Myself say. However, My Scripture speaks in time, and My eternal Word is not subject to the course of time, because My Word exists in eternity equal with Myself. Those things that you see through My Spirit, I see also, and those things that you speak by My Spirit, I speak also. Yet, while you see those things in the course of time, I do not see them in time, and while you speak them in time, I do not speak them in time."

CHAPTER 30 — A False Dualism

I HEARD You, O Lord my God, and I imbibed a drop of the sweetness of Your Truth. I understood that there are certain men to whom Your works are displeasing. And such men say that You were forced by necessity to make many of these works, such as the fabric of the heavens and the arrangement of the stars.

They say that You did not make them from Your own resources, but that they had been created elsewhere from another source and that You merely drew them together, and compacted them, and framed them. They aver that You did this after overcoming Your enemies, and from them You erected the ramparts of the world, so that they, being bound down by this structure, might no longer be able to rebel against You.

Furthermore, in regard to other things, such as all those of the flesh, those extremely small living creatures, and whatsoever is rooted in the earth, they claim that you did not actually make them or even fit them all together. They assert that a certain mind, hostile to You, and of another nature, which You did not make, but which was opposed to You, did beget and frame these things, in the lower parts of the earth. Men who say these things are clearly insane, for they look not upon Your works by Your Spirit, nor do they recognize You in them.

CHAPTER 31 — The Gift of Knowledge

WHEN men observe these things through Your Spirit, it is You Who see in them. Therefore, when they see that these things are good, it is You Who see that they are good, and whatever things are pleasing because of You, it is You Who are pleasing in them, and whatever things through Your Spirit please us also please You in us.

For who among men knows the things of a man save the spirit of a man that is in him? Even so the things of God no one knows but the Spirit of God. Now we have received not the spirit of the world, but the Spirit that is of God, so that we may know the things that have been given us by God (1 Cor 2:11-12). Clearly I would be remiss if I did not say: "Truly no one knows the things of God save the Spirit of God."

How then do we know what things are given us by God? I answer that the things that we know by the Spirit, even these *no one knows but the Spirit of God.* Just as it was rightly said to them who were to speak in the Spirit of God, *It is not you who speak* (Mt 10:20), so it is rightly said to those who know in the Spirit of God, "It is not you who know." And no less rightly is it said to them who see in the Spirit of God, "It is not you who see," so that whatever they see to be good through the Spirit of God, it is not they but God Who sees that it is good.

Therefore, it is one thing for a man to think what is good to be evil, like those men mentioned above, and another thing that what is good a man should see to be so, even as Your creation, because it is good, may be pleasing to many men to whom, however, You Yourself are not pleasing in it. For this reason, they would rather enjoy Your creation than You.

It is another thing again, when a man sees a thing to be good, that God should see in him that it is good, namely, that God may be loved in that thing which He has made, yet Who cannot be loved save by the Holy Spirit Whom He has given. *The love of God is poured forth in our hearts by the Holy Spirit Who has been given to us* (Rom 5:5). By the Spirit we see that whatsoever exists in any degree is good, for it comes from Him Who Himself does not exist in degree, but He is what He is.

CHAPTER 32 — A Brief Account of the Works of God

THANKS be to You, O Lord. *We see Heaven and earth,* whether the corporeal portion, upper or lower, or the spiritual and corporeal creation. And in the adornment of these parts, whereof either the whole bulk of the world or the universal creation consists, we see *light* made and separated from the darkness.

We see the firmament of Heaven, whether that primary body of the world, between the spiritual upper waters and the lower corporeal waters, or this space of air—since this also is called heaven— through which the birds of the sky wander, between these waters which are borne as vapors above them, and on clear nights fall down again as dew, and those *waters* that, being of more weight, flow upon the earth.

We behold a surface of waters gathered together on the fields of the sea, and the dry land both bare and formed so that it may be visible and in order, the mother of herbs and trees.

We see the lights shining from above, the sun to serve the day, the moon and the stars to comfort the night, and by all those are times made known and signified.

We see on all sides a watery element, which is fruitful in fish, beasts, and birds, because the density of the air that bears up those birds in their flight thickens itself by the exhalation of the waters.

We see the face of the earth beautified with earthly creatures, and *man, created after Your own image and likeness,* who even through that very image and likeness, i.e., by the power of reason and understanding, is made superior to all non-rational creatures. And as in his soul there is one power that, by giving counsel, governs and another that is made subject in order that it may obey, so also for man in the corporeal order there was made woman.

By virtue of her reasonable and intelligent mind, she would have an equal nature with him, but in the sex of her body she would, in like manner, be subject to the sex of her husband, even as the active appetite must be made subject to reason, that it may conceive correct and prudent conduct.

These things we see, and considered individually they are good, and all together they are very good.

CHAPTER 33 — Praise and Love

*L*ET *Your works praise You* (Ps 145:10) so that we may love You, and let us love You so that Your works may praise You. Those works have their beginning and their ending in time, their rising and setting, their growth and decay, their beauty and their privation. Therefore, they have a sequence of morning and evening, in part secret, in part apparent. For they were made from nothing by You, not out of Yourself, not of any matter that was not Yours, nor of any that existed previously, but out of matter that was concreated, i.e., out of matter at the same time created by You, because without any interposition of time You gave form to its formlessness.

For since the matter of *Heaven and earth* is one thing, and the form of Heaven and earth another, You made the matter wholly out of nothing, and the form of the world out of that formless matter. Yet You made them both together, so that the form would follow the matter without any interval of time.

CHAPTER 34 — The Church

WE HAVE also considered what You willed to be manifested by the making of these things in such an order, or by having them written about in such order. And we have seen that things individually are good, and all together very good, in Your Word, in Your Only-begotten, both Heaven and earth, the Head and Body of the Church, in Your predestination before all times, without morning and evening.

And You began in time to put into execution Your predestined things, so that You might reveal hidden things and put in order our disordered parts. *For our sins hung over us* (Ez 33:10), and we had departed from You into the abyss of darkness, and Your good *Spirit was borne over us* to succor us in *due season.*

Then did *You justify the ungodly* (Rom 4:5) and separate them from the wicked. And You made firm the authority of Your Book between those above, who would be obedient to You, and those below, who would be subject to them. And You gathered together the society of unbelievers into one conspiracy so that the zeal of Your faithful might become apparent and they might bring forth works of mercy, distributing their earthly riches to the poor with the hope of obtaining riches in Heaven.

After this You enkindled certain *lights in the firmament,* Your holy ones, having the Word of life, and shining with the sublime authority of their spiritual gifts. Then again, for the conversion of unbelievers, You produced out of corporeal matter the Sacraments and visible miracles, and voices and words according to the firmament of Your Book, by which also the faithful were to be blessed.

Next You formed the *living soul* of the faithful through their passions well-ordered by the virtue of continence, and after that You renewed after Your own image and likeness the mind, subject to You alone, having no need to imitate any human authority, and You submitted its reasonable actions to the excellence of the understanding, as is the woman to the man. To all officers of Your ministry who are necessary for the perfection of the faithful in this life, You willed that such good things should be given by the aforesaid faithful as might be of profit to them in the life to come.

All these we see, and we realize that they are very good, because You see them in us, You Who have given to us Your Spirit, whereby we may both see these things, and in them may love You.

CHAPTER 35 — The Peace of Eternity

O LORD God, give us peace, for You have granted us all that we have—the peace of repose, the peace of the Sabbath, a peace without any evening. All this most beautiful order of things that are very good, when its course shall be finished, is to pass away, for in them has been made both a morning and an evening.

CHAPTER 36 — The Sabbath of Eternal Life

B UT the seventh day has no evening, nor has it any setting, because You have sanctified it to endure for all eternity, so that because You rested on the seventh day, having completed all Your works, which were very good, although You even created them in unbroken rest, the voice of Your Book may proclaim to us beforehand that, after our works, which are very good because You have given them to us, we also shall rest in You on the Sabbath of eternal life.

CHAPTER 37 — Eternal Rest in Heaven

FOR then shall You also rest in us, even as now You work in us, and so shall that rest of Yours be in us, even as now these works of Yours are through us. But You, O Lord, always work and are ever at rest. You do not see for a time, nor are You moved for a time, nor do You rest for a time. Yet You make all things that are seen in time, and the very times themselves, and even the rest that comes subsequent to time.

CHAPTER 38 — Two Ways of Seeing

THEREFORE, we see these things that You have made because they exist, but they exist because You see them. And we see outside ourselves that they are, and within ourselves that they are good. But You saw them as already made, even there where You saw them as yet to be made. At one time we were inclined to do well, after our heart had conceived this out of Your Holy Spirit, whereas formerly, having forsaken You, we were moved to do ill. However, You, O God, the One and the Good, never did cease to do good. There are some good works of ours, done as a result of Your gifts, but they are not eternal. After them we hope to find rest in the greatness of Your sanctification. But You, the Supreme Good that needs no good, are ever at rest, because You Yourself are that rest.

And what man is there who can make another man understand this? Or what Angel can do so to an Angel, or what Angel to a man? Let it be asked of You, let it be sought in You, at Your door let us knock for it. So shall it be received, so shall it be found, so shall it be opened (cf. Mt 7:7-8).